MANAGING CHANGE

172

£6.95

MANAGING CHANGE
Reflections on equality and management learning

Russ Vince

First published in Great Britain in 1996 by

The Policy Press
University of Bristol
Rodney Lodge
Grange Road
Bristol BS8 4EA

Telephone (0117) 973 8797
Fax (0117 973 7308
e-mail: tpp@bris.ac.uk

© Russ Vince, 1996

British Library Cataloguing in Publication Data
A catalogue record for this book is available from the British Library

ISBN 1 86134 037 0

Cover design: Qube, Bristol.

Printed in Great Britain by the Alden Press, Oxford.

Contents

Acknowledgements

My main acknowledgement is of Linda Martin for her love, ideas and northern humour. Much of what I feel and know has been formed from the dialogue between us.

Various other people have also helped me to start and to finish this book. Robert French and Peter Simpson listened to me as I talked the book into shape; they also provided excellent commentary on early drafts and considerable friendship. I have appreciated the support and comments of other friends and colleagues from the Research Unit for Organisational Learning and Change at Bristol Business School. I would also like to thank Paul Hoggett, Hannah Hurst, Lillian Kitusa, Munira Thobani, Lynne Greenaway, Laura Woodruff, Claudia Heimer and Judi Marshall. The Local Government Management Board funded the review of the diversity literature in Chapter 7 as part of a research project on Equalities and Organisational Design. I have very much appreciated the hard work of the staff at The Policy Press, and in particular Alison Shaw for encouraging my initial motivation to submit an outline.

The book is a jigsaw of my thinking, writing and practice as it has developed over the past 10 years. Parts of the book have been published previously, sometimes with similar words, either as academic papers or as chapters. These include articles in *Management Education and Development* (with Linda Martin), *Management Learning, Organisation Studies* (with Mike Broussine), in the *Journal of Management Education* and a chapter in *Rethinking Management Education* by Robert French and Chris Grey (published by Sage).

"Happily I woke one morning with a revelatory insight – that I would never get it right, that seeking to do so was a futile waste of energy, that I should proceed with this 'truth' in mind and allow myself to be more playful in my explorations". (Marshall, 1995, p 29)

Introduction

There are three main themes in this book: change, equality and management learning.

Management learning is the academic discipline within which the book is situated. Burgoyne (1994) provides one definition of this discipline when he talks of "managing by learning". He points out that practitioners interested in management learning want to achieve a better understanding and integration of the two notions of managing and learning whether their practice is as managers or as management educators/developers. A key aspect of management learning is a reflection on the underlying theories, models and frameworks that managers or management educators/developers apply in practice. At the centre of this definition is the notion that practitioners attempting to manage, to learn, to educate and to develop need to be 'reflexive', to continually theorise their practice and practise their theory.

I have attempted to structure this book as an exercise in management learning. In Part One I develop my own perspective on and definitions of management learning through reflections on the research process, on experiential learning and on organisational change. I consider and discuss a number of theories, models and frameworks that underpin my current practice. The particular issue that has influenced and driven my evolving definition of management learning has been my conviction that management thinking is mostly dominated by "naive humanism, based on a simple notion of an individualised self with a true nature which can be the source of personal, interpersonal and organisational purpose" (Burgoyne, 1994, p 45). Such a perspective ignores the complexities of power and emotion in organisations. My own desire is to place greater emphasis on a social self, on psychodynamic relations, and on the emotional and the political aspects of processes of managing and learning. Most of Part One is an exploration of these issues.

In Chapter 1 I discuss the relationship between learning and the research process. This allows me to introduce the key issues of relatedness, emotion, power and unconscious dynamics and to set them within the context of processes of human inquiry (Reason, 1988), which seems to me to be the predominant methodological standpoint within management learning. In Chapter 2 I concentrate on the critique and development of two well known and well used theories of experiential management education and management development, the Action Learning approach of Revans (1983) and Kolb's Learning Cycle (1984). I attempt to develop both of these approaches by introducing emotional and political perspectives into the original models. In this way I hope to provide a broader model of learning from experience, one that includes an approach to emotions in organisations and, at the same time, is adequate for engaging with social power relations in organisations.

In Chapter 3 I move into the area of organisation and the management of change. I construct a framework emerging out of psychodynamic theories which attempts to move beyond the view of change as a planned process, towards a method which focuses on organisational members' emotions and relations, on forces of uncertainty and defensiveness. In this way I am both advocating a dynamic view of change and pointing towards issues for engaging with change that are often avoided.

In Part Two I explore aspects of equality in organisations as a context for, and one example of, working in practice with the thoughts and reflections of Part One. This theme has not been the only aspect of my work, it is not the only form of practice that has influenced my thinking and theorising. However, in Part Two I highlight different ways that I have thought about and engaged with various aspects of equalities and inequalities in local government organisations over the past 10 years. I have found that being involved with struggles over issues of equality in organisations has provided an opportunity for me to engage with emotional and political processes of learning and change, both for myself and with others.

Chapters 4 to 7 outline my various attempts over the past 10 years to explore the relationship between equality and organisational learning and change. In Chapter 4 I describe an action research project undertaken in the mid-1980s on equal opportunities in organisations, which sought to regulate organisational behaviour and to set a context for both improved individual learning and organisational change. This action research helped me to identify some of the various avoidance strategies that managers use to defend against the impact of equal opportunities within their organisations. In Chapter 5, I develop the idea of 'management by avoidance' as a result of interventions in three local government organisations. This exploration allowed me to be clearer about the day-to-day expression of (particularly white, male) power in local government. In Chapter 6, I continue to consider the nature of management by avoidance, although this time in terms of exploring everyday relationships between organisational members involved in either promoting or defending against equality. In Chapter 7 I offer a critique of the idea of 'managing diversity', which is currently seen as a method for developing equality in organisations, and reflect on the broader range of issues that need consideration if organisational change is to occur.

In Part Two of the book I therefore highlight the successes and failures of different strategies for intervention around the development of equality in organisations. I do not attempt to provide a coherent or fixed definition of equality. As Adam Phillips (1995, p 104) says: "Too much definition leaves too much out". However, I do use the words *equality* and *equalities* to mean slightly different things, and I do try to explain (below) why equality is integral to management learning. When I refer to 'equality' I am mainly talking about a concept that is expressive of a perpetual aspect of organisational life. I do not think of equality as an achievable organisational state, but rather as an idea that has continuous potency for exploring the relational and political in organisations. I use the word 'equalities' to express the diversity of voices, positions, practices, issues and relations that are played out within organisations. Both of these words seem to find and lose definition as they are continually contested in the everyday practice of organisation.

When I began the work that is represented in this book I thought of equality as an outcome of planned strategies, and as a possible and desirable position for organisations to adopt. My view has changed, and my perspective now is that inequalities are a consistent aspect of organisational life, that the desire for and impossibility of equality constitute a continual paradox of organisational life. What is important about working with this paradox is that highlighting struggles over equality and equalities offers insights into emotions in organisations, organisational politics, management learning and organisational change.

I think of equality as a powerful metaphor within which to explore the nature and development of manager and management learning in public (and probably private) organisations. Everyday struggles around equalities in organisations provide considerable insights about the nature of both organisational learning and change, particularly if one is interested in the relational, emotional and political processes affecting organisational learning and change. Viewing the organisation through struggles over equality provides a perspective on the possibilities and difficulties of providing management learning. It is therefore possible to reflect through this metaphor on how processes of management education and management development might be created and sustained.

Struggles over equality are not solely metaphorical. Inequalities between differing socially positioned groups are an integral and ever present aspect of organisation. Real inequalities exist in relation to differential positions of power between socially defined groups as a political fact of life in organisations. Inequalities also have a powerful impact on individual members of an organisation, whether from the desire to experience greater equality or to avoid it. The existence of inequalities inevitably produces engagement with the power and politics created within and between people in the organisation, as well as through the effects on people of complex, external power relations. Equality therefore provides an important context within which to understand power relations in organisations more completely.

In the final part, in one final chapter, I attempt to draw some very open conclusions about management learning from my thoughts, frameworks and experiences. My experiences in terms of equality and management learning have been full of emotion, connection and conflict, as I have interacted with and against others in their organisational roles and from our differing identities. In addition, there are two short pieces within the book, called 'Reflections', one at the start of Part Two and the other at the start of Part Three, which are written in a style that is (even) more personal and self-absorbed. I have included these in order to highlight fragments of my own processes of learning and change. As Denzin (1994, p 503) says: "The other who is presented in the text is always a version of the researcher's self".

I think that there are two intersecting experiences from which I personally approach equality and management learning. The first is my experience as a white man and the second is my experience as a white man whose work is about management education and management development. I share the feelings of many managers I have met who believe that, on the surface, change is 'a good thing'. Underneath, they and I both recognise a fear and denial of change. This paradox needs to be held and worked through if learning and change are to occur. Working with the paradoxical tensions of our desire for and denial of equality is a continual aspect of both my inquiry and my learning. This book is about what my experience and inquiry has led me to believe about equality and management learning. My work is part of a process of understanding that began before the book, and will continue after it. It is a mechanism of reflection and dialogue which has allowed the creation of a number of temporary theoretical positions, given rise to a series of individual and collective understandings, and supported my evolving practice.

Throughout the book I explore the relationship between equality, learning and change. At the beginning of my explorations I thought that, since white middle class men were responsible for the mobilisation of our particular bias within society, we needed also to take responsibility for change. This view has now altered, and my previous perspective looks to me like just another form of control (don't worry, the white man will take care of change). I now see that equality is a continual political and psychological force that, when it is not denied, avoided or suppressed is an essential part of change for all of us. I still accept that as a man I have to work with the ways in which I reinforce and perpetuate inequality as an integral part of the regimes in which we live. I have learned that I need to refuse to do this in isolation from the social and political reality of organisations. As a man my struggles will be different to the struggles of black people and of women, but as men and women, white and black we are all caught up in those struggles and therefore have to work together to challenge them. We all have to do different types of work on equality because equality is an essential aspect of learning and change.

Our inability (as managers and management educators/ developers) to sustain a creative and interrogative attitude towards social reality often seems to derive from our fear of disturbing our own internal establishment (Hoggett, 1992, p 153). Learning arises from such disturbance, and therefore involves us in experiencing rather than denying our internal politics and emotions. It would be wonderful if such experience was a consistent and practical possibility, rather than a fleeting aim, sometimes held and sometimes lost. However, side by side with the genuine desire to learn sits the genuine desire to flee from learning, from the difficulties posed for us by internal and external politics and emotions. Critical thinking in the field of management learning can provide a lead in the development of a practice of management education and development that fully addresses the complexities – emotional, political and rational – that are involved in the learning process.

This book is an attempt to provide the reader with a perspective not only on equality, learning and change but also on the processes that are necessary to ensure that such concepts can develop as an integral part of the everyday life of organisations and an everyday part of management. The learning processes that managers either employ or avoid are central to their understanding of their continual engagement with everyday practice. The contribution I feel I have made to the development of management learning is based on my commitment to and interest in the following:

- Exploring the emotional and relational dynamics of management learning and organisational change, particularly organisational defences and managerial avoidance strategies. Partly, this involves exploring the complex internal and external inter-relations that go into the continual construction of self and other, for individuals, within groups and in organisations.

- Working with an unending and evolving perspective on power as it is created, enacted and translated in everyday relations, and from the social construction of our relations.

- Bringing the psychological and the political together, in order to be thoughtful and insightful about the theory and practice of management learning, management education and management development.

- Continuing to find myself challenged and surprised by the unforeseen consequences of undertaking and writing about my work.

Part One

one

Action research and management learning

In this chapter I explore what may be distinctive about management research undertaken from a learning perspective. I suggest that there are some general principles that influence research in the field of management learning, and I set these in relation to various key issues that have a particular influence on the learning process. The objective of this chapter is therefore to present a framework of questions which might represent particular aspects of research within the field of management learning. The general phrase I use to depict this framework is the notion of 'research as learning'.

The approach I am describing when I use the phrase 'research as learning' involves the integration of specific dynamics that underpin both research and learning. It is my aim to identify these dynamics, and to describe how they can be explicitly incorporated in the process of management research. I am therefore attempting to produce a more specific definition of the meaning of learning in the context of research into management learning and to emphasise the practical implications of this definition for such research.

Assumptions about research as learning

In order to provide clarity and some sense of containment, I will explain the assumptions that lead me to the notion of research as learning. First, I am assuming that most people who are researching in the field of management learning are doing so primarily from a broadly phenomenological standpoint, and not from a positivist one. Comparisons between positivism and phenomenological approaches abound in both the general research literature, and the literature on management research (Burrell and Morgan, 1979; Heron, 1981; Lincoln and Guba, 1985; Dainty, 1991). I will not be discussing the differences, strengths and weaknesses of either of these paradigms. I am also assuming that the reader of this book subscribes to the notion that research in management learning tends to be concerned with theory as the outcome of inductive analysis, rather than testing theory through deductive processes (for a comparison of deduction/induction see Gill and Johnson, 1991, pp 28-37).

My second assumption, which is linked to the first, is that research in management learning tends to be at the 'action-oriented' end of the various approaches available. Bennett (1991) identifies six approaches in management research:

- Pure basic research: resolving, illuminating, exemplifying theory.

- Basic objective research: general problems of knowledge application.

- Evaluation research: assessing the performance of an enterprise.

- Applied research: solving specific problems in an organisational setting.

- Action research: making learning and change self-generating within the research process.

- New paradigm research: inquiry into people and relations between people.

In this book my primary concern is with the last two approaches identified above, because they are both concerned with working explicitly on the integration of learning and research. My reflections on methods and approaches in this book centre on what I will refer to as action research or human inquiry (ie, new paradigm) based ways of researching.

There is a wide variety of approaches that escape from the constraints of a positivist research tradition into methods that are seen to be more suitable to the complexities of human inquiry. In fact, this has been a theme in social science writing for more than three decades. These broadly qualitative or action-based approaches include 'grounded' theory (Glaser and Strauss, 1967; Turner, 1981); participatory research (Hall, 1975); action science (Argyris, Putnam and Smith, 1985); action research (Susman and Evered, 1978; Brown and McIntyre, 1981; Elden and Chisholm, 1993); action inquiry (Torbert, 1991); qualitative evaluation and research (Marshall and Rossman, 1989; Patton, 1990); feminist research (Stanley and Wise, 1983; Griffin, 1986; Mies, 1993); ethnomethodology (Hassard, 1991); social research (Morgan, 1983; Hammersley, 1993); reflexive research (Steier, 1991); naturalistic inquiry (Lincoln and Guba, 1985; Guba and Lincoln, 1990); and various 'new paradigm' and collaborative research approaches (Reason and Rowan, 1981; Torbert, 1981; Reason, 1988, 1994).

As the previous paragraph suggests, the choice of approaches is wide-ranging. However, in this chapter I do not want to compare them or to explore their relative merits. Instead, I draw a range of general principles from action research and human inquiry perspectives.

General principles underlying research as learning

Action research is a methodology which intends to bring about learning and change and is therefore also likely to bring out defences against learning and change. I am interested in ways of researching that reveal both the possibilities and the barriers to learning and change. In addition, action research considers that collaboration with and participation from the people who are being researched is a vital element of the sense-making process. Together these two ideas provide a contextual focus that makes research relevant to future organisational action and development as well as to the avoidance of change. Thus,

> ... contemporary forms of action research also aim at making change and learning a self-generating and self-maintaining process in the systems in which the action-researchers work. (Elden and Chisholm, 1993, p 125)

Action research acknowledges the value of the interchange between "the tacit and explicit knowledge of insiders plus the formal frameworks and concepts of outside researchers" (Chisholm and Elden, 1993, p 294). The idea of this method is to bring the feelings and reflections of people inside the system to the surface so that both researcher and researched contribute to the generation of contextually relevant or 'local' theory.

One of the main propositions in action research is that: "the process is as important a product as the solution to a scientific and practical problem" (Elden and Chisholm, 1993, p 128). But, what does 'the process' mean? I suspect that 'the process' will mean different things in different contexts, and I would suggest that there has been a tendency to define 'the process' very generally, such as "adding to the stock of knowledge about change processes" (Gill and Johnson, 1991, p 9), rather than making any specific attempt to say what is meant by it.

One of the most powerful influences on an understanding of 'the process' in the field of management learning is Argyris' (1982) distinction between 'single-loop' and 'double-loop' learning. Argyris elaborates a conception of the process of learning as the extension of knowledge. He demonstrates that there is a powerful underlying level of learning that can be experienced and analysed through questioning how the learning was learned. Single-loop learning promotes 'self-sealing and self-fulfilling' practice, because it does not address how the learning was learned. Double-loop learning promotes a self-reflexive understanding of the interaction between the experience and the structure of learning. Research which acknowledges this distinction, recognises the radical significance for learning of a self-reflexive perspective. It therefore seeks to understand how the very process of knowledge production affects the knowledge produced. Another way of expressing this would be to describe such research as a critical theory, one that is suspicious of its own suppositions (Gergen, 1992).

Reflecting on these considerations and on some of the approaches that I have noted above, it is possible to abstract and draw out some general principles which seem fundamental to research in the field of management learning. These are:

• Research is a *developmental* process, a learning process, which engages both researcher and researched in the possibility of change.

- Research is a *personal* process motivated by the individual desire and willingness to expand personal knowledge and understanding. Therefore it contributes towards personal learning and change.

- Research is *experiential,* the lived experience of both researcher and researched has value and impact. This experience is constructed socially, politically and inter-personally.

- Research is a *reflexive* process. It acknowledges the continuous relationship between theory and practice as it creates and shapes individual and organisational knowledge, behaviour, structure and systems.

These four statements form the basis of my sense of the *general principles* that underpin 'research as learning'. In addition, there are four *key issues* that intersect with these principles.

Key issues in research as learning

I think that it is possible to give more specific meaning to the process of learning how to learn in the context of 'research as learning'. I intend to do this by discussing four issues that influence 'the process', and which might particularly encourage self-reflexive or double-loop research practice: relatedness, emotion, power and unconscious dynamics. *Relatedness* can be seen in two ways: relatedness between various individuals, groups and organisations within the research; and relatedness that is grounded in the emotional substrata of experience evoked by the research process. This second aspect of relatedness is concerned with the impact on the research of individual and collective *emotion.* The third area for discussion is the political or *power* issues that are present for individuals and within an organisation and, finally, the *dynamics,* or unconscious processes that both influence and are set up by the interaction of behaviour and structure in organisations.

Defining the self-reflexive process of research in terms of relatedness, emotion, power and unconscious dynamics makes the link between learning and research explicit in various ways. Both learning and research can then be perceived as areas in which the interaction or engagement between individuals, groups and organisations is fundamental to the process. Such engagement evokes anxieties and is not always conscious or controllable. The interaction between behaviour and structure suggests a dynamic process within which they both continually shape and constrain the individual and the organisation. Neither learning nor research is detached from human emotion, nor are they detached from the social power relations that impact on all human interaction and engagement.

Before exploring these four key issues in greater detail, I want to show how the general principles I have described intersect with these issues. This is represented in Table 1.

Along the top of the grid are the four general principles I identified, suggesting that research concerned with learning will be a developmental, personal, experiential and reflexive process. Along the side of the grid are key issues for research as learning based on four issues that clarify and represent the process of research. The spaces in the grid give an indication of the way in which the principles and the issues relate to each other. These questions (offered as an example rather than a rule) will I hope both highlight and clarify issues involved in the design and development of 'research as learning'. The 'research as learning' grid is not an approach to management research in itself. It is intended as a way of looking at, a way of questioning, research approaches and as a way of integrating learning into management research.

Table 1: 'Research as learning' grid

	Research as learning: general principles			
Key issues for research as learning	Developmental	Personal	Experiential	Reflexive
Relatedness	How do the researcher and researched relate with the whole research process? What are the consequences for learning and change? How do our respective roles promote or defend against learning and change?	What does my position in the research mean to me and others and for the research as a whole?	What exactly are the lived experiences of the people involved in the research? How can the experience of relatedness within the research process be included?	How are processes of reflection set up within the research project to change and develop it as it happens? What are the mechanisms for checking back?
Emotion	What are the underlying emotions in the research process as they evolve and what impact do they have on the development of all aspects of the research? What fantasies are affecting the research, and how do these organise understanding and pattern behaviour?	How can the impact of emotion be captured/bracketed? What have I brought with me emotionally? What are the underlying emotions stimulated by the research process?	How do previous and current emotional experiences impact on the research process? How does the research work with these?	To what extent are decisions made in the research of an avoidance of emotion? How can (eg) dependency be acknowledged and worked with?

Key issues for research as learning	Developmental	Personal	Experiential	Reflexive
Power	What external patterns of difference, disadvantage and discrimination are impacting on the research and to what effect? What bias(es) exist in the context of the research and how can they be worked with?	How do I define and communicate my role and identity in the research? What is the impact of my authority as researcher? What power is being invested in me in the research process?	What does individual and collective knowledge of discrimination mean in the context of the research? How is discrimination reinforced in the research process?	To what degree is difference allowable/ acceptable? How can difference be worked with in a non-defensive way? How is action to counter discrimination integrated into research?
Unconscious dynamics	What is happening to the transference on to the researcher? What splits are there in the groupings? What are the inter-group dynamics? How is individual and group anxiety managed?	How does my behaviour impact on the research group? What projections/ splits/assumptions are taking place and why? What are my defence mechanisms?	How is the experiential dynamic captured by/in the research group? What aspects of experience are/are not being acknowledged/ included	As the research process unfolds, what is it saying about the researcher/ researched, the context, the methods, etc?

An illustrative example

In this section I give a brief example which is used to explore and explain the framework I have proposed.

A researcher wished to inquire into spirituality in management. Her approach was to ask respondents to discuss, in small focus group settings (six to eight people), the spiritual side of their work as managers. She initiated a pilot group to clarify her research approach. This group talked very openly about their experiences for one hour, and the researcher (who sat outside the group) was able to record a variety of very rich and personal data, containing a diverse range of experiences and interpretations of spirituality at work. These included strong views about the nature of human existence, about religious beliefs, and experiences of life and death. The discussion was remarkable in various ways, not the least because this was a group of near total strangers.

In the feedback session to review the pilot focus group it became clear that the researcher had not thought about the consequences of getting individuals to talk about such profound personal experiences. The simple 'thank you' she had imagined, was not enough, the researcher had a responsibility for what she initiated in terms of the feelings and emotions shared by respondents. The researcher had not understood either the emotional or structural power of her role in the research process. She had set a context within which the individuals in the focus group could make themselves vulnerable by sharing personal experiences, and then not honoured the depth of their vulnerability. From their vulnerable position, respondents within the group were asking themselves – was it OK to say what I just said, to share what I shared? – and there was no element in the research process which allowed participants to debrief from at least some of these feelings.

In this example, the researcher wanted the participation of the individuals in the group without considering what their participation might mean and involve. She took a non-participative stance in her role, which was not made explicit or negotiated with the group. She withheld her own perspective on spirituality (in order not to influence unduly the focus group and as a way of 'managing' the effects of bias) while expecting others to share and engage from their experience.

The researcher's conceptualisation of her role was to get something from participants, some experiential data for her project. She had not imagined that her impact on the focus group from her powerful role as 'researcher' might be an integral and important aspect of the overall data available for analysis. Such a realisation makes it more likely that the research can itself both represent and be a learning experience. Setting up a process for bringing out and reflecting on such data is a legitimate and essential part of 'research as learning'. However, the richness and complexity of engagement between people in a research process requires the researcher in such situations to be critical and self-reflexive about their process, as well as concerned with capturing experience. I maintain that this critical and self-reflexive stance can be enhanced through consideration of the questions that arise at each intersecting point of the research as learning grid. It is to the further explanation of the framework that I now turn.

Further elaboration of the key issues

The proposed research as learning framework is designed to assist the researcher who is interested in the question: what enables learning to take place as an integral part of research? I shall now discuss the four key issues in detail, relating them to my example.

Relatedness

The different relationships between researcher and researched are not based on relationship in the sense of how they get on with each other in the research, but rather on the issue of relatedness, that is the issues and implications of relations within the whole process of the research. Among other things, relatedness particularly implies the need for an acknowledgement of and working with different roles in the research. Part of capturing the research process will involve both researcher and researched needing to address how their respective roles might promote and/or defend against learning and change.

Relatedness is an important issue in research as learning because one of the basic aspects of action research and human inquiry models is the breaking down of traditional relations between researcher and researched. In more positivist forms of research, the relationship between the knower and the known must be a cautious one in which the researcher remains somehow 'outside' the research (Lincoln and Guba, 1985). It is held that if the researcher is detached from the researched, if she or he does not engage, then the research remains free from values and bias. In research as learning the idea of a detached researcher is rejected. Instead, the researcher attempts to assess interaction from within as a collaborative and/or participative process (Reason, 1988; Whyte, 1991). This means that the roles of the researcher and the researched are not as clear cut, and that the relatedness between the roles of researcher and researched is a key process issue that needs to be managed.

In the above example, the researcher had a fairly limited perception of her role in the focus group. She found that it was difficult to manage the consequences of the procedure she had adopted for the inquiry, in relation to the experiences of the people within the research. In order to do this effectively she needed to examine more closely her own feelings and perspectives on spirituality and their place within the organisation she belonged to. In such instances it is important for the researcher to have worked on and recorded his or her own positionality or role, and to have refined the research process on this basis, so that the underlying meanings between "me, them and us" (Reason and Marshall, 1987) can be utilised. This involves a pre-group, reflective stage on the following aspects: (i) thinking through and recording personal experience of the subject; (ii) the imagined and known experiences of the researched; (iii) an understanding of the role that is being taken in the research; and (iv) how the processes within the research affect the `here and now' of research groups.

Emotion

Another way of perceiving the concept of relatedness is in terms of the "emotional substrata of experience" (Krantz, 1990a) which is evoked by involvement in action research and human inquiry for both the researcher and the researched. The emotions aroused in people involved in the research will be varied, but will certainly reflect both the anxieties inherent in working on a particular subject, and the anxieties that emerge as a result of collaborating with others.

In the example that I have given, there were many anxieties, some of which were an integral aspect of the emotional reality of the experience (ie, a group of people coming together for the first time), and others emerged as the process progressed (ie, was it all right to say what was said here, did it go too far?). Sensitivity to the process of research as learning involves an analysis of underlying emotions and their expression through emerging patterns of experience, understanding and behaviour. These will be imported into the research as personal or collective dependency and/or bias, and will be expressed both in terms of their enactment and their avoidance.

Acceptance and inclusion of the underlying emotions that are brought to and stimulated within the process of research as learning mean that the researcher has to work with the impact of that emotion on the research as it evolves. As such, underlying emotional experience offers an important additional layer of data. The researcher has to consider how such emotions can be captured or "bracketed out" (Reason, 1988) from the research, both in terms of her or his emotions, and in terms of those that are stimulated within the research process. In addition, research as learning asks the researcher to reflect on how decisions about methods might affect the emotional complexity present within the study.

Power

One of the basic propositions of research as learning is that "research can never be neutral" (Bennett, 1991, p 76), and that power is a constant issue within research. It is, therefore, a critical theory which is "tied to an emancipatory interest" and which "seeks to free individuals from domination both by others and from forces that they do not understand or control, including those ones that are created by and between people" (Giddens, 1993, p 67).

One assumption, often made by students in relation to action research and human inquiry, is that the interchangeability of, and collaboration between, the roles of researcher and researched in some way neutralises the power differences between them. In fact, such an acknowledgement explicitly brings to light the power issues present in research, in terms of both the practice and the understanding of different research roles. In many approaches to management research, the ways in which a research process might itself render people either powerful or powerless, is not an insignificant question. In research as learning it is one of the most important.

In the example I have given, the researcher's strategy for managing her role (detached observation) was based on the assumption that this stance would enable her to keep her 'bias' (ie, her own emotional and political predispositions) out of the group. This position was shown to be naive, because her stance was experienced by the participants as withholding, insensitive and detached. Whatever the researcher's stance – the level of involvement or detachment; the patterns of difference and disadvantage; the issues surrounding different identities – it will reflect the social power relations present in, and created by, the research. research as learning will involve noticing, capturing and considering such power relations as an integral aspect of self-reflexive practice. In this way, it can clearly define and investigate the *context* of power and powerlessness in the research as an integral aspect of the study. The complexities, uncertainties, values and emotions underlying research within its context can be brought to light through explicit engagement with the power relations present within a research project.

In research as learning there can be no such thing as bias free inquiry. Instead, it is appropriate to pursue actively the question of bias, because the identification and recording of emotional and political predispositions makes it possible to separate out different levels of engagement and analysis. The differences, disadvantages and discrimination underlying research within its context can often be brought to light through explicit attempts to capture individual, group or organisational bias. It is also necessary to consider how bias is 'mobilised' (Lukes, 1974) as a form of power in the external context of a research study. For example, it is not unknown for research to be 'mobilised' in support of organisational directions that have already been decided upon.

Unconscious dynamics

Research as learning acknowledges that the research process is shaped by unconscious processes (Berg and Smith, 1988) which connect to the issues of relatedness, emotion and power. The approach is therefore concerned to work with the 'here and now' of learning within the research, as well as the research within management learning. This concern emerges from a recognition of the importance of unconscious material in promoting and knowing about management and about organisational learning and change (Kets de Vries and Miller, 1985; Hirschhorn, 1990).

A variety of questions arise at this point. How is it possible to work with those unconscious tendencies between researcher and researched that are present in research projects? What function do the researched serve for the researcher (or vice versa)? How are individual and group projections acknowledged, recorded and managed? How are participants engaging with each other and the researcher in terms of previous relationships, dependencies or attachments?

One way to answer these questions is to consider how clinical approaches to research (Berg and Smith, 1988; Kets de Vries, 1990) can inform research as learning. There are many psychodynamic concepts that can be utilised in understanding the dynamics of the research process. For example, defence mechanisms (Oldham and Kleiner, 1990; Argyris, 1989); parallel process (Berg and Smith, 1988); and self–object relations (Diamond, 1990). However, the two I wish to concentrate on here are transference and countertransference.

The concept of transference is central in clinical work. It is important to separate its meaning as a psychoanalytic concept, and as an everyday occurrence (what Spero, 1994 has referred to as "big-T Transference and little-t transference"). In psychotherapy, Transference is an organising activity indicating the continuing influence of a person's early formative experiences. It involves repeated behaviour patterns that are based on specific relationships, usually parental ones. Although Transference is most noticeable in psychotherapeutic settings, transference occurs to some extent in every relationship. Everyday transference has been well researched, for example, in terms of the leader/follower relationship (Kets de Vries, 1989a and 1989b). The researcher therefore, in his or her role, is likely to be the subject of transference that impacts on the research process.

This type of everyday, organisationally situated transference involves a recognition that the individual (group or organisation) evolves and perpetuates not solely as a result of its own identity, but *in relation* to others' perceptions and fantasies of that identity. Self-perception and others' perceptions are locked together, creating a 'dynamic' engagement which continually positions, defines and shapes the individual (group or organisation). This dynamic is not just a process between individuals, but also between individuals within a group; between groups within the organisation; and between organisations.

The researcher is prone to being experienced and positioned in many ways, for example, as the expert, as the enemy or as some form of saviour. Similarly, the researched are prone to being positioned and experienced in various ways, for example, as a set of opinions without feelings. Such dynamics have a profound impact on the construction, management and development of the research process. In the example I have given, the difference between her expectations and her experience of the focus group was so powerful that the researcher abandoned her study altogether (and retrained as a plumber). Powerful feelings and projections are likely to be evoked in methods of action research and human inquiry because they are explicitly related to the study of human engagement. In addition to this, there are underlying forces (competition, envy, defensiveness) that are characteristic of the external context of management research. An analysis of the underlying or unconscious dynamics as an integral part of the process of research as learning will lead towards a more comprehensive knowledge of the reasons for individual, group and organisational behaviour and action.

Issues of validity in research as learning

In this short section I discuss research as learning in relation to research validity. I intend to do this by highlighting a variety of cross-validating processes. The concept of validity from a phenomenological viewpoint centres around the question: "has the researcher gained full access to the knowledge and meanings of informants?" (Easterby-Smith et al, 1991, p 41). This requires an approach which explicitly seeks to bring multiple layers of knowledge and meaning to the surface, involving engagement with the underlying processes in the research. Research as learning as I define it, therefore, is an attempt to show how 'full access' can be gained, not only to the knowledge and meaning of the researched, but also to the intersecting knowledge and meaning of the researcher, and to the dynamic created between them.

A broad sense of sufficient "richness and complexity" (Patton, 1990) in phenomenological approaches emerges through the use of a variety of cross-validating techniques. These might include:

- A wide variety of different types of data and data sources. I have emphasised that a specific understanding of 'the process' of research enables the researcher to plan and capture more varied levels of data. For example, to capture both conscious and unconscious process; emotional as well as rationalised experience; and different levels of power and powerlessness. This might also involve an inter-organisational component, "linking organisations together in networks of development projects" (Engelstad and Gustavsen, 1993).

- Utilising the interpretations of a variety of researchers. The interpretations of the researcher need to be contextualised effectively in order to ensure their validity. This can be achieved through inviting multiple interpretations of the data from within and outside the organisation(s) studied. As Reason and Rowan (1981) point out, "valid research cannot be conducted alone". This also applies to multiple theoretical interpretations and multiple methods of study.

- Seeking reactions to written descriptions. The responses of research participants to interim written descriptions, or to the actual material from which the analysis was undertaken, provides additional layers of interpretation which can be used comparatively within the overall research. The researcher is seeking both to maintain clarity within his or her role, and at the same time to promote the collaboration and engagement of participants.

- 'Falsification' processes. Torbert (1991) emphasises the importance of undertaking a 'negative analysis' within action research. Conscious attempts by the researcher(s) to deny, contradict and disprove the data provide opportunities for highlighting problematic elements of the approach.

- Finding ways of checking back. Action research and human inquiry are concerned with experiential knowing, with the everyday development of learning and change within a context. If researchers want to move beyond impressionistic conclusions, then it is important for them to build in processes for checking back on the data, on the design, on the methods, and in relation to categories for analysis. This notion is at the heart of research as learning because it implies continuous development and the impermanence of knowledge and meaning. The systematic use of processes designed in relation to 'double-loop' learning will ensure that all frameworks become interim, and that they allow for the possibility of change.

Although these processes assist in working with the issue of validity within action research and human inquiry approaches, the clearest way to relate to this concept is as a continual question that needs to be posed at all stages of a research process.

Concluding reflections

My argument to this point has been as follows. A learning perspective in management research explicitly engages with questions that arise out of the examination of principles and processes of research as learning. I have identified and explained four key issues that seem particularly important as a description of processes of research as learning. All four issues point the researcher towards a need to reflect consciously and skilfully on their experience within the overall learning context of the research. I assert that research as learning requires engagement with the self, with social and political issues, with organisational contexts, and with organisational dynamics as an integral part of any study and analysis.

The application of the questions within the research as learning grid provides a mechanism for access to distinct layers of knowledge and meaning. My own values are both subjected to and subject to the issues that emerge from the social and political context within which the work is based.

> All research is grounded in consciousness, because it isn't possible to do research (or life) in such a way that we can separate ourselves from experiencing what we experience as people (and researchers) involved in a situation. There is no way we can avoid deriving theoretical constructs from experience because we necessarily attempt

> to understand what's going on as we experience
> it. (Stanley and Wise, 1983)

The subject of this research in this book is learning and change, the subject in the research is learning and changing. The action research projects that I describe in Part Two of this book provide an illustration of the practice of research as learning as it has evolved for me over a 10-year period. The action research I have undertaken was designed to engage with the relatedness between different levels of understanding and commitment to equality in practice, as well as with different perspectives and strategies on equality within organisations. Latterly, I have become more and more interested in capturing the emotional experiences relating to the individual, the group and the organisation, as well as exploring the everyday politics of equality. The designs I use have emerged as a part of my attempts to acknowledge the emotional and political predispositions on equality that exist at different levels of power within an organisation.

In this chapter I have been exploring what may be distinctive about management research undertaken from a perspective on management learning. I use a variety of broadly phenomenological approaches to abstract some general principles that influence research in the field of management learning, and I set these in relation to various key issues that seem to me to have a particular influence on the learning process. The ensuing matrix, the research as learning grid, presents a framework of questions which can be used to define a context for research within the field of management learning. The grid is also an attempt to highlight and define the specific dynamics that are part of the processes of both research and learning. I have attempted to identify these dynamics, and to describe how they can be explicitly worked with in the process of management research.

I perceive the grid as supportive of management research with an emphasis on learning, and as a way of framing my own evolving perspective on research in the field of management learning. However, I expect and hope that the framework itself is interim, and that the continuing process of research will bring to the surface and change the ways in which learning and research are brought together, both for myself, for other researchers, and in terms of management and organisational research.

Learning occurs between a fear and a need. On the one hand, we feel the need to change if we are to accomplish our goals. On the other hand, we feel the anxiety of facing the unknown and unfamiliar. To learn significant things we must suspend some basic notions about our worlds and ourselves. That is one of 'the most frightening propositions for the ego. (Kofman and Senge, 1993, p 19)

Paradoxically, anxiety prevents learning, but anxiety is necessary to start learning as well. Managing learning or a change process means managing these two kinds of anxiety. (Schein, 1993a, p 89) *two*

Management learning: thinking about learning from experience

In this chapter I explore some of the thinking behind management learning by discussing some of the theories that have informed my own view of management learning. I place a particular emphasis on learning from experience, in terms both of a theoretical body of work and of my own intellectual engagement with the processes involved.

I focus on the experiential because the notion that managers learn best from reflection on their own experience has provided a very powerful underlying model for the practice of management learning, particularly through the work of Revans (1971; 1983) and Kolb (1984). I reflect on and rethink how these approaches have been used in practice, thereby identifying three key problems. First, I believe there has been an overemphasis on individual experience and that this has led to an insufficient analysis of the social and political context of that experience. Second, there has been an overemphasis on the rational and intellectual aspects of learning from experience, as a result of the difficulty of managing and working with the emotions involved in learning and change. Third, existing models are inadequate for dealing with the social power relations of management learning, and how power relations within and outside learning groups contribute to the social construction of individual and group identity.

I highlight some of the political and emotional issues that are often omitted in approaches to experiential learning, in order to move towards a broader, more inclusive picture of learning from experience. Thus, my emerging definition of management learning is very bound up with rethinking experiential learning.

Learning and change

The starting point of my analysis is an acknowledgement of the relationship between learning and change, whichever way round you look at them:

- "The word learning undoubtedly denotes change of some kind" (Bateson, 1973).

- "The factor most likely to influence our capacity to change is our capacity to learn" (Plant, 1987).

My conceptual framework for management learning has been particularly influenced by three approaches. First, the work of Bateson (1973) which provides a general framework for understanding different 'levels' of learning. Second, the work of Freire (1972) who offers a perspective on the relationship between learning and power. Third, a range of literature which explores the psychodynamics of organisation (Jaques, 1990; Menzies-Lyth, 1990; Hirschhorn, 1990; Kets de Vries 1990; Hoggett, 1992).

Bateson (1973) identifies four levels of human learning and looks at their implications for change (Table 2).

Bateson's categories provide a framework that can be applied to an understanding of management learning, particularly in the tension between methods that encourage *reinforcement* (LI) and methods that encourage *change* (LII). Learning II is the theoretical site of experiential learning since it is here that experience and the development of knowledge meet. Learning and change may take place where it becomes possible for managers and organisations to break free from the constraints of habit, and develop new ways to apply experience in the context of management.

Table 2: Bateson's levels of learning

Levels	Implications
Zero learning	Zero learning is based on predictable or specific responses which are not subject to trial and error. Zero learning does not signify the capacity to reflect in any way to enable change, it is simply about response. Even the recognition of a wrong response would not contribute to any future skill.
Learning I	Learning I implies a change as a result of trial and error, within a set of alternatives. Correction does therefore have an implication for future action. In other words, this level has moved from stimulus/response to stimulus/response/reinforcement. Learning I is, therefore, about a process of habituation.
Learning II	Learning II implies some flexibility in the potential to act as opposed to reinforcement of action. It is therefore a change in the set of alternatives from which choice is made. Learning II implies a capacity to 'learn how to learn', in other words, a shift of the frameworks from which choices are made.
Learning III	Learning III is a shift in the underlying premises and belief systems that form frameworks. Level III Learning involves a capacity to 'make a corrective change in the system of sets of alternatives from which choice is made'. In other words, the capacity to examine the paradigm or regime within which action is based.

Source: Vince (1996)

Management learning is a field of knowledge that attempts to include the promotion of learning how to learn. It challenges processes of habituation. Change occurs through an acknowledgement of, and an interaction with, current habits and 'attachments' (Marris, 1986) as an integral aspect of the learning process. It is the result of the implementation of actions that emerge from the acknowledgement of being caught in some form of dependency. Change is not a potential outcome of learning, but is integral to it. If it is possible to learn how to learn by questioning our habits and attachments, then it is also possible to envisage that to learn this as a skill would have significant implications not just for our understanding of change but also for our ability to change. This then leads me to question how our habits in relation to learning are formed.

How we learn to limit learning

Our education system defines for us, as well as with us, what is 'useful' knowledge. The initial process of schooling implies, for example, that it is more useful to acquire the technical skills necessary for our role within various industries and professions than it is to acquire the political skills that allow us to assert our perceptions of what we want from such a role (Illich, 1971). As the subjects of the schooling process we are mainly required to be actively unquestioning. We are encouraged to be the recipients of knowledge predominantly defined for us rather than with us. The consequence of this is that:

> Many people learn not to think their own thoughts, to speak their own language i.e. to unlearn their own culture. People are, in a sense, being forced not to see the truth of their reality any longer. (Fritz, 1982, p 6)

Our schooling into society affects us as learners by promoting a dependency on other people's knowledge, and providing little support for the evolution, from an early age, of either political or emotional skills, critical or reflexive thinking.

The legacy of schooling and the consequent dependency we develop on particular learning processes, affect our adult understanding of how to learn. We can become defensive about ways of learning if what we are used to is challenged. Our familiarity with some forms of learning can act as a block against the exploration of other forms. Claxton (1984) describes such blocks in relation to the individual adult learner and characterises them as a personal defence system against non-familiar or threatening forms of learning, ie

- I must be COMPETENT
- I must be CONSISTENT
- I must be IN CONTROL
- I must be COMFORTABLE

The need to feel competent, consistent, in control and comfortable for ourselves and with others sets a boundary around our capacity to learn and to change. This boundary is built as a protection against anxiety and uncertainty, a protection against the unfamiliar. Claxton's analysis is useful in explaining the ease with which individuals create learning environments as places for the reinforcement of existing knowledge and experience (LI) rather than as opportunities for change (LII). At every opportunity for learning there are powerful emotions (eg, fear and anxiety) that can either promote or discourage change:

> Change is an excursion into the unknown. It implies a commitment to future events that are not entirely predictable as to their consequences, and inevitably provokes doubt and anxiety. (Menzies-Lyth, 1990, p 451)

Anxiety can be seen as a starting point of individual and group defences against learning and change. Individual 'defensive techniques', like depersonalisation and denial of feelings, easily become institutionalised within a group and become characteristic of its resistance to change (Jaques, 1955). Menzies-Lyth (1990) and Jaques (1990) have both undertaken studies which discuss how the social structure of an organisation is built and maintained as a result of anxiety, and how this creates social defences against change. Jaques' (early rather than current) work suggests that individual responses to a shared social situation combine, producing a common psychological response to organisational history and restraints, and that these interact with conscious goals. He sees this as an "unconscious use of institutions", to be conceived of dynamically:

> There is therefore a constant movement between shared social experiences of the institution, the meshing of individual responses into a common psychological response, and the dynamic and

evolving unconscious of the institution. (Samuels, 1993, p 281)

Any initiative where there is an intention to produce organisational learning and change must therefore work with the largely unconscious needs of individuals to manage anxiety. I will be returning to and developing this theme in greater detail later in the chapter.

The struggle to learn and to change can be both complex and uncomfortable, involving strong feelings and prolonged uncertainty. Paradoxically, individual and group defences are both helpful, because they contribute to the manageability of learning and change, and unhelpful, because they place restrictions on them (Schein, 1993b). Such defences create an outline within which change can be managed, but they also create a boundary within which change can be avoided. Management learning involves simultaneously thinking about the provision of opportunities for learning about change and for changing the way we learn. This means that those of us who are practitioners within this discipline will need to acknowledge and work with the educational and organisational boundaries that are perpetually and unconsciously created as an integral part of individual or organisational avoidance of change.

In addition to psychological issues, there are also political issues that limit learning, and which need to be considered in the development of experiential learning. One of the most fundamental propositions informing experiential learning is the notion that the review and development of individual experience forms the basic resource for learning (Smith, 1980). It often seems that such learning, because it focuses on the individual, is somehow detached from the social and political context of experience. Both individual and collective experience are invariably products of a social system, and in turn contribute to the capacity of that system to resist change. In other words, our experience is both conditioned by, and an exercise of, power (Roberts, 1996).

Learning and power

In order to explore the political context of experiential learning I want to discuss aspects of the work of the Brazilian educationalist,

Paulo Freire. The importance of Freire's work is that it takes into account the issue of power on two levels. First, it acknowledges the power of personal motivation towards change, activated and perpetuated through a process of experiential education. I would say that this is one part of the system of management education we are familiar with in the UK.   Second it acknowledges the educational importance of challenging oppressive and/or paternalistic societal values and norms as an integral aspect of the educational process. This aspect is often ignored by the system of management education we are familiar with in the UK.

Freire's work highlights a dual relationship between the learner and power. He explores how powerful it is for individuals to reflect on their own experiences in such a way that new perceptions about themselves and their world can be formulated. He also explores the tools that people need in order to interact within the society that exploits them. The forms of learning that we are primarily familiar with, in the many different scenarios of management education, consistently ignore this second, more political aspect of the learning process.

To expand on this I will look more closely at some of the issues Freire raises about learning and power. In *Pedagogy of the oppressed* (1972) he describes two types of learning. The first is "the banking concept of education":

> ... in which the students are the depositories and the teacher is the depositor. Instead of communicating, the teacher issues communiqués and makes deposits which the students patiently receive, memorise and repeat. (Freire, 1972, p 45)

Freire's concern in describing this 'banking' model is to demonstrate that such learning is an 'exercise in domination'. He proposes instead a 'problem-posing' form of learning, a balance of action and reflection of people upon their world explicitly in order to change it. Such a shift is a step towards confronting one aspect of the hegemony of the banking model. Learning requires engagement with the educational process (in addition to content) as a fundamental part of the evolution and development of contextually relevant knowledge. Such action struggles with the boundary of the educational process, seeking to redefine it as a clarification not just of available knowledge, but also of its oppressive and/or liberatory nature. Therefore:

> Whereas banking education anaesthetises and inhibits creative power, problem-posing education involves a constant unveiling of reality. The former attempts to maintain the submersion of consciousness; the latter strives for the emergence of consciousness and critical intervention in reality. (Freire 1972, p 54)

Table 3 explains the relationship between the 'banking' and the 'problem-posing' models in more detail.

Table 3: Freire's banking and problem-posing models

The banking model	The problem-posing model
1. The Teacher knows The Student doesn't know	1. Student and Teacher exchange knowledge through 'dialogue'
2. The Teacher talks The Student listens	2. A process of reflection and action for both: 'a process of becoming'
3. The Teacher chooses The Student complies	3. 'Critical intervention' ie, consciousness of and within the learning environment
4. The Teacher's experience is primary, the Student's is secondary	4. Begins from the Student's experience/expertise
Therefore the Student is: – Passive – An 'empty cup' – A spectator not a participant	*Therefore the Student is:* – Active – A 'full cup' – A participant not a spectator

Source: Vince (1996)

In the banking model, the relatedness between teacher and taught is not constrained by a desire to generate, develop or change knowledge, merely to exchange it through deposits and withdrawals. My role as teacher can be defined in simple terms: I know and you don't, I speak and you listen, I choose what and how you learn, and you comply, because the idea of praxis (Freire, 1972, p 60) is anathema. In the problem-posing model teacher and taught are both in a 'process of becoming', a process whose success depends on the 'dialogue' between us. Thus, my consciousness of the role of teacher, your consciousness of the role of taught, is constructed and enacted through a dialogue, that is, as a result of the relatedness between these two roles in terms of both the content and process of learning. Such a model opens up the politics of learning, by recognising the social and contextual construction of consciousness.

The banking model relies on the individual authority of the teacher and the individual passivity of the student. To maintain this relationship, power must be excluded as an issue within learning. In the problem-posing model, experiential learning is not about an individualised experience. Rather, it concerns related experience, involving the individual, the group and the system. Power is thereby acknowledged as an ever-present and dynamic force, helping to define and redefine the experience of learning.

The main concept used by Freire to propose a way forward is that of 'dialogue'. The word dialogue signifies that the relationship of power between learners in a learning process (whether they are the teachers or the taught) is not an individualistic one, that is, "knowing is a social event with nevertheless an individual dimension" (Freire and Shor, 1987, p 99). The 'educator' enters into dialogue with the social reality of the student as well as with their individual reality. In this way the problem-posing model is a challenge to those who dominate the individual as much as to the individual themselves. Therefore:

> ... the teacher has the right but also the duty to challenge the status quo, especially in the question of the domination by sex, race or class. What the dialogical educator does not have the right to impose is his or her position. But the liberating teacher can never stay silent on social questions, can never wash his or her hands of them. (Freire and Shor, 1987, p 174)

Freire's work provides an approach to understanding the nature of management education not simply in terms of the experiential reality of the individual, but in relation to the social reality in which the learning process is itself situated.

In experiential learning environments it is possible to work explicitly with the social and political nature of learning. Such a perspective involves working with various issues. First, it is necessary to acknowledge socially constructed and reinforced differences (class, race, gender, disability differences). Active engagement with the consequences of such differences has to be an integral rather than suppressed aspect of educational process. The suppression of this social reality in much experiential learning contributes to the alienation of individual and group identities from the learning process.

Second, there are complex processes of power at work in management education. To an extent these can be explained as processes of 'structuration' (Giddens, 1976; 1984). Giddens' theory of structuration asserts the 'duality of structure': structures are not only produced by human action but are also the medium of human action. People draw on various material and authoritative resources in the course of their interactions, and in doing so maintain "regularised relations of autonomy and dependence" (Giddens, 1984, p 16). Giddens depicts power as being bound up in relations of reciprocal autonomy and dependence, which he terms "the dialectic of control". A learning environment is a powerful and contained arena for viewing negotiations on autonomy and dependence. This is particularly focused on expectations and feelings about the respective roles of tutor and student.

Finally, a political perspective on experiential learning provides the connection between management learning as a here-and-now experience, and the experienced reality of politics or power in organisational life. Therefore, the boundary or the 'margin' between what is happening in an experiential group now, and its mirror image in experience of management and organisation, becomes the focal point for both learning and change. It is the learner's capacity to work with marginality as the site of experiential learning that will create possibilities for learning and change:

> I am located in the margin. I make a definite distinction between the marginality which is imposed by oppressive structures and that marginality one chooses as a site of resistance – as location of radical openness and possibility. This site of resistance is continually formed in that

segregated culture of opposition that is our critical response to domination. We come to this space through suffering and pain, through struggle. We know struggle to be that which pleasures, delights and fulfils desire. We are transformed, individually, collectively, as we make radical creative space which affirms and sustains our subjectivity, which gives us a new location from which to articulate our sense of the world. (hooks, 1991, p 153)

At this point I would like briefly to review and bring together the perspectives I have mentioned. Initially, I discussed Bateson's distinction between different 'levels' of learning in order to establish that experiential learning aims to encourage change through processes of reflecting and acting on meta-levels of experience – what Bateson refers to as learning how to learn (and therefore, learning how to change). From here I introduced the idea of learning and change as emotional as well as rational experiences, influenced and blocked by individual and collective anxiety. According to writers like Jaques and Menzies-Lyth, a powerful and dynamic organisational unconscious is created through the interplay of: individual anxiety that can structure an organisation, and the structure of an organisation that can promote anxiety. This psychological dynamic is also attached in organisations to a political dynamic, a dialectic of control. I used the work of Freire to explore the impact of social power relations in educational processes and to explain the social reality within which learning processes are situated. Finally, I referred to the importance of the boundary or margin as a place where individual identity meets the experienced reality of power in organisations. These perspectives provide a picture of what I feel experiential management learning involves.

I now want to look in more detail at some of the dominant theoretical models underpinning current approaches to management learning, and at how they might be developed to express a practice which perpetuates both learning and change.

Learning and management

Many of the approaches which provide the theoretical basis for the education of managers are firmly rooted in the experiential reality of the individual in the context of the group. 'Learning from experience' has been a strong theme in management education since the 1950s and 1960s, through such mechanisms as 'T-Groups' or 'sensitivity training'. Although T-Groups arise from the work of Lewin (1951) the term became a generic one for a range of development methods which sought to enhance individual and group learning (Handy, 1985). The methods used might vary considerably, but the aim in relation to individuals within groups can be generally expressed as:

> An approach ... which, broadly speaking, provides participants with an opportunity to learn more about themselves and their impact on others, and in particular to learn how to function more effectively in face to face situations. (Cooper and Mangham, 1971, p 23)

The primary mechanism for such learning is feedback from other members of a group, prompting individual self-examination, the consideration of new values, attitudes and behaviour. Such approaches emphasise that issues like disclosure, which have an emotional content or 'risk-factor' are often subverted or avoided in management and organisation. Since much of management is undertaken within groups or teams, these and other inter-personal skills enhance (or at least clarify) the relationships between people engaged in management tasks. The idea of learning as a process integral to everyday management experience is a strong theme in the literature which underpins management learning. Revans' (1971; 1983) 'action learning' process and Kolb's (1984) work on 'learning cycles', are influential models.

Although both of these models have arisen on the basis of a challenge to rationalistic approaches to management and organisation, I want to argue that they both fall short of providing a way of integrating the emotional and political into management learning. I have explained elsewhere (Vince and Martin, 1993; Vince, forthcoming) that the application of these models has often tended to encourage the rational/intellectual skills of managers in interpreting and working with their experience. This has led in some cases to reflection on experience being constructed or interpreted as managers 'thinking about their experience' (Mifsud, 1990), emphasising the rational nature of the reflective process. If, as I outlined earlier, part of learning from experience is about working with the emotional and power dynamics generated in the learning processes, then the reflective process also needs to occur through a combination of the rational, the emotional and the political.

Models like those of Revans and Kolb can only be helpful if there is an explicit recognition of the relationship between an individual's capacity to integrate rational, emotional and political experience. Our tendency as learners to avoid and deny the emotional and political aspects of management learning means that thinking about experience tends to dominate. In this chapter I suggest developments in both models in order to encourage and extend the possibilities for exploring emotionally based experience and for representing the politics of experiential learning. Such an exercise is important in rethinking management learning because it has proved very easy to over-emphasise the rational/intellectual aspects of learning from experience. In turn, this has led to problems for managers and management educators in fully representing the change process within our work.

Revans and action learning

I want to explore this representation of change processes in detail through the development of the Action Learning Cycle. Action learning was developed as an approach for managers to work on real work tasks as learning experiences (Revans, 1971; 1983). Action learning is constructed as an approach to individual development, but it is also important in the strategic task of integrating learning into the everyday working lives of managers, and consequently of creating organisations where learning, and therefore change, are taken seriously. The original features of action learning have been summarised by Mumford (1992) and developed in a variety of ways by others (Pedler and Boutall, 1992; McGill and Beaty, 1995).

Within the action learning process Revans perceived learning to be based on the interaction between two kinds of learning, programmed knowledge (P) which is the introduction of knowledge or skills, and questioning (Q) which is the process of exploring such knowledge in practice. This allowed him to formulate the equation: $L = P + Q$ or, learning occurs when programmed knowledge meets questioning insight. Revans (1983) emphasises that behavioural change is more likely to occur as a result of reflection on experience (questioning insight) than on the acquisition of programmed knowledge. Reflection with other managers, who may well be engaged in similar issues of management practice, therefore affords the most practical and effective learning process. Management learning is achieved both through focusing on real work problems, and as a result of managers learning from and with each other.

The structure of the action learning approach to reflection on experience has five successive stages: observation, provisional hypothesis, trial, audit and review. This can be represented as a 'cycle' or developmental loop, returning again and again to different situations and phenomena (see Figure 1). Revans (1983, p 17) describes these five stages as "the intellectual structuring of experience to achieve a command over the world", in essence an intellectual process of reflection and action which affects everyday practice.

Figure 1: The action learning cycle

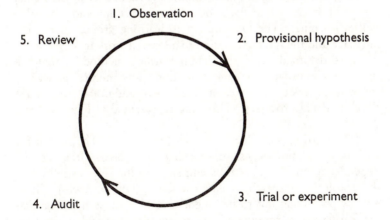

1. Observation

5. Review

2. Provisional hypothesis

4. Audit

3. Trial or experiment

The emphasis of Revans' model is on the use of intellectual processes to review experience. He uses the phrase 'the scientific method' to describe action learning. The model concentrates on the rational aspects of learning, providing a map of the intellectual processes involved. However, it does not, I feel, explore or offer models for the understanding of those emotional or political processes that also underpin learning. In his writing on action learning, Revans does discuss the emotional and psychological implications of the approach, but in general and rather dismissive terms:

> ... exercises such as sensitivity training, non-directive counselling and other excursions into group psychotherapy are but rarely anchored to the here and now demands of business. (Revans, 1983, p 64)

His views seem to create two problems. First, the model or method does not openly consider the effects of emotional resistance to or avoidance of learning. Implicit in the model is an assumption that emotions such as fear and anxiety are managed separately from the issue of addressing the work task. This exclusion effectively dismisses the process of individual and group defensiveness against learning which is always present within learning and working groups. Second, the rationality of the model does not make an analysis of power and oppression possible within learning. The bias present in learning groups shapes the language and the interaction used to address a work task.

In order to develop the action learning method so that the underlying approach recognises emotional and political as well as rational processes I have outlined two additional five stage developmental processes. These are represented in Figures 2 and 3.

The starting point for both cycles is anxiety. The reason for this is that approaches to learning that break free of the dependency on a teacher thus emphasising the responsibilities of the learner and thereby create anxiety (Claxton, 1984). It is anxiety-provoking not to be taught or told because it means that the learner is confronted with the responsibility for what and how they need to learn. Such responsibility has both psychological and political implications: psychological because the individual may need to overcome fears, for example 'getting it wrong' or 'taking a lead' and political because getting it wrong or taking a lead always have an impact on the social system within which the learning is taking place.

Figure 2: Cycle of emotions promoting learning

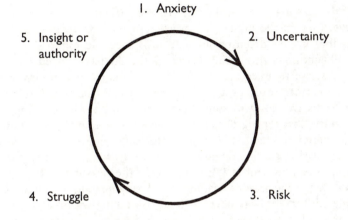

1. Anxiety

5. Insight or authority

2. Uncertainty

4. Struggle

3. Risk

Figure 3: Cycle of emotions discouraging learning

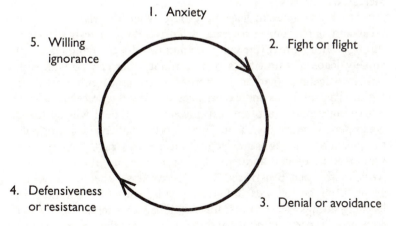

1. Anxiety

5. Willing ignorance

2. Fight or flight

4. Defensiveness or resistance

3. Denial or avoidance

The emphasis of Revans' original model leans strongly towards what managers *think* about their experience, rather than what they *feel* about their experience. Such an emphasis allows anxiety to be denied and discarded. A dependency on the rational aspects of the model deny the emotional reality that is constantly present in learning groups.

If the starting point in the rational cycle (Figure 1) is what we observe, then in the underlying cycles it is what we fear – those things that inspire defensiveness and resistance. In Figure 2 (the cycle of emotions promoting learning) the anxiety created from fear gives rise to uncertainty. Some participants in experiential groups are more ready or able than others to be challenged, or to move themselves towards some new or revised knowledge. Their uncertainty, that feeling of being on the edge of change, does not get the better of them, rather it creates the conditions for risk-taking. Risks are many and varied in learning groups: the expression of powerful feelings like anger; the risk of speaking or not speaking; the risk of leading or of staying out. Individuals struggle with the consequences of their risk-taking within a group. They may have to struggle through other people's reactions, or with their own emotions at having aired something long suppressed. The result of this cycle of uncertainty, risk and struggle is a feeling of empowerment involving either an insight or increased authority.

There are times in learning groups when the risk seems too great and our intuition towards defensiveness and resistance win through. In Figure 3 (the cycle of emotions discouraging learning) anxiety leads not to a form of uncertainty that can be withheld, rather to feelings that set in motion reactions of either fight or flight. The emotions and experiences an individual receives within a learning group can often feel unwelcome. There will be times when people in groups are not ready to be challenged or not able to question existing knowledge. Invariably, such feelings are supported by denials and avoidance strategies and, if these do not work, with open resistance and defensiveness either towards the group itself or towards individuals within it. It is common in learning groups for example, for individuals to attempt to create a scapegoat in order to avoid and defend against their own need to change. As individuals set up denials, defences and avoidances so they are creating the right conditions for their own willing ignorance.

The following examples of managerial behaviour, drawn from my work with action-learning groups, help to explain these models further:

An individual manager is working on her problem, the difficulty of relating to a member of her staff. One of her colleagues in the set notices that the manager seems to be avoiding her competitiveness with her subordinate, and questions her on it. Our manager's immediate feeling is to deny the competition, yet something in what her set colleague has said rings true. She feels suddenly on the spot, uncertain, as if she would rather be elsewhere. However, because she felt some truth had been acknowledged she talks about envying her staff member's ability to be liked by the rest of the team. Through their questioning, the set help her to struggle through her own feelings of difficulty in being in the managerial role. The experience in the set eventually provides her with the insight that her envy is a block to her effectiveness both with the specific individual and with her team. She resolves to undertake some practical actions which she imagines will overcome this particular problem.

A senior administrative manager is working on his difficulty with delegating to his staff. He manages a team mostly of women, and some set members have begun to question him about his difficulty passing his work on to his women staff. The things he is saying about the women who work for him seem to be both controlling and rather paternalistic. When challenged, he insists that this is not the issue, and resists this 'irrelevant' questioning, emphasising that he always treats everybody equally in his team. He feels as though he has to fight off this line of questioning by the set in order to get to the 'real' issue. Some set members see this as an avoidance of issues that would make a difference if he could take them on board. Our manager becomes more and more defensive about the problem he is addressing, he feels that the women in his set are being 'bloody feminists'. The experience in the set convinces him that he doesn't have a problem and is a much misunderstood person. To shut the group up he says he will talk to his staff and see what they say.

The two cycles of emotion illustrated here attempt to describe that point in a learning group where an individual, a part of the group, or even the group as a whole has the (largely unconscious) option to move in the direction either of self-empowerment or self-limitation, of change or non-change. An awareness of the separate emotional forces that promote or discourage learning will provide improved opportunities for experiential groups to manage and make sense of processes of change, both personal and organisational.

The application of experiential models in isolation from emotions that either promote or discourage learning, supports and perpetuates two complementary difficulties for managers: their over-reliance on the intellectual experience of their work, and their fears about emotions at work. Thus, managers can quickly come to value the task-oriented or problem-solving aspects of the Revans or Kolb models without addressing their own emotional experience of work. The feelings generated (feelings that might produce learning and change if the manager could own up to them) become detached or 'split' from the objectives of the group. The same process that banishes emotion from work organisations affects the learning group. In other words, the learning group begins to mirror the constraints on knowledge and understanding present in the manager's work.

It is possible, therefore, that the models which commonly underpin management learning and which are explicitly designed to work with managerial experience, can also help an individual to deny what such experience means, especially its emotional meaning. The danger is that an experiential group can develop the same self-limiting structure characteristic of the organisation it comes from, where emotional meanings are suppressed as a result of managerial fears about their consequences. The potential for understanding and working with change in such circumstances is considerably lessened.

To accept the notion that emotional meanings are suppressed allows for a clearer understanding of the politics of experiential learning. In order to highlight this the two cycles of emotion promoting or discouraging learning (Figures 2 and 3) have been combined to create Figure 4.

Contact between people in experiential groups suggests contact between differing emotional realities, different systems of meaning, different types of bias. The encounter between people in a learning environment is, therefore, necessarily a political process. The word 'political' signifies social power relations both at the institutional and interpersonal levels and their effects on the individual and the group. People are positioned unequally in and by organisations and groups as a consequence of social constructions of their identity. Consequently, women and men, black and white, disabled and able-bodied, gay and straight people have to address differential experiences of power and powerlessness as aspects of their organisational practice and of management learning.

The power and powerlessness of individuals within learning groups is an integral aspect of the group process. Both power and powerlessness can be avoided or denied; they can become fixed, or they can change and evolve. The impact of the relationship between power and process constantly shapes the agendas and the practice of experiential management education. Consequently, it is important to consider how power relations are acknowledged and worked with. All educational contexts represent and replicate, within their own internal processes, external social power relations. Transactions between individuals in learning groups can also serve to act out or re-stimulate power struggles, and the intense emotions associated with power and difference, that is, fear, hatred, rage, contempt. The intensity of these emotions, and anxiety about how to deal effectively with power relations in groups and organisations, means that educational or learning groups have an interest in defending against and avoiding these issues. Group members, at various stages in their interactions within learning groups, move backwards and forwards between positions or roles as the powerful and the powerless. Such positions are a reflection of the politics of learning in groups.

Thus we can see that the emotions which promote or discourage learning are affected by the internal politics of a learning group, and it is the struggle between these two emotional states which underpins and explains the nature of the political struggles within a learning group (see Figure 4).

The political nature of experiential management education is expressed through the strategic choice available to learning group members to move in a direction that promotes learning, or a direction that discourages learning. In other words, movement towards either risk or denial/avoidance is often a political, as well as an emotional, act on behalf of the individual.

Figure 4: The politics of action learning

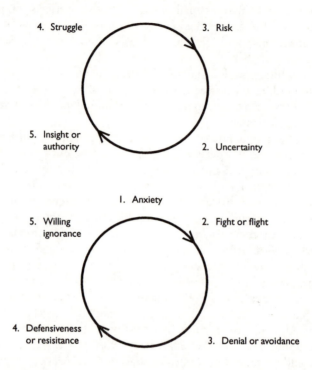

The examples above, already used to clarify both cycles, can be referred to again. In the example of the 'senior administrative manager' the political motivation for his behaviour is clearly to defend his power against the assumed or actual threat posed by either his female staff, by female colleagues, by the notion of equality in practice, or by a combination of all three. The manager's defensiveness or silence is strategic, it is a political mechanism employed to defend authority. In the example of the 'team leader' there is an advantage to this manager in accepting herself as a block to her own effectiveness. Her choice to risk working through this emotional material can also be seen as strategic, as it may increase both her standing in the team (because she can admit to being human) and the general effectiveness of the team. This manager takes such a risk because there is a good chance it will strengthen her authority.

Kolb and experiential learning

Kolb's learning cycle is one of the most well known illustrations in management education, and has become the key theoretical model to express the nature of experiential learning (Cunningham, 1994). The cycle is represented in Figure 5.

Figure 5: Kolb's learning cycle

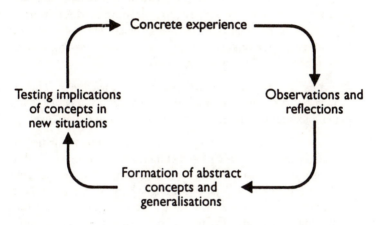

Kolb (1984, p 26) maintains that "learning is the process whereby knowledge is created through the transformation of experience". He offers six propositions that characterise the transformation of experience, and these form the theoretical basis for the cycle.

1. *Learning is best conceived as a process, not in terms of outcomes.* Ideas are continually formed and reformed through experience and this process stimulates inquiry and skill in 'knowledge getting'.

2. *Learning is a continuous process grounded in experience.* "If the education process begins by bringing out the learner's beliefs and theories, examining and testing them, and then integrating the new, more refined ideas into the person's belief systems, the learning process will be facilitated". (Kolb, 1984, p 28)

3. *The process of learning requires the resolution of conflicts between dialectically opposed modes of adaptation to the*

world. "In the process of learning one moves in varying degrees from actor to observer, and from specific involvement to general analytic detachment". (Kolb, 1984, p 31)

4. *Learning is a holistic process of adaptation to the world.* It involves the integration of thinking, feeling, perceiving and behaving.

5. *Learning involves transactions between the person and the environment.* This suggests a dual meaning to the notion of experience such that internal experience (eg, of joy and happiness) inter-relates with external or environmental experience (eg, 20 years doing this job).

6. *Learning is the process of creating knowledge.* This is achieved through interaction between subjective life experiences and more objective human cultural experience.

The model or cycle emerges in Point 3, from the polarities of actor/observer and involvement/detachment. This is then linked to various ideas that constitute the key human processes of shaping or developing the self, that is, becoming whole, being in context, creating knowledge. At the heart of the approach is the idea that the individual can manage his or her own learning through reflecting on experience, and can therefore be in control of his or her own self-development.

Over the past 20 years the learning cycle has influenced both research in and the implementation of management education and management development (Gill and Johnson, 1991). Part of the attraction of the cycle is that it accommodates both deductive (moving from abstract concepts to testing their implications) and inductive (concrete experience leading to reflective practice) approaches to theory in management education, thereby providing a bridge between objectivity and subjectivity, positivism and phenomenology.

Within organisations and on management courses the learning cycle has been used as the basis for helping managers to understand the notion of learning from experience. Exploration of the cycle has helped managers to see that learning can occur either from an individual's rationality or their emotional reality. The four stages of the cycle imply: (i) a direct experience where either thoughts or feelings or both are generated; (ii) a process of reflecting on thoughts or feelings; (iii) drawing rational conclusions or emotional insights about experience; (iv) implementing, testing and initiating action from the experience (see Figure 6). The cycle encourages managers and other learners to perceive a whole process of learning and to identify those parts of the process where – for whatever reason – individuals are dependent on, or stuck in, particular parts of experiential awareness.

In management development contexts, the popularity of the learning cycle arises in part from its accessibility to managers, both as a way of comprehending the processes of individual and organisational learning and development, and in terms of perceiving aspects of the process that may currently be omitted (eg, managers often say something like 'I jump to conclusions without spending time thinking about what I have just done'). The learning cycle has been widely used as an expression of the process of learning for managers within organisations.

The learning cycle is an accessible way of expressing both the importance of experiential knowledge, and the link between theory and practice. However, whenever I come across the learning cycle (which I do with amazing regularity) I do feel uneasy because it seems to me that there are other aspects to experiential learning that remain unexpressed in the current model.

Figure 6: Kolb's cycle expressed specifically in relation to experience

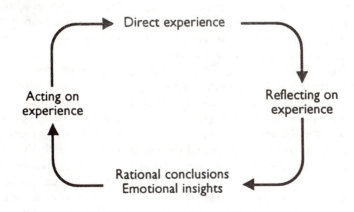

The emphasis of Kolb's model is on individual experience and how this affects and is affected by social reality. Experience is not seen as being constructed, shaped and contained by 'social power relations'. (In using this term I refer to the idea that people are positioned unequally in and by organisations and groups as a consequence of social constructions of their identity). The effect of this is that the learning cycle appears to be rather a-political, assuming that people are able to speak about their experience in their own voice. This is sometimes possible. Equally possible is that the reality of people's experience is denied and called into question, which is a particular dynamic of oppressive relations (Martin, 1994).

Consequently, there is a need to look beyond Kolb's learning cycle for an integration of a *political* dimension to experiential learning which is not currently contained in the model. There are two aspects to this, reflecting the workings of power on both external and internal experience. First, all levels of experience in the cycle are constructed, shaped and contained by social power relations. Second, complex and unequal relations around knowledge are constructed between people as an integral part of the learning process. This means that learning groups continually reproduce and renegotiate unequal relations among their members and that this corresponds to emotional and unconscious levels of experience. The emphasis of Kolb's model is on the direct experience of the individual, but including power in the model will involve a shift of emphasis whereby direct experience needs to be seen in relation to *subjectivity* (Flax, 1993) not individuality. Subjectivity refers here to the creation and maintenance of individual identity within groups that are formed in society through unequal social power relations.

The effect of power is to define categories of people as particular kinds of subject. Thus, "power does not directly determine identity but merely provides the conditions of possibility for its self-formation" (Jermier, Knights and Nord, 1994, p 8). Clearly, individual experience is not detached from a network of power relations and discourses (Fraser, 1989) that at the same time help to form and to resist both the organisation of the self and the organisation containing the self. "The experience of power is inescapable whenever there is effective organisation, binding independent agents together, yoking them to the pursuit of a purpose made common" (Clegg, 1994b, p 164).

Subjectivities are achieved in organisations through inter-personal transactions of power (Martin, 1994), through the mobilisation of bias (Lukes, 1974) and through key episodes representing contextually specific aspects of power within an organisation (Vince, 1990). Power is a mobile and dynamic process which can offer the possibility for agency at the same time as restricting it. Learning, therefore, is in the possibility of being an agent, in being able to act in diverse ways; it is in the capacity of individuals to be an agent in the construction of the self as well as in the disciplining of the self (Hardy, 1994).

In terms of developments in relation to Kolb's learning cycle, this suggests the importance of attempting to extend the model from one that captures the evolution of individual learning from experience, towards a model that can acknowledge both the construction of that experience through complex and varied power relations, and the role that subjectivity plays in creating new relations of power and powerlessness. It is this complex and paradoxical ability to act from a space which is both bound by the shifting constraints of power (open to the challenge of inner creativity) and which stresses the central importance of relations with others (or the repression of such relations) that provides a more complex picture of the constitution, structure and ongoing experiences of a self within the wider context of social relations. It seems to me that experiential learning may become possible in the very play of power on the subject as well as through subjective transformation of relations to power.

The concept of experiential learning is in need of review because, contextually, things have changed since the learning cycle was developed. To an extent, Kolb's learning cycle can be seen as a reaction against research, education and development processes in the past that emphasised some fairly rigid and directive attempts to generate and to impart knowledge. The learning cycle was a crucial contribution to an understanding of the importance of experiential knowing. However, there will always be some things that are best not learned from direct experience. In general, these include such things as terminal illness, torture and extreme physical or psychological pain. In a more specific managerial or organisational context, examples may include sexual or racial harassment, the feelings engendered by managerial bullying, and (in most organisations) attempting one's own induction programme as a new member of staff, or leaving the implementation of health and safety to the discretion of each organisational member. Regardless of how much responsibility we take for learning from our own experience and learning with others, we still have to rely a great deal on learning from the experience of others. In the context of management education and development, when I say 'from the experience of others' I am not speaking about expert knowledge or traditional lecturing methods, I am referring to the complex and unequal relations around knowledge that are constructed between people and which are an integral part of the learning process.

Learning from experience in Kolb's model implies learning from something that has passed. The process involves generalising from memories that prompt future action. What it does not encourage is work with "here and now" (Yalom, 1985) experience in the present. This is a particularly important issue in management education and management development contexts where looking back on experiences in the past is sometimes a convenient way of avoiding what is in the present. The here and now provides an immediate and social context for past experience, a container within which past experience is both reflected upon *and* transformed. In practice, working with the collective or social context of here and now experience encourages managers to see how their behaviour and participation in the learning environment 'mirrors' their behaviour and participation within organisations. Working explicitly with this mirroring process gives managers the opportunity to risk new ways of behaving and participating within a (relatively) safe learning environment, and then to put these into action within the organisation (see Vince, 1995a,b,c).

Approaches to learning in educational institutions often recreate the learning environment in ways that defend against certain emotions. The apparent need, wherever possible, to exclude unwanted emotions from management education places limitations on both the extent and intensity of learning. As I have already shown, fears, anxieties and doubts are very common emotional experiences in the process of learning and change. The challenge for management education is therefore to work with those underlying emotions that can (at the same moment) encourage the possibility for learning or alternatively engender defensiveness and discourage learning.

Experience is not always conscious experience. There is an assumption behind Kolb's learning cycle (see Point 2 above) that people are open to experience, not defended against it. People's behaviour, inside and outside of organisations, emerges out of deeply held patterns and unconscious processes which both encourage *and* discourage learning from experience. It is the defensiveness or the denial of experience which is often ignored in the educative environment. People in learning groups, for example, do not just interact thoughtfully and respectfully with each other. They also create and recreate each other, as representatives of past relationships, as gurus or idiots, as good or bad, as judge or judged, etc. All these feelings, or similar ones, are present in any management education or management development context. To ignore this type of experience risks missing the potential for learning, yet to engage with it allows in the fear of conflict and an anxiety about the destruction of learning.

Another issue in relation to Kolb's model is that experiential learning is portrayed as "very first-order orientated" (Cunningham, 1994). Learning is also a meta-level process. This means that in addition to, for example, reflecting on experience in order to transform it, there is a need within the educative environment to reflect on our reflections in a way that calls our process into question. In this way we will be able to engage with the madness in our method as well as the method in our madness. This shift may emerge if the practice of experiential learning includes ways of venturing beyond reflections on experience in order to create an integrated personal, social, political process, one that can be provocative of reflections within reflections.

I have identified five issues which constitute both a critique of Kolb's learning cycle and a description of areas where developments associated with the cycle might occur. These are:

1   Experience needs to be seen as constructed, shaped and contained by social power relations.

2   Complex and unequal relations around knowledge are constructed between people as an integral part of the learning process.

3   The need to focus on here and now experience, and the 'mirroring' process between people within the educative environment and the organisations they represent.

4   The need to find ways of working with underlying and unconscious processes, particularly defence mechanisms.

5   The inclusion of second-order or meta processes relating to each aspect of the cycle.

The first and second of these points are reflections on the lack of a political perspective within the learning cycle. They point towards the need to review the model in the light of social and organisational power relations.   The third and fourth are reflections on the need to consider further the psychological, and particularly the unconscious, processes as an integral aspect of the learning cycle.   The final point suggests an additional area for development that is beyond the reflection–action loop, and which encourages managers and management educators to gain an insight into the living experience of thinking, into the nature of our tacit thought, and to our experience of this in action (Isaacs, 1993).

My perspective on Kolb's model of experiential learning acknowledges the anxiety, fear and doubt that is so characteristic of the beginning of a learning process, what could be called an *unconcrete experience*. As with action learning, the emotions at this point can take the learning in one of two directions, one that promotes learning and the other that discourages it.   If an individual or group is capable of holding the anxiety then they can, to a sufficient degree, contain these difficult emotions. This notion of 'holding' is one way of expressing an *observation and reflection* process whereby learners take the risk of remaining in an uncertain state, maybe feeling incompetent, in order to undermine what they currently know and to entertain something new.   The process of holding or risking the unknown often leads towards some form of *generalised insight*, although not necessarily one that is understood, as it may be that the learning happens later.   It is through the rejection of defences against the turbulent unknown of the process of learning that effective experiential learning can be achieved.   Such turbulence is characteristic of the continual need to learn once again how to learn, thereby *including unconscious experience.*

Our unconscious defences are there to serve a useful function as well as to promote avoidance of difficult situations (Oldham and Kleiner, 1990).   The difficulty faced by the learner (whether in the role of student or teacher) is working with this paradox.   In addition, there is a need not simply for an individualised attention to learning but also for a collective one, where individual and social experience both contribute to the continual evolution of the underlying structure through the very process of action. The importance of Kolb's learning cycle has been that it has encouraged managers to accept the interlocking nature of reflection and action. The cycle provides little assistance in encouraging managers to comprehend the reflexive processes that underlie individual reflection and action. Such a model would need to propose a radical shift in managerial understanding of learning. The aim of such a model would be to support people in "discovering a capacity to doubt the validity of perceptions which seem unquestionably true" (Palmer, 1979); to utilise this capacity to interact across internal organisational boundaries; and to relate more effectively to ever shifting visions of the whole.

An individual's or a group's risks and struggles, defences and avoidance strategies are political acts as well as emotional responses. They are the product of different levels of power and powerlessness within organisations and groups. If the model of management education being used denies such forces then it cannot be an adequate model for learning, because it contributes to the reinforcement of managerial experience that is willingly ignorant of power issues. It is important to have a political perspective on management education so that managers can reflect on the personal and institutional significance of different managerial experience (eg, black/white, female/male, disabled/able-bodied, gay/straight) for the very practice of change within their work.

Rethinking the practice of management learning

So far in this chapter I have suggested that the practice of experiential learning might be enhanced if managers and practitioners address, with equal importance, the rational, emotional and political levels inherent in both learning and change. At present, processes of management learning can seem either to be excessively rational, in the sense that they focus on managerial 'problem solving' or strategic development, and/or to be excessively humanistic, in their reliance on the 'person-centred' form of 'openness' in groups. The tendency in both of these approaches is to avoid a range of highly significant psychological and political dynamics, thereby mirroring and reinforcing the avoidance of the same dynamics in organisations.

This 'management by avoidance' (see Chapter 5) is shaped both by internal responses to learning and change and by external, socially constructed processes of interaction particularly around power and powerlessness. In this final section of the chapter, therefore, I want to propose three particular areas for the development of a revised practice in experiential management education that take my analysis into account. These are:

- working with the emotions of avoidance;

- working through the avoidance of power issues;

- working through the avoidance of underlying dynamic processes.

Working with the emotions of avoidance

Fineman suggests that: "We could regard all organisations as having zones of expressive tolerance which are likely to vary according to organisational type and part" (1993, p 218). Similarly, I think that specific organisational contexts of experiential learning (eg, groups of managers from the same organisation; organisationally tailored management competences) have characteristic and largely hidden "zones of expressive tolerance" that signify boundaries of individual and group learning and change. The challenge for management learning is therefore to identify and work with the student and tutor roles on the emotional boundaries of learning, and within their organisational context. This means working in ways that clarify what these unspoken, unseen, yet powerfully present boundaries are.

One boundary I have already identified, is that anxious place within a learning group where it is possible to move in a direction that promotes, or one that discourages learning. The ways in which anxiety impacts on the learning process are seldom acknowledged as an overt issue in management education. Anxiety can promote learning through risk and it can discourage learning through defensiveness, avoidance and denial. The effectiveness of experiential learning will be enhanced where work is done overtly with these and other key emotional processes. Such work requires those of us who assume responsibility for the education of managers to be highly sensitive to our own emotional states, and to hold and work effectively with those feelings that are projected onto us in our role as staff in the learning environment.

Working through the avoidance of power issues

Power and powerlessness in organisations are shaped and practised through the interplay of interconnecting and significant transactions (Martin, 1994) between individuals, groups and systems. There are many ways to describe the exercise of power (Hardy, 1994: see also Chapter 4 below) and these combined descriptions testify to the complexity of the issue. It would be insufficient to say that power can be expressed solely as the hierarchical authority one manager has over another; or as the legitimacy given to particular groups; or as the mobilisation of bias; or as a self-perpetuating phenomenon created from the interface between structure and action. Power is all of these and more.

In experiential learning, the ways in which power impacts on the learning process are often avoided. The primary mechanism of this avoidance is an unhelpful but pervasive humanistic myth that different individuals come equally into experiential groups. As a result, despite the clear differences between people, it is held to be possible to work together, without needing to work on the impact of difference. An emerging approach to experiential learning involves the acknowledgement of this avoidance of differential positions of power between individuals and groups in the learning environment. This means that processes of experiential learning will need to address the inter-personal and inter-group politics involved in the processes of learning, which reflect socially constructed power differences.

Power and powerlessness find expression in two particular areas. First, in the many avoidance strategies and habits which encourage educators to ignore socially and politically constructed inequalities. Second, through the difficulties educators have in working with challenges to the power of their own role. In the first instance, avoidance may be promoted by fear, hatred or guilt; in the second, through the anxiety that surrounds the possibility of losing face and/or control. It is possible for the practice of experiential learning to be enhanced where work is done explicitly on different expressions of power in the learning context. This will involve both managers and management educators in developing their abilities to hold and explore differential positions of power and equality as an integral aspect of understanding their subject.

Working through the avoidance of underlying dynamic processes

Another way of seeing avoidance in managers and organisations is as 'defence mechanisms', or processes through which resistance to change is brought into being. Kets de Vries and Miller (1985) offer six types of defence mechanism which they consider "play a major role in obstructing or inhibiting organisational change":

- *Repression:* certain memories, desires, emotions, thoughts and wishes are made unconscious and thereby divorced from awareness.

- *Regression:* attempts to revert to earlier ways or to actions that have previously provided some security.

- *Projection:* ascribing to another person or group an attitude or quality that one possesses but rejects in oneself. An attempt 'to keep the self conflict free'.

- *Identification:* thinking, feeling acting as one conceives another person to think, feel, act. Adopting the behaviour, values, attitudes of a significant individual.

- *Reaction formation:* one of a pair of contradictory attitudes or traits is kept unconscious and hidden by emphasising the opposite. Hate is replaced by love, selfishness by over-generosity, etc. The opposite, non-observable attitude persists unconsciously.

- *Denial:* attempting to exclude the existence of an unpleasant or unwanted piece of external reality, the truth being too anxiety provoking. The individual creates a delusion that nothing has changed.

The decision to work with and through the defence mechanisms that promote avoidance opens the door to a significantly different level of engagement with change. Psychodynamic insights provide the context for a reframing of traditionally humanistic words like 'participate' and 'collaborate'. Such concepts no longer have to contain a denial of the regressive and defensive characteristics that underlie all group and organisational dynamics. Psychodynamic theories are important in the development of thinking about experiential learning because they extend the definition of 'learning from experience' away from both the problem-oriented rationality of many change initiatives; and from the sharing-our-feelings oriented humanism of many traditional experiential learning approaches.

Developments in experiential learning can occur where there is a shift of emphasis from the 'sharing' of experience to 'working through' experience. This requires the educator to develop particular abilities. First, the ability when working with organisations, with groups and within individual practice, to focus on what is being avoided. Second, the courage to engage with the underlying dynamics through interpretative interventions (see Pines, 1993). This involves interpreting transference and counter-transference, individual defences and avoidances, and those forces that have shaped individual and group identity. An interpretative stance also brings into the open the key dynamic of role differences between tutor and student.

In the same way that managers in their organisations consciously and unconsciously block the working through process, so managers in educational settings use various mechanisms to block processes of working through experience. These include:

- The tendency to blame others or to redirect their anger.

- The inclination to escape into rationality or to deny emotion.

- The capacity for self-blame or positioning the self as a victim.

- The desire to take control, to take responsibility for providing solutions.

Refusal to change is both caused and reinforced on a day-to-day basis in organisations and learning groups by defence mechanisms such as these. As a result of this 'mirroring' process between two separate environments (ie, the organisation itself is reflected and acted out in the learning environment) the educator can assist managers in understanding their own working groups as a reflection of processes taking place in the wider organisation.

The practice of experiential management education can be enhanced where the educator takes seriously that aspect of their role which demands that they are responsible for identifying and working with the underlying organisational dynamics reflected in student groups. As Alderfer (1990) points out, this is by no means an easy task.

> The requirements for people who accept staff roles for experiential group dynamics learning events are substantial. They call for extensively developed emotional and intellectual capabilities ... for the flexibility to adapt to changing circumstances while attempting to remain whole as human beings and realistically responsive to the events that occur. (Alderfer, 1990, p 275)

If experientially based forms of management learning are to continue to be employed as a method for approaching individual, group and organisational change, then educators will also need to change. I suggest that the starting point for such change, and for a rethought-out practice of experiential learning, emerges from a deeper exploration of three areas that are currently replete with avoidance strategies: (i) work with emotions that are avoided; (ii) the avoidance of power and equality as ever-present process issues; and (iii) the avoidance of the complex underlying dynamics of working groups.

three

Management learning and organisational change

In this chapter I continue to explore my understanding of management learning. I move on from my reflections on processes of experiential learning and focus more on the learning organisation, organisational learning and change and my understanding of the nature of management learning.

Initially, I describe the components of the learning organisation or learning company with reference to the work of writers in the USA and the UK. I focus briefly on the notion of dialogue in order to illustrate the way that particular aspects of the general theory of the learning organisation have been developed. This leads me into an exploration of emotion and the management of change. I discuss ways of moving beyond problem-solving or planning based approaches to change, towards a method which focuses primarily on organisational members' emotions and relations, and on forces of uncertainty and defensiveness. In this way I am trying to reinforce a dynamic view of change, and to point towards some key issues for engaging with aspects of change that are often avoided.

The learning organisation and organisational learning

The idea of a learning organisation or learning company is now a well established metaphor for management thinking in the 1990s. The theories and practices associated with the learning organisation are not new (Ulrich, Von Glinow and Jick, 1993).

They have emerged as a result of other approaches that can be traced into the 1950s, 1960s and 1970s (see Dodgson, 1993) and which culminated in the work of Argyris and Schon (1978). I have discussed some of the thoughts and theories of this period in the previous chapter. It is, however, the work of Senge (1990; 1991) in the USA and Pedler, Burgoyne and Boydell (1991) in the UK, that has motivated current explorations into the theory and practice of organisational learning. In this section, I briefly discuss this work and look towards the future of the field.

Senge (1991, pp 6-12) identifies five 'disciplines', each of which are seen as dimensions in building an organisation that can learn.

- *Systems thinking:* involving a shift from seeing problems as caused by something 'out there' to seeing how our actions create the problems we experience. 'Each has an influence on the rest, an influence that is usually hidden from view'.

- *Personal mastery:* 'the discipline of continually clarifying and deepening our personal vision'. The organisation's commitment to learning depends on the commitment to learning of its individuals.

- *Mental models:* these are 'deeply ingrained assumptions, generalisations or even pictures or images that influence how we understand the world and how we take action'. Individuals need to learn to unearth our internal pictures of the world and hold them up for scrutiny.

- *Building shared vision:* the need to move towards creating shared pictures of the future that foster commitment rather than compliance.

- *Team learning:* this involves suspending assumptions as a process for collective thinking. Individuals need to learn how to recognise (defensive) patterns of interaction in teams that undermine learning.

Systems thinking is the 'fifth discipline', the discipline that integrates the disciplines into a coherent body of theory and practice (Senge, 1991, p 12). Although Senge is exploring the ways in which individual actions create the problems we experience, his view remains focused upon the individual manager within the individual organisation. As Lessem (1993) points out,

Senge stops short of viewing managers, organisations and whole societies as being interconnected.

In the UK, Pedler, Burgoyne and Boydell (1991) have deliberately used the word 'company' rather than 'organisation' because organisation "is a mechanical sort of word", and company "is one of our oldest words for a group of people engaged in a joint enterprise" (Pedler et al, 1991, p 1). Their starting point is that organisational learning "is not brought about simply by training individuals; it can only happen as a result of learning at the whole organisation level". They define the learning company in the following way: "A learning company is an organisation that facilitates the learning of all its members and continually transforms itself" (Pedler et al, 1991, p 1).

There are 11 processes or characteristics that support the evolution of learning companies, and these constitute a 'blueprint' for organisational learning (Figure 7).

These characteristics, set alongside the principles outlined by Senge, have established the fundamental point that learning organisations attempt to combine the facilitation of individual learning with the learning of the whole organisation. As Hawkins (1991; 1994) points out, however, there has been little attempt to tackle the issue of *how* these processes connect? Understanding the processes by which collective systems learn is far more complex than understanding individual processes.

Given the approaches I have described it might be easy to imagine that the learning organisation is created from a coherent set of general ideas or principles that become specific when they are applied in different contexts. One way to see how wrong this is, would be to read two key US papers in the field that offer very contrasting perspectives. In the first, Garvin (1993), writing in the *Harvard Business Review*, proposes a rational "framework for action", a description of how to create and sustain organisational learning. He wants to move away from the "far too abstract" ideas (of Senge) towards something more 'concrete', which he refers to as the "three M's": meaning, management and measurement. This paper situates the learning organisation within mainstream management thinking, represented in the slogan: 'if you can't measure it, you can't manage it'.

Figure 7: The eleven aspects of the Learning Company

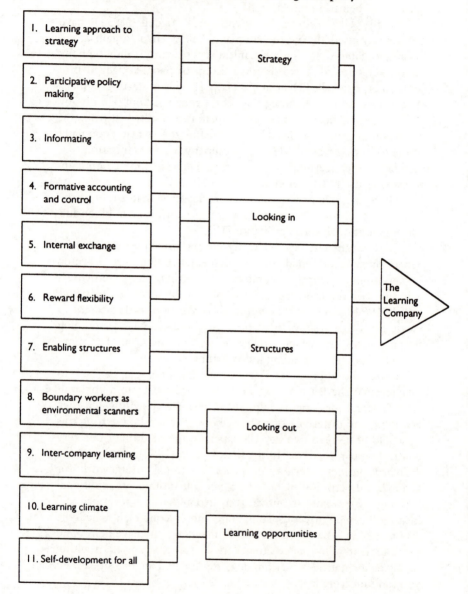

Source: Pedler et al (1991)

In the second paper, Kofman and Senge (1993), writing in *Organisational dynamics*, contend that there is nothing more practical than a good theory:

> The problem with seven-step methods to success, keys to successful organisations and similar how-to's is that, ultimately, they aren't very practical. Life is too complex and effective action too contextual. (Kofman and Senge, 1993, p 7)

Their approach, in marked contrast to Garvin, explores paradoxes, uncertainties and meta-level issues: the primacy of the whole, the community nature of the self, and language as a generative practice. The only area of similarity between the two perspectives is their use of slogans (in Kofman and Senge): "it's not what the vision is, but what the vision does that matters". These two papers represent very different and competing notions of what constitutes the learning organisation, with both claiming to be 'practical' in relation to the influence of their perspectives on successful companies.

Marsick and Watkins (1994) have identified a range of barriers to the development of the learning organisation:

- An inability to recognise and change existing mental models.

- Learned helplessness (the learning organisation "demands a curious, proactive, self-directed learner").

- Tunnel vision (an inability to take a perspective on the entire system).

- Truncated learning (learning efforts that never take root because they were interrupted or only partially implemented).

- The lingering power of individualism (which tends to undermine the collaborative characteristic of learning organisations).

- A culture of disrespect and fear (respect is seen as the foundation of an intrinsically motivated and continually learning workforce).

- Entrenched bureaucracy (organisational structures that are the antithesis to learning and change).

- The part-time, temporary and overtaxed workforce (a low commitment workforce means difficulties in implementing high-commitment changes).

- The struggle between managing and capitalising on diversity ('managing' diversity carries the connotation that we will continue to control others – to keep this new voice from disrupting and challenging the norm).

Such barriers are likely to exist in many organisations, particularly in public service organisations where bureaucratic structures continue to be the norm, despite several years of decentralisation and fragmentation into smaller units and networks. In such organisations it may prove useful to focus on *organisational learning* as well as *the learning organisation*.

Lundberg (1995) differentiates between these two terms. He sees the learning organisation as a specific metaphor for organisations and organising. Organisational learning however, describes certain processes or types of activity which may occur at one of several levels of organisational analysis. "Thus we can talk about organizational learning as something that takes place in organizations, whereas the learning organization is a particular type or focus of organization in and of itself" (Lundberg, 1995, p 10). This distinction is based on the identification of specific processes within an organisation, which may contribute to either the promotion or discouragement of learning (and therefore of change).

One such process concerns the interplay between individual and organisational learning (Fiol and Lyles, 1985; Kim, 1993). Torbert (1994, p 66) has identified four particular blocks to the simultaneous development of individual and organisational learning. First, he thinks it unlikely that there will be many individual managers with sufficient authority in the organisation to initiate such a process. Second, even with such authority, organisational learning would require repeated "non-coercive but confrontative interventions and few managers exercise such behaviours as a part of their regular practice". Third, "there are, simply, no actions or organisational designs that will unilaterally and reliably cause transformational managerial or organisational learning". Torbert, however, sees this as an important condition of transformational learning because it retains the uncertainty and doubt necessary to fuel the learning process. Fourth, the type of organisational structure that might create the simultaneous development of managerial and organisational learning "is radically unfamiliar to virtually all managers and scholars".

Torbert's (1991) contribution to organisational learning is aimed at working with and through such barriers by analysing and identifying developmental stages of management knowledge and being. These are set in the context of different types of power and different processes for action.

Hawkins' (1994) suggested agenda for organisational learning attempts to map out some of the key issues within the field. His agenda is in seven parts:

- The need to develop a new understanding of the nature of the systemic learning of whole organisations.

- The development of an integrative model that shows the inter-connection of the various approaches.

- Revisioning our basic metaphors for describing learning.

- Positioning the learning organisation in relation to other approaches to organisational understanding and development.

- Producing company wide case studies of organisational learning.

- Moving beyond a 'Social Darwinian' view of organisational learning (ie, beyond the idea that organisational learning is primarily important in terms of organisational survival or competitive advantage) towards collaborative learning.

- Moving beyond organisational learning.

Organisational learning and dialogue

Approaches to organisational learning have tended to "take too little account of the ... complexity and problems involved in learning" (Dodgson, 1993, p 384). Dodgson points out that organisational learning can be conservative as well as generative, and can sustain existing organisational structures of belief. This idea is developed from the work of March (1991) who makes a distinction between 'exploration' and 'exploitation' in organisational learning.

> The essence of exploitation is the refinement and extension of existing competences, technologies and paradigms.   Its returns are positive, proximate and predictable.   The essence of exploration is experimentation with new alternatives. Its returns are uncertain, distant and often negative.   Thus the distance in time and space between the locus of learning and the locus for the realization of returns is generally greater in the case of exploration than in the case of exploitation, as is the uncertainty. Such features of the context of adaption lead to a tendency to substitute exploitation of known alternatives for the exploration of unknown ones. (March, 1991, p 85)

Organisational learning can be inhibited through a tendency to reinforce existing power relations (often referred to as organisational 'values') emerging from the difficult emotions that surface in the context of both individual and organisational uncertainty. The struggle between exploration and exploitation is an integral aspect of organisational learning, and there is often a very fine dividing line between the two.   Given this interplay between politics and emotions in organisations, there is a need for internal processes of communication to allow individual members of an organisation to contain uncertainty and suspend their inclination to revert towards existing power structures and relations.

Since the initial work on organisational learning, various aspects of theory have been developed. Team learning has been explored, particularly in terms of different ways of communicating within teams or organisations to promote "collaborative learning" (Hawkins, 1994). The focus of this thinking about new ways of communicating has been on the process of dialogue as distinct from debate or discussion.   The interest in finding different processes for communication stems from an assumption (Schein, 1993b) that organisations are at present more likely to be broken down into sub-units of various sorts, and these are likely to develop their own subcultures.   Current organisational designs increasingly involve communication across subcultural boundaries in order to develop a common language and common mental models. The evolution of new, shared mental models is inhibited by existing cultural rules about interaction, particularly "mutual face-saving" (Schein, 1993b) and defensive routines (Argyris, 1990).

In large group psychology, the process of dialogue is seen to provide access to the varied individual *and* social meanings that the context of a large group creates (de Mare, Piper and Thompson, 1991). This metastructural level provides decipherable individual and collective meaning which is at the same time a translation of experience. Dialogue is therefore seen to provide simultaneous access to both individual experience and the translation of that experience through a social context. This has led to a definition of dialogue as:

> ... a sustained, collective inquiry into the processes, assumptions and certainties that compose everyday experience. Yet this is experience of a special kind, the experience of the meaning embodied in a community of people. (Isaacs, 1993, p 25)

Dialogue is therefore an attempt to set individual managerial experience and action within the context of collective thought and shared assumptions, and the living social processes that sustain them. The importance of the practice of dialogue, in terms of organisational learning, is as an attempt to offer managers access to a meta-level of management learning (Isaacs, 1993). It invites managers to ask 'what is leading me and others to have a predisposition to learn in this way at all?' Both Schein and Isaacs believe that such a perspective is crucial if managers are to transcend existing, inhibitive 'rules' about interaction across subcultural boundaries, in order to develop common languages and mental models, and to work effectively within increasingly complex and uncertain forms of organisation.

The importance that these writers place on dialogue comes from their realisation that increasingly managers might need to develop their awareness of the living experience of thinking, not reflection after the fact about it. Dialogue suggests a different process of communication and interaction from discussion or debate. In terms of managing the difference between dialogue and debate, managers are asked to *contain* immediate responses, to let the issue (our perceptions/feelings/judgements/impulses) rest for a while in a state of 'suspension', to see what more will come up for ourselves and from others. In this way it becomes possible to experience both the individual reaction, and the reaction of the whole.

Evolving ideas about dialogue in organisations provide one avenue of inquiry that extends current conceptualisations of organisational learning. They imply the need not simply for an individualised attention to learning but also a collective one, where individual and social experience both contribute to the continual evolution of underlying structure through the very process of action, and in order to relate more effectively to ever shifting visions of the whole.

Part of the focus in this work on dialogue has been on accepting and working with *emotional* responses: with underlying assumptions and defences that inhibit opportunities for collaborative learning and organisational change. One effective way of working with emotional as well as rational responses is to concentrate on the 'here and now'. I am not only using the phrase 'here and now' as a way of expressing the importance of engaging with immediate experience; I also use it as a phrase which forms a central element of a whole methodology for working with unconscious processes: in therapeutic groups (Vinogradov and Yalom, 1989); in the general field of group relations (Colman and Geller, 1985; Gillette and McCollom, 1990; Trist and Murray, 1990); and in terms of management and organisation (Hirschhorn, 1990; Hoggett, 1992).

In their work on dialogue, Schein and Isaacs emphasise the difference between reflective attention to past experience and "proprioception" (Schein, 1993b), which is attention to and living in the moment. Proprioception involves becoming conscious of how much our thought and perception is both a function of our past experience *and* the immediate events that trigger it. In terms of managerial and organisational learning, such a process necessarily involves perpetuating a critical stance towards the self in context, in order to determine whether past ways of acting remain appropriate. Such a practice will involve self-examination of our emotional state as well as our opinions. In this respect, there is a particular need to highlight and explore further the relations between emotion and the management of change.

Emotion and the management of change

One intention in this book is to try and add to the different ways of looking at and working with change in organisations. The suggestions I make are based on a set of working propositions that move away from problem-solving or planning based approaches to change, towards a method which focuses primarily on organisational members' emotions and relations, and on forces of uncertainty and defensiveness. In this way I am trying to reinforce a dynamic view of change, and to point towards some key issues for engaging with aspects of change that are often avoided.

In Britain, during the 1970s and 1980s, new theoretical models of organisational development and change began to highlight the dynamic processes through which change unfolds (Pettigrew, 1987). The context, content and process of change became central to explanations of organisational change, especially when looked at longitudinally (Dawson, 1994). This shift of emphasis focused on the relationship between the content of a specific change strategy, the context in which the change takes place and the process by which it occurs. It provided explanations of the processes managers use to mobilise and reconstruct contexts in order to legitimate their decisions to change. Contexts could be examined on two levels: the 'inner' – the culture, structure and politics of an organisation – and the 'outer' the economic, political and societal contexts within which an organisation operates. The advantage of this theoretical shift was that it reminded practitioners not to exclude the complex social and political issues that intersect with individual and inter-personal behaviour in organisations.

Such a shift pointed towards the complexity of organisational change. Increasingly, the challenge of managing and organising change will not be faced by finding solutions but by finding different ways of engaging with uncertainty and paradox, with the emotional and the irrational in organisations.

Various writers have produced overviews of approaches to change: Goodman (1982), Wilson (1992) and Burnes (1992). An overview is given by Schein (1985) who highlights five different processes and perspectives on change. He proposes that the management of change has been seen as:

- *an evolutionary process* arising from natural and irresistible forces;

- *an adaptive process* achieved through environmental manipulation;

- *a therapeutic process* where change happens inside a group but as a result of interaction between the inside and the outside;

- *a revolutionary process*, where power is the key variable;

- *a managed process*, one which assumes forces can be both under the control of and beyond the control of managers at the same time.

Clearly, my own theoretical starting point is firmly set within the context of 'therapeutic' change processes, and particularly so in relation to psychodynamic approaches to organisational change (Miller and Rice, 1967; Kets de Vries and Miller, 1985; Hirschhorn, 1990; Kets de Vries, 1991; Hoggett, 1992; Diamond, 1993). I am particularly interested in the everyday unconscious and emotional processes that impact on the management of change, and in identifying and working with emotions in organisational change. However, organisations continually shape and are shaped by social power relations and my standpoint is that both emotional and political forces are occurring together in organisations, and that such forces are particularly relevant in relation to the possibilities for and defences against change.

Fineman (1993) believes that the central question for research concerned with investigating emotions in organisations is 'to discover how people come to know they have hit a boundary'. This suggests the need to ask how people can realise (in both senses of that word: to comprehend and to accomplish) their responses to change. How, therefore, do people within organisations comprehend and act for or against the shared emotional experiences that underlie relations between different levels of the organisation. My interest is in exploring and demonstrating how managers respond at the boundaries of their roles and relations, and also in identifying the extent to which managing the boundaries can offer new opportunities for organisational analysis and action.

The term 'boundary' is used to describe a "rule about relatedness between things" (Smith, 1982). The boundary is an essential element in individual, group or organisational identity. It provides not only a sense of being an entity, but also contains the sense-making processes that continually shape and redefine the individual, group, organisation in practice. This relatedness is seen as central to organisational change. Thus:

> ... to work analytically in institutions is to use one's alertness to the emotional experience presented in such settings as the medium for seeking to understand, formulate and interpret the relatedness of the individual to the group or the institution. It is understanding that relatedness, I believe, which liberates the energy to discover what working and being in the group or the institution can become. (Armstrong, 1991, p 4)

The boundary is a transitional space (Hoggett, 1992), a bridge between the internal emotions of individuals and their social and political context, a space where the possibility exists to discover or develop creative ways of relating, and creative ways of interacting with what surrounds us.

> It is unlikely ... that a comprehensive programme of specific changes can be planned for any organisation. Change is more likely to be brought about by attending to favourable boundary conditions, that is primarily favourable patterns in the exercise of power. (Stacey, 1993, p 206)

The boundary is therefore one place where it is possible to identify the intersection between individual experience and social power relations (hooks, 1991). The boundary is also a difficult space because the relatedness between things is often confusing, uncertain, shifting and paradoxical. Boundaries imply barriers or defences that may have to be crossed or breached for change to occur, they imply a framework of meaning or attachment that provides coherent identity to something, and therefore a difference from something else. All these aspects of the boundary often discourage an analysis of the disorganised relations between, for example, people, groups, parts of an organisation, organisations, social groups. The tendency to ignore the emotional and the relational aspects of change in organisations is a result of the strength of perception in management education that change can be managed rationally.

There are many models of change in organisations that are based on the idea that change is a problem to be solved through appropriate diagnosis, often of forces of 'resistance', followed by appropriate readjustment or strategy. This usually involves a given number of 'steps', for example, in the literature of resistance to change: "10 critical factors" (Matejka and Ramona, 1993), "8 basic patterns" (Conner, 1993), "4 distinct stages" (Reynolds, 1994), "10 key principles" (Kyle, 1993) and "5 common causes" (O'Connor, 1993), these being just the recent additions. Such perspectives on change in organisations are based on the idea that change is primarily a strategic issue, shaped by internal politics and individual interests (Kotter and Schlesinger, 1979). Change can be planned for and resistance dealt with through a variety of possible strategies on a continuum (in Kotter and Schlesinger's (1979) model ranging from communication to coercion) and the underlying assumption of these approaches is that there will be an appropriate strategy to fit an identified problem of change.

The difficulty with problem-based models of change is that they over-emphasise the rational and consequently do not take into account the complexity, ambiguity and paradox acknowledged to be an integral part of organisation (Morgan, 1986; Johnson, 1987; Dawson, 1992). Rationality is often the driving force behind managerial thought, action and training. In such circumstances emotional reactions to change are often seen as less important. There are several reasons for this. First, the overly rational manager can easily dismiss emotional complexity simply because it is 'irrational': what is paradoxical and contradictory is deemed irrelevant. Second, organisational cultures are often created as a defence against emotions like anxiety (Menzies-Lyth, 1990), and this makes it difficult for organisational members to express feelings within the organisation. Third, managers absorbed into organisational cultures dependent on task completion and strategic problem solving invariably find emotions and feelings difficult to articulate. Fourth, organisations give little space or opportunity for organisational members to access and understand their own and others' conscious and unconscious feelings about organisational life generally, and organisational change in particular.

Change depends as much on comprehending and managing emotional relatedness as it does on employing rationality or logic to solve problems. It is important to move away from an over-emphasis on the rationality that underpins the management of change in order to integrate the emotional with the rational.

Paradox and defensiveness

Berg and Smith (1990) argue that overly rational attempts to either reconcile or categorise change tend to suppress the *paradoxical tension* that could give meaning to the change process. In Chapter 6 I provide an example of paradoxical tension in an organisation when I highlight the tendency within local government organisations to be active and yet also avoid equality. Staying with such paradoxes makes it possible to discover a link between opposing forces and opens up the framework that gives meaning to the apparent contradictions in the experience. This framework is not built on a structural premise, but on a relational one. Change does not only occur as a result of outlining a set of problems to diagnose and solve. It can also be approached through identifying patterns of relatedness and through containing the paradoxical emotions and relations that challenge the ways in which we think about ourselves and others. Such patterns are constructed by both unconscious and conscious processes in organisations or individuals.

There are many instances in organisations of paradoxical tensions, where the idea of change is built on one set of strategically orientated feelings and relations, only to lead towards another underlying set, characterised by personal anxieties and prompting very defensive responses. As Krantz (1990b) points out, managerial reliance on problem solving and technical skill is itself an expression of the (defensive) wish in the business community that uncertainty can be controlled.

Thus, any attempt to work with change needs to take into consideration those individual and organisational defence mechanisms against anxiety that, at a largely unconscious level, structure and form managerial and organisational responses to change (Kets de Vries and Miller, 1985; Oldham and Kleiner, 1990). Defence mechanisms are used by all of us to some degree, they are an aspect of everyday behaviour. Their function is to assist in the management of situations that threaten the ego. It is important to have such boundaries around the self, but, as Oldham and Kleiner (1990) point out, they can be either an asset or a liability, depending on how they are used. Individual defensiveness can become habitual and over-used, creating defensive group patterns that institutionalise through competitiveness, denial and avoidance as underlying organisational processes. Defence mechanisms not only refer, therefore, to the protection of an individual ego, but to the maintenance and perpetuation of an organisation's culture, created out of inter/intra-personal and inter/intra-group relatedness.

An understanding of change can emerge from the identification of relations as well as problems, and this offers two opportunities for working with change. First, the paradoxical tensions that arise within individuals and between different individuals and systems can be contained rather than excluded as unimportant. The tensions implicit in paradox need to be lived and worked with at individual, group and organisational levels. In practice however, such tensions are more often resolved through intra/inter-individual and group defence. Second, defences can be seen as various ways in which the contradictions of paradox, and the emotional discomfort that such contradictions imply, are repressed, denied or projected, often unconsciously. An analysis of defensive relations creates the possibility of holding onto what is paradoxical and ambiguous, as an integral component of organisational change.

Attachment to meaning: psychological and political deep structures

In addition to paradox and defence, a third area involved in individual or organisational change is the attachment of an individual or organisation to a particular frame of meaning. Different aspects of meaning within change processes have been identified by Marris (1986). In his book on the relationship between loss and change, Marris outlines the nature of *attachment* as a process fundamental to people's ability to manage change. Marris sees attachment neither as an emotion nor a purpose, rather as a condition from which emotion and purpose arise. Both loss and change can undermine a person's trust in his or her attachments, that is, in those factors holding deep patterns in place. In other words, attachments provide individuals with a basic framework for meaning and relatedness.

Marris identifies three principles in the management of change. First, an engagement with what is 'mine', what change means to me, emotionally as well as intellectually. Second, an engagement with (and valuing of) different kinds of experience and interest. This can be seen as a social expression of, and interaction with, meaning through individual identity (see Giddens, 1991). Third, an engagement with individual attachments or the 'essential continuity in the structure of meaning' for individuals. For Marris, the deepest struggle with change is about a fundamental resistance we feel as people to battle against the tide of attachment, within which we frame our meaning of ourselves.

Marris' reflections are useful in this context because they point to different stages and intensities in the management of change as a process. His principles on change imply that individuals or groups will be required to engage at three levels: (i) with individual dependency or attachment (ie, what belongs to me, perpetuates me and restricts me); (ii) with the social context and social power relations that shape and are shaped by individual meaning (ie, my bias, and the developmental consequences of those opportunities I have to implement within social power structures); and (iii) with organisational boundaries (ie, the largely unconscious regime created by individual and organisational attachments).

This view intersects with a policy related perspective put forward by Benson (1982) who suggests three different structural levels to power in organisations. The first of these is the 'administrative structure' of an organisation which describes what can be experienced on the 'surface' level of everyday tasks and procedures. Second, an 'interest structure', a level expressing overt and covert conflict between competing interest groups. Finally, the 'rules of structure formation', a level of organisational life that constrains and directs activity, but is largely beyond the conscious comprehension of people within the organisation.

At a fundamental level, change is avoided and made possible through a complex intersection of both psychological and political issues. Attachment is not only about a continuity in the structure of meaning within the individual, but also involves the ways in which the current order, and the routines that support it, is reinforced by the ontological security that it provides for individuals and for groups. Organisational change needs to be perceived and worked with both as a psychological and as a structural/political phenomenon which is shaped through an attachment to individual and organisational histories as they are enacted, through engagement between people, in organisational settings.

The above discussion can be summarised by describing three connected strands that are important to the surfacing of emotional and relational aspects of change in organisations. These are expressed below as three inter-connected propositions:

- *Paradox: the tensions between clarity and uncertainty, the 'self-contradictory' nature of individual emotions and organisational action, are constantly present in any process that attempts to deal with change.* Most organisations are pervaded by a wide range of conscious and unconscious emotions, thoughts and actions that their members experience as contradictory. Attempts to unravel these contradictory forces (paradoxically) create stuckness. The more that members seek rationally to pull the contradictions apart, to separate them so that they will not be experienced as contradictory, the more they become enmeshed in the self-referential binds of paradox (Smith and Berg, 1987).

- *Defence: various individual and social defence mechanisms against anxiety are unconsciously utilised by individuals and within the context of organisation in order to defy change.* Individual and social defence mechanisms serve the function of protecting both the person and the organisation from anxiety (Jaques, 1955; Menzies-Lyth, 1990). Some of these mechanisms will be appropriate to maintaining clear boundaries, but others will signify the use of habitual and self-limiting responses to the change process.

- *Attachment: there will exist a variety of attachments to meaning and identity, formed from an interaction of unconscious individual and organisational processes and through social power relations, that create shape and construct the basic structures within which change is possible.* Unconscious psychological drives and dominant political forces interact to define the boundaries of an organisation, and legitimise certain behaviours while invalidating others. These will reflect, for example, power structures or inequalities present in the social construction of reality. Such attachments relate to both individual identity and organisational culture.

These propositions provide a context for a shift of focus in organisational analysis of change away from the rational into the relational. This can encourage a starting point for working with organisational change that is both emotionally and politically focused. My perspective attempts to acknowledge the patterns of relatedness, within the organisation or the individual, between psychological or emotional aspects of potential change (eg, denial, dependency, anxiety) and the intersecting political aspects of potential change (eg, power differentials, competing policies, external interests and constraints). Working with organisational change from this perspective will involve deeper inquiry into the relatedness between the self and the system and a more active engagement with differences that are currently covered over.

This framework was developed and applied in a paper in which myself and my colleague, Mike Broussine looked at emotional responses to organisational change in the context of local government (Vince and Broussine, 1996). The paper addresses the difficult area of how internal and external practitioners of change can work with the emotional as well as the rational material that influences everyday work. We conclude that any attempt to engage managers in the emotional experiences that underlie relations between different levels of the organisation involves four issues. These indicate four aspects to change processes:

1   *Working with complexity and uncertainty in the change process:* managers can learn to stay with the uncertainty long enough not to automatically deny or avoid the feelings associated with it. Managers are given the opportunity to hold on to the complexity of their work experience in order to find what is stimulating rather than oppressive about it.

2   *Reviewing the boundaries:* managers perceive the boundaries between different groupings within an organisation as more clear and separate than they actually are. This is because emotions are more visible at the boundaries between groups. Managers need to reflect more fully on the issues that exist on the boundary between organisational groups.

3   *Relatedness:* once managers have become aware of an emotional level of interaction existing underneath their everyday perspective on inter-personal behaviour, they are able to assess the extent to which feelings about change are

based on defensive reactions or actual differences. This promotes greater tolerance of difference within and between organisational groupings.

4   *Working through:* the realisation of underlying emotions or processes between groups does not seek to deny or shift managers away from their actual feelings about the change process. The capacity to work through an issue is most powerful when it is done in the political context of real work experiences within each organisation.

These four processes provide a tentative model for working with change, and emerge from explorations of the propositions that underpin a relational approach. In practice, the process of working through will come up against barriers, defences or avoidances. Kets de Vries and Miller (1985) identify four barriers to the process of working through, in the direction of insights and change. My own reworking of these gives the following four barriers: (i) blaming others (redirected anger), (ii) escaping into rationality/the denial of emotion, (iii) blaming the self (taking up a position as victim), and (iv) taking over responsibility (or being positioned into responsibility by others).

In this chapter I have provided a general discussion of the learning organisation and organisational learning. I focused on the notion of dialogue as an example of how organisational learning has been developed in practice. I then explored aspects of relations and emotion in organisations in order to develop a framework for understanding and analysing management learning and organisational change from a psychodynamic perspective. I have particularly attempted to move away from individualist and rationalist notions of change towards a framework where there is an emphasis on relations and relatedness, and where the emotional complexities of change are included. I imagine that this will provide increased opportunities for insights that contribute to the practice of management learning.

Part Two

"Any theory is also the autobiography of the theorist." (Chatwin, 1989, p 5)

"Memory is where the self is held captive. Telling one's story is a means of becoming." (quoted in MacKeracher, 1995, p 2)

Reflections: one

In Part Two, over the next four chapters, I provide a description of a process of learning and change. The learning and change that I describe covers my own exploration of the relationship between change, equality and management learning, and my unfolding understanding and experience of the meaning of words that give this book its title. I have been searching for, finding, discarding and agonising over my relationship towards the subject of equality and management learning for ten years, and I imagine that this will continue. I have learned that there are few concrete answers, but that inter-connected stories like the ones I outline in this book do have an impact on action and practice in the ever-shifting relations that constitute organisational learning and change. In this first section of reflections I talk a little about my own experience of this journey towards understanding the nature of change.

The reason why I got into this issue in the first place was because I wanted to change the world.

In 1985 I began an action research project which aimed to identify the attitudes of managers towards race and gender equality, and to suggest ways in which managerial prejudices against black people and women could be confronted. The project also sought to identify ways of promoting organisational change. In an interview with the director of a training organisation I sat and listened to him say that black people were lazy, not prepared to work outside of their own community and that they needed a "major re-education process, so that they can get the right attitude to work". I asked him to repeat some of what he had said so that I could write it down verbatim. He actually repeated it. After the interview I felt angry with him, and I felt upset and uncomfortable about this experience.   When the report had been written and made public, the organisation he worked for were obliged to call this manager's attitudes into question. He got the sack. I was not sure whether this was the type of change I had imagined or wanted.

Before this, when I was a community worker, I was in and out of groups of people organising.   They organised against bureaucracy and they organised for pleasure.   A belief in the creative power of groups mixed with a vague sense of injustice brought me to my starting point. My practical education emerged as I moved in and out of contact with self-help and self-development groups.

Using what I had learned from these experiences, and relying on my enthusiasm, I was searching for a grail of sorts: a process of change that people could accept. Suddenly things would make sense.   I was searching for a process that freed 'them' from the self-imposed prison of their prejudices.   I imagined that I could gradually persuade, that if I remained committed to the possibility that individuals could change then they would change. All that needed to happen was that somehow myself and other white men would become conscious of our prejudices, and through this find a clearer and more human understanding of the relationship between equality and management.   From here, I really cannot imagine what it was about me at the time that wanted to take on such a task, or why I was approaching it with such naiveté and pomposity. What was I trying to prove? I imagined that I was out there and having to put up with other people's bias, pushing against the world. Now I understand much better how much they had to put up with mine.

I was in control. I remember the excitement I felt at planning change programmes, particularly analysing the diagnostic tools and interventions and creating the appropriate programmes for those specific change issues. Working with my co-trainers, or with internal organisational change agents, this stage of the intervention was wonderful. So many opportunities for creative interaction, for serious discussion, for laughter and invention, for playing with ideas and ways of working. It was working together with the like-minded that gave me my energy.

My initial style was to be challenging of individuals and groups. Sometimes this worked well, at other times it didn't work well at all. I wanted to make people change at the same time as wanting them to change themselves. My values were telling me that I had to learn about how to make change possible, not that I had to make it happen. But I also wanted to force people to change, I just didn't want them to know that I thought like this. Also, at the time, I didn't think that I thought like this.

Looking back it seems clear to me now that I had built my initial approach out of my own anxiety, the anxiety of not feeling competent and confident that I could make change happen, of trying so hard to be right. As a consequence I was prone to defensive expressions of control.

Once I had taken the risk of not looking for solutions I found a way of working that felt somewhat less dependent on defensiveness, fear and conflict. I came to think that what I could achieve would be to learn about one aspect of management learning. This is why my focus became the barriers and possibilities for learning, and on processes of defensiveness and avoidance, which seem particularly played out around equal opportunity. They are about me and the other, about our struggle for change.

In a nightmare I once had, I agreed to be an internal trainer on an anti-racism training workshop for staff in the part of the University where I was then working. The hostility I managed to generate towards myself from some of the academics and support staff who attended this event was ferocious. Was this a dream or did I really do this foolish thing? It's better to remember it as a dream.

In 1989 I suffered a severe and painful problem with my digestive system. Lying in hospital, reflecting on the reasons why I was in such a condition, I was struck by the knowledge that my way of working was probably one of the causes. My management developer role involved me in attempting to contain my own and other peoples' powerfully felt confusion and conflict around change. I had attempted to digest a great deal of emotion on the issues of equality, learning and change, as I attempted to work with and through my own and other people's hostility, struggles, resistances and anger. I think (and I had a lot of time to think about this) that I internalised too much of these emotions, kept them inside, thinking that I was immunised against their effects. I would be able to gradually digest them, gradually make sense of them, and in this way to develop the skills of working with them towards both individual and organisational change. I was wrong.

My way of working changed as a result of this experience, and I changed my way of supporting myself to do my work. My perspective now is this: no organisation is worth destroying yourself for.

When I started out on the work I describe in this book, I believed that I was an agent of change, a person who could go into organisations and make change happen. I see it very differently now. I have learned enough about both myself and the change process to know that mirroring organisational power relations creates no change. Now I experience more and more that change happens in connection with others, through friendships and collaboration, it happens as a result of uncertainty and risk, through organisational politics, and it happens for reasons I cannot fathom. Under these uncertain conditions and relations it seems better for me to try to speak from my position, to have some courage to hold onto my own voice long enough to imagine what might change and what might remain.

It is very strange sometimes, the timing of these things. Just when I had decided that I had finished working on the relations between management learning and equality (after the work described in Chapters 4 and 5) I got a telephone call. A local government manager that I had never met called and said: "Could I have a reprint of your paper on management by avoidance? The one I've got has been used so much that it's fallen to bits." Such moments are irresistible, they are full of hope. I could feel my enthusiasm as we talked: "Just out of interest, how have you used it?.... Really ... have you thought about bringing a group together ... you already have one, I'd love to meet them...." And so it goes. These days my fervour for learning is based much less on a pompous desire to convert people. Now I take pleasure in meeting people who want to collaborate in learning, and in the struggle to communicate our differing, changing and evolving experiences of both theory and practice.

Nothing could be more detrimental to organisational learning than this process of elevating individual defensive tactics to an organisational routine. (Argyris, 1994, p 77)

four

Organisational responses to the practice of equality

The action research outlined in this chapter was the starting point (developed in the following three chapters) of an investigation of organisational action and inaction on equality, and of the relationship between equality and the management of change. In this research, which was conducted in the mid-1980s, I concentrated on issues concerning the implementation of equal opportunity policy within various organisations. My aim was to explore and reveal responses to the practice of equal opportunities. At this stage of my investigation into equality and management learning I thought that the perceptions, skills and knowledge that were necessary to manage change could be seen within the struggle to develop and implement equal opportunity policy and practice. I imagined that the implementation of equal opportunities would lead to greater equality in organisations.

During the 10-year period represented by the four chapters in Part Two, I have moved from attempts to highlight ways of promoting equal opportunity, towards a perspective on equality as a continual and contested aspect of everyday organisational life. The consistency in my perspective over this decade emerges from my awareness that actions in relation to equality, both for and against, tend to generate strong feelings. Everyday contests over equality bring to the surface the underlying emotions that are continually present between people with different positions in organisations. Actions for and against equality engender strong reactions in individuals, often giving rise to behaviour that is motivated by defensiveness and anger. Such emotions and the fears they inspire contribute to the defensive structuring of the organisation against the development of equality. Despite the relative failure of equal opportunities to make an impact on organisational structure and behaviour, equality remains a challenging issue.

In the specific action research project that makes up this chapter I was attempting to combine and integrate aspects of research, consultancy and training into a project designed to encourage the organisations involved to develop an active stance on the implementation of good practice. I imagined that, as a result of their own involvement in challenging existing individual and organisational practices on equal opportunities, the participants within the action research might become more familiar with ways of organising that promote equality. They would then have an opportunity to include emotional, social and power issues (as well as rational perspectives) within their understanding of their work and how to change it. This in turn might make it easier for them to accept and understand change as an integral and omnipresent part of their work, rather than a vague and distant goal which it is very easy to be cynical about. In addition, the project was concerned to identify organisational responses to the practice of equality and to develop a framework for further action and research.

Background to the action research

The action research was undertaken within organisations funded by central government through the (then) Manpower Services Commission (MSC) and responsible for providing places for young people through a programme called the Youth Training Scheme (YTS). These schemes included private and voluntary organisations as well as public service organisations.

The YTS was launched by the Manpower Services Commission in September 1983. It was designed originally as a one-year programme of training on work-based skills and competencies for young people. In April 1986 the duration of YTS was changed from one to two years. Trainees generally received a programme of training and work placements throughout their two-year involvement with the scheme. Organisations that provided YTS places were required to satisfy the MSC on 10 criteria (including equal opportunity) before they could become Approved Training Organisations (ATOs). The assessment of competence in each area was done by MSC staff to a set of guidelines. From 1983, the MSC promised a firm commitment to the provision of equal opportunities. This commitment was established on the recognition that even though "equal opportunities ... may not be a reality in working life" the MSC itself "would not replicate that inequality" (De Sousa, 1987, p 66). Despite this commitment there was considerable evidence at the time to demonstrate that both race and gender discrimination were prevalent within schemes (Commission for Racial Equality [CRE], 1984; Fenton et al, 1984; Avon Accredited Training Centre, 1985; Pollert, 1985; Wickham, 1986; De Sousa, 1987) and that the MSC had great difficulty dealing effectively with its consequences.

The MSC's definition of equal opportunity at the time of this part of the research covered four different areas of discrimination: race, religion, gender and disability. The action research project highlighted in this chapter concentrated on two areas, race and gender. The reason for this was that YTS demonstrated different reactions towards race and gender than they did towards other issues (Avon Accredited Training Centre, 1985). Whereas organisations were open to the idea (if not the practice) of finding ways of supporting the inclusion of disabled people within their organisation, scheme staff seemed less willing to accept the need for action on racism and sexism. Also, organisational members could make connections between race and other issues like gender, class, age, but found it difficult to include race when discussing those other issues. One of the reasons for this may have been that there were very few black staff involved in the delivery of YTS in the Avon area.

There were three stages to the action research project:

- An investigation of the current practice of the 12 major schemes in the (then) County of Avon.

- Direct consultancy work with selected schemes in order to monitor and encourage good practice.

- The development of an approach relevant to all the participating organisations which would bring them in line with requirements laid down by the MSC that: "YTS is an equal opportunities programme, and is open equally to all eligible young people regardless of race, religion, sex or disability" (MSC, 1987).

Each of the three stages had different objectives which were reflected in different methods of research. The methods of the different stages of the project varied as follows:

- The first stage established the general organisational perspective on equal opportunity policy and practice within YTS. This was done through a process of direct contact and interview with key organisational staff. Individual perspectives on key questions were recorded and the information collated into an initial report (AATC, 1987).

- The second stage reflected the need to build on stage one through the identification of specific problems and ways of challenging them. This was achieved through a process of consultancy within selected organisations. Using a framework which invited the possibility for change, key individuals were encouraged to acknowledge organisational and individual problems and begin to work on ways of challenging them.

- The third stage reflected the need to build on stage two through the development of specific ways of changing previous bad practice on equal opportunities demonstrated either by individuals or within organisational groupings. There was a need, therefore, to propose and test a strategy for future development. A more comprehensive study was initiated through the introduction of a pilot system for monitoring how effectively identified problems and issues were addressed.

In November 1984, the Chairperson of the Avon Area Manpower Board, the governing body of the MSC in the Avon area, wrote a letter that was distributed to all Youth Training Schemes in Avon expressing the board's keenness that schemes "are seen to provide equal opportunity for all and we intend to promote positive action to avoid any form of discrimination". In addition, the Board asked schemes to "report the steps you have taken, or will take, to implement a policy of equal opportunity within your scheme". Of the 120 schemes operational in Avon at that time, the MSC received 15 replies, most of which indicated that the providers thought that they were already equal opportunities employers. The need for research and development began here.

Results: stage one

In order to clarify the understanding, or lack of understanding, of local schemes on equal opportunities, the most senior managers of the 12 largest schemes (in terms of number of trainee places) in the Avon Area were interviewed. A set of interview questions were developed using CRE guidelines. The questions covered issues of both policy and practice. The people who answered these questions were, in each case, the individual who at that time held the position of scheme manager, or a similar position in terms of their own ability to influence the development of policy within the organisation. The research sought the individual perspectives of managers within the sample on five key areas:

- their personal attitudes to equal opportunity (as an influence on policy and practice within the organisation);

- the policy of the organisation;

- the recruitment practices of the organisation;

- the monitoring practices of the organisation;

- the training on equal opportunity they have received or have given to staff

Below I highlight the significant aspects to emerge from the overall process of interviewing.

Personal attitudes related to policy development

Schemes were not familiar with and did not use any basic information relating to codes of practice on equal opportunity in YTS. For example, the CRE and the Equal Opportunities Commission had available (at the time the interviews were conducted) a variety of publications dealing specifically with good employment practice and equal opportunities within YTS. In most cases when the interviewer showed these documents to the scheme respondent it was the first time that they had come across them.

Schemes did not feel that they had a problem with equal opportunity. They therefore were ambivalent on the question of change and reluctant to prioritise equal opportunity in any way. The data indicated a range of overtly discriminatory responses, but respondents mostly saw equal opportunity as something which was unimportant.

Where there was concern about equal opportunity, it tended to be concern about the scheme's image on equal opportunity rather than the issues of equal opportunity.

The policy of the organisation

Those people responsible for the development of policy were often:

– unaware of what a policy implies and involves;

– hostile to the issues of racism and sexism;

– putting the blame on the victims of discrimination;

– aware that equal opportunity is an emotive issue *and*

therefore concerned to smooth it over.

Policy was envisaged as something infused into general organisational culture rather than a form of documentation designed to clearly portray specific actions. Staff assumed that a 'professional' organisation recruits 'professional' staff who will not discriminate because they work 'professionally'. As a rule, schemes interpreted equal opportunity policy as an equal opportunity statement linked to advertising for staff.

The recruitment practices of the organisation

Schemes could see no obstacles within their own recruitment practices preventing black trainees or young women from getting and keeping a place on their scheme. They found it hard to comprehend, for example, that their application form, through asking for 'nationality' might offer the opportunity for staff responsible for shortlisting to discriminate.

Schemes did not find it easy to connect the consequences of their attitudes within recruitment procedures (eg, interviewing) to recruitment practice. Their philosophy ranged from blame (ie, it was 'their' fault for not coming); an automatic assumption of openness to anybody; financial constraints on recruitment resources; or the importance of having 'the right attitude' or image.

There was evidence of 'first-line recruitment' in some schemes, whereby the YTS intake was used to select permanent employees into the organisation. If, as was clearly established in each case, the YTS scheme was under-represented by, for example, black people, then the organisation as a whole would be under-represented by the recruitment procedures of the training scheme.

The monitoring practices of the organisation

As a result of equal opportunity being given such a low priority, schemes had no procedures enabling them to review and develop policy and practice. About one third of the schemes monitored the number of black people who came into the scheme, but they only did that because they knew MSC required them to keep that information. In some cases the information itself was useless because the scheme kept no record of the number of black trainees who left after a short period of time on the scheme.

Schemes were reluctant to consider reviewing and changing training programmes in order to meet the needs of disadvantaged trainees. Only one scheme (an engineering project) had made changes to their programme on the basis of gender differences between trainees. They had changed the requirements of a young woman's programme of learning in order to include the use of lifting gear since she had less physical strength than other trainees. Most schemes considered such moves as 'discrimination in reverse'.

Even where schemes were given information about the type of monitoring practices it was possible to employ, there was little idea of how such information could be used to change and develop recruitment practices. For example, monitoring the number of completed applications received from black people and female applicants against the number who received trainee places would provide a clear indication of any discrimination within the selection process.

The training on equal opportunity that they have received or provided for staff

The lack of interest schemes demonstrated towards equal opportunity issues gave rise to ambivalence towards training. Schemes generally felt that there was not the 'time' available to give to training, and that staff did not see it as a need. Where training was seen as a need it was the type of training that 'told' the scheme what they should be doing. Schemes wanted to be instructed not facilitated.

The incentive to train or be trained in relation to equal opportunity did not exist because schemes did not see equal opportunity as a problem.

The interviews provided a picture of the levels of non-existent policy and practice within YTS schemes at that time; they gave an insight into the attitudes of policy makers within schemes and they formed the basis of stage two of the action research, which related to the establishment of a consultancy framework from which schemes would be encouraged to both perceive and act on, a need to change.

Stage two

The second stage of the action research used a consultancy framework within a sample of sixteen schemes. The YT schemes were selected for one or more of the following reasons:

- They were representative of a particular training area (ie, banking, construction, retail). A cross-section of training areas was felt to be important.

- They were a large and/or prestigious project that could provide reasonable employment opportunities.

- They had, at least through their senior manager, demonstrated an interest or motivation in the development of their practices on equal opportunity. (Note: this did not mean that the schemes were chosen because change was more likely, rather that some initial motivation would allow a certain level of access within the organisation.)

The method used in this stage of the action research was constructed on the basis of the information from stage one. It represented a model for planned change that was seen to be potentially effective in ensuring development as well as getting information from schemes. There were three aspects to the model:

The initial interview

The questionnaire devised for stage one of the project was revised and developed for use within the second stage. Although the questionnaire formed the basis for the interview, different schemes required different questions depending on:

- the way the scheme was organised;

- the type of scheme;

- the level of existing understanding of or openness to the issues;

- the level of conflict generated by the questioning.

I wrote down information within the following broad areas:

- relevant statistical information (eg, number of black trainees);

- the written or 'assumed' policy of the scheme;

- the publicity/recruitment/interviewing practices;

- the induction/development/staff training practices;

- the monitoring and evaluation practices;

- the needs that schemes could identify for their own development related to equal opportunity.

The initial interview lasted generally between two and three hours and was again conducted with one or more people on the scheme staff who were responsible for the development of policy. Although some schemes in phase two were the same schemes as in phase one, the initial interview was still conducted. During this time the following opportunities were additionally being sought:

- To reflect on the schemes own practices with the interviewee in such a way that the person could see any of the shortcomings of existing practice.

- To challenge, where possible in the context of the interview, the assumptions of interviewees.

In summary, the initial interview stage was mainly concerned with drawing out and recording the interviewee's perceptions of existing policy and practice and their personal attitudes and perceptions.

Discussion within a support group

I provided a brief written report to a support group of people selected as a result of their involvement with YTS and equal opportunity. The areas covered in the report were:

- the policy of the scheme;
- the gaps between policy and practice (if there was no policy then a résumé of practices);
- the key people and the assumptions they had communicated;
- specific areas where attention seemed necessary;
- any initial recommendations.

The support group discussed this information, making decisions and recommendations regarding the next stage of the process. The support group was comprised of an equal number of black and white members. Members of the support group undertook some of the interviews themselves so that they had personal experience of scheme attitudes and could relate to the action research process.

Follow-up with schemes

Having discussed the information in the support group I attempted to 'follow-up' the scheme in some way. Follow-up was very varied. Schemes were, for example, asked to undertake a task, write a policy, devise a strategy, establish direct contact with relevant community projects or certain local people. In all cases the point of the follow-up was to encourage some action from the schemes which could be monitored at a later stage. The schemes that entered into this work began to perceive that having a policy means having a process of continual action, monitoring and development.

Types of follow-up included:

- revisiting schemes to continue working with key individuals or groups;
- developing small groups of staff from schemes with similar needs;
- matching or pairing schemes;
- providing courses and training days.

Below I highlight some of the implications for change that emerged from the action research.

A heuristic approach: managers in the organisations involved would have preferred to be informed or taught about what a good policy looks like. The development of equal opportunity policy was seen as an inconvenience and a distraction from the real work. The main strategy towards equal opportunity policy was to avoid tasks, and as far as possible to encourage either more junior staff, or me as 'the expert' to develop a policy. In addition:

- the equal opportunity was seen as 'a low priority';
- the subject of equal opportunity was highly emotive, offering considerable scope for defensiveness, avoidance, justifications and prejudice;
- equal opportunity was a frightening idea to many people interviewed either because managers felt their power or person to be threatened by it or because they did not know how to act in relation to equal opportunity.

The action research process encouraged the view from the support group that in relation to the development of good practice on equal opportunity, it was important to have a continual re-invention of the wheel. In this way, those people who did find the process difficult could experience and acknowledge their difficulty as an integral part of what they were attempting to learn. In some cases this did encourage more appreciation of what was involved in equal opportunities, in other cases it only helped to harden attitudes. This shift away from task orientation/delegation of task, into the arena of value orientation/ownership of task reduced defensiveness to a level where those individuals could accept the need for change. This meant that they had begun to work not just on the development of a policy but also on its implementation.

The approach was heuristic, in the sense of providing a clear frame within which self-managed learning might take place. This approach was seen to promote:

- The establishment of ways of learning and development that minimised collusion and tokenism.

- The establishment of clear evidence about those who were prepared to change and those who were not. Different strategies for different people could therefore be justified.

Wider issues involving equal opportunity training: looking back at the evolution of race training up to the mid-1980s there were two distinct stages. The first was Racism Awareness Training (RAT) an adaptation in this country of work by Judy Katz (1978). Racism Awareness Training linked the attitudinal to the institutional, in training sessions that were of two or three days duration. The training often began by examining individual attitudes and where they come from, moving into the ways in which these attitudes exist in, and are perpetuated by, institutions and organisations.

The second stage, Anti-Racism Training (ART), evolved as a critique and development of RAT. The difference was that in ART much more emphasis was placed on the actions that were taken as a result of individual 'awareness'. The training process also developed to include follow-up work intended to make the individuals who had been through ART more accountable for their future actions. One problem with RAT and ART (and there are many more – see Gurnah, 1984) is that although they often began to address the issues of monitoring future action, training workshops rarely gave enough time to look at that future action in more than a tokenistic way. Therefore one could ask what was the point of raising awareness if nothing was going to be done about it?

Another problem with such training was that, in giving people the language of anti-racism, they were given opportunities to be more subtle in their discrimination. The shift from attitude to action in ART was a constructive theoretical change but one that was difficult to monitor in practice. The issue of monitoring the actions that individuals develop, of making them accountable, became crucial. The full implications of these problems remained largely unaddressed by ART. This study, in process and intent, attempted to make the issue of monitoring an integral part of the work. The third phase of the action research developed this

notion further.   In addition, awareness training raised a key
paradoxical tension within the learning process, training was
successful in helping people to learn how to act *and* to avoid equal
opportunities.

Various recurring issues: in this particular context of managers
involved in YTS, a variety of personal and organisational issues
emerged:

- It was more often the organisation that was problematic and
  not the young person/trainee.   Questions about why the intake
  of black people or young women (in areas of work
  'traditionally' associated as male) were so low got a standard
  response: 'they don't apply'.

- Individual managers did not understand the need for or
  importance of positive action.   Positive action was seen as
  'reverse discrimination'.   There was a general misconception
  that equal opportunity meant treating everybody equally.   If
  the individual accepted the existence of racism and sexism in
  society then they accepted that, as a result of discrimination,
  black people and women are treated unequally.   To attempt to
  treat everyone equally in their organisation would serve only
  to reinforce and perpetuate discrimination, by denying the
  consequences of its existence.

- The study and subsequent investigation showed that many
  schemes only had one black trainee.   The action research
  suggested that schemes knew how to 'cope' when they had
  only one black trainee ("He works harder than the white
  lads") but not when there was more than one black person
  ("They group together and create a problem").

- A variety of individual justifications for inaction emerged:

  – we don't have the time, we're busy you know;

  – it's not us it's the placement providers (careers office,
  schools, parents, etc);

  – it's too big a risk;

  – it's opening up a can of worms.

- Defensiveness and avoidance were key issues to deal with in
  order to encourage individuals to a point where they could act

effectively. The issue of time was a common justification. Schemes found it difficult to understand that if their time was used up implementing ineffective practices, then they were indeed wasting their time.

- Individual managers assumed that the language they used was value free. They had little sense of why language was an issue (see Bhavnani, 1984).

Common elements of good practice: the study demonstrated and that there were elements of good practice that could be common to all schemes:

- A written equal opportunity policy document and policy statement. The statement covers overall intent, the policy covers specific practice.

- Recruitment and selection practices needed to be re-assessed from the perspective of equal opportunity. This included publicity; contacts; the image of the scheme; selection criteria; interview techniques; tests; the application form; what was said to potential trainees.

- The development of ways of dealing with the equal opportunity issues that emerge during YTS. This included having an equal opportunity content in induction programmes; appropriate training for staff and in training programmes; dealing with racism and sexism (ie, trainees, staff, placement providers); knowing how to raise issues.

- A complete range of statistical and developmental monitoring needs within a scheme. Statistical: applications to the scheme; acceptances; rate of drop out; numbers, male and female, black and white; occupational areas. Developmental: review and development group; contacts with other agencies; consistent training; openness on equal opportunities.

- An understanding of positive action as a continuous responsibility for the development of better policy and practice in relation to both equal opportunity and scheme effectiveness.

The action research highlighted some of the problems associated with implementing equal opportunity policy and practice in YT schemes.

- Policy
  - few written policies;
  - little policy implementation;
  - poor communication of policy;
  - no support for staff to understand how to implement policy;
  - no plans of action;
  - avoidance of the reasons for having a policy.
- Recruitment and selection
  - ineffective publicity;
  - no thought about relevant contacts;
  - a white/male image ;
  - no clear selection criteria;
  - no training on interview techniques;
  - irrelevant tests;
  - complex and patronising application forms;
  - no thought about how to deal with equal opportunity openly in recruitment.
- Equal opportunity during YTS
  - no evaluative mechanisms for assessing progress;
  - no equal opportunity content on induction;
  - no monitoring of the placement provider or guidelines on equal opportunity relating to them;
  - no staff training or development;
  - ineffective management of implementation and instances of discrimination.
- Monitoring
  - insufficient information to assess the development of equal opportunity within schemes;
  - unclear or non-existent records;

- no understanding of why monitoring is important;

- no internal mechanisms of development.

- Positive action

  - positive action was seen as reverse discrimination;

  - no knowledge of what to do;

  - no commitment to/reluctance to prioritise equal opportunity.

Competences for the internal change agent/active manager: reflection on the process of the action research gave rise to the identification of a range of competences, attributes and insights that might be useful for internal change agents or managers involved in the attempt to work with organisational members on the development of equality.

Knowledge about equal opportunity

- An ability to see how equal opportunity issues affected their life and work on a day-to-day basis, and how discrimination takes place in organisations.

- An ability to speak from actual experience.

- An ability to identify and deal with a range of avoidance strategies (see later in this chapter).

- An understanding of policy and practice as developmental, rather than legal.

Change skills

The study demonstrated that the development of equal opportunity in organisations is an issue that produces strong reactions. The following skills in working with change might be a part of such development:

- An ability to take risks and to be uncertain.

- An ability to recognise and work with anxiety, fear, defensiveness, avoidance, vulnerability, anger, guilt. These feelings constitute the most significant individual blocks to the development of learning on equal opportunities.

- An ability to refrain from being punitive or attacking.

The process of questioning

The aim of the action research on equal opportunity in YTS was tangible changes of policy and practice. The most effective changes were the ones that an individual worker or group perceived and implemented for themselves.

In addition, the internal change agent and/or manager involved in attempts to make change happen would need to have a formal process for themselves that assists in the continual questioning and reflection on their personal practice. This might be achieved through a variety of well boundaried processes, for example: role analysis, supervision, counselling.

The support and development of learning

The change agent needed to resist becoming the one who could provide the answers. Managers in the study would often attempt to put me in this role. It was not an effective strategy to respond directly to a manager who said "you tell me what I should be doing" since he or she would invariably go away and not do it. My responsibility was to work with the knowledge and action that people could develop for themselves.

I adopted a particular focus on initiating processes for monitoring how effectively individuals or groups act to manage their own learning and development. This involved highlighting any possibilities for learning, however minimal. Practical tasks were encouraged that could be assessed with the individual or group concerned. Understanding was then measured through individual levels of action and avoidance of the tasks set.

Monitoring and evaluation

Monitoring was the aspect of equal opportunity that seemed to make a difference to the development of good practice. I was responsible for devising an effective method of recording what was expressed. The individual manager or group was then left with a summary of actions to be undertaken. The most effective strategy was to identify and work with the key people on the scheme. The 'named person' was not always the person who made the most difference in terms of developing or changing policy and practice. (Note: at the time, MSC required each ATO to have a named person who was designated as responsible for equal opportunity.)

The end of an interview/discussion was often a very significant time. The individuals involved frequently said things that represented their actual feelings right at the end. In relation to the schemes in the study, visits normally ended with a review of the actions to be undertaken between the present meeting and the next meeting.

The Manpower Services Commission

At the same time as the action research sample described in stage two was put into effect, the MSC had local staff assessing the competences of schemes on all 10 areas that make up the submission document for becoming an ATO. This included equal opportunities. Two problems emerged in the action research that reflected directly on the MSC.

The first was that the MSC's concern was not so much for what was actually being implemented on equal opportunity within schemes, rather for what the schemes said they were implementing. In this way the MSC helped organisations to cover-up bad practice. For example, here is a record of what was on the submission document of one scheme in relation to equal opportunity:

> The Company has an excellent record for producing equal opportunities. Subject to satisfying recruitment requirements any person is eligible for this scheme. The training process is designed to provide equal opportunity and continuous assessment and ensure that individuals receive maximum benefit. All schools in the area are informed of training opportunities and a close link with schools operates through the schools liaison programme. (AATC report, 1985)

The action research view of the scheme was quite different. The scheme's intake statistics were:

September 1984   50 engineers, all male, 1 black trainee
37 clerical, all female, 1 black trainee
September 1985   50 engineers, 1 female (who left after 2 weeks) 1 black trainee
34 clerical, 1 male, no black trainees

The scheme's recruitment procedures were ineffective because most of their recruitment was unsolicited. They made no attempt at positive action to redress the imbalances demonstrated by their recruitment statistics. Only certain individuals 'receive maximum benefit' from the scheme because the training process is set up with an assumption that all training is equal for everyone.

The second problem identified by the action research concerned the documentation produced by the MSC both during and after the ATO process as it placed greater importance on information than it did on implementation. The effect of this was that schemes could see clearly what it was they should be doing, but they had little or no idea of how to do it.

Stage three

Stage one of the action research was designed to establish information relating to the nature of discrimination in YTS. This information underpinned the process used in stage two, a framework for communicating and developing good practice. The lessons learned through the process of the action research were then applied to the third stage of the process – ways of implementing and monitoring good practice.

I have identified implementation and monitoring as the two areas (at that time) in which the least work had been done and the most work was needed. The issues of implementation and monitoring received less attention because they required more effort. They were mechanisms for change that went beyond individual control, they posed a threat to YTS organisations and staff because being properly monitored meant being properly accountable. The issues that showed the greatest potential for change were also identifiable as the issues that gave rise to the greatest avoidance strategies.

In terms of implementation, the organisations involved showed a consistent difficulty in knowing what to do about equal opportunity. There were general and individual value positions which imposed barriers beyond which, staff would maintain, it was not possible to go. This point was often shown to be (at least in the first instance) the issue of positive action, which is to say, the key implementational area of development.

Monitoring also highlighted individual and organisational values. It posed a notion of wider accountability that many scheme staff found difficult to accept. Monitoring can be defined as an evaluation of the attempts that staff might make, individually or collectively, to ensure better policy and practice in their organisations. The task of such evaluation was to ensure that the actions staff attempted to implement were implemented in a way that went beyond tokenism. The data suggested that if strategies for avoidance were a prominent element of the individual's and the organisation's relationship to change on equal opportunity issues, then monitoring was a necessary aspect of working with these avoidance strategies.

In this third phase of the action research the focus of the study concerned testing ways of developing the understanding and willingness of individual staff to change. In addition, it was an attempt to provide people with a of framework which would enable them to develop their thinking about the relationship between management and equality. This framework would also help to maintain the motivation for continually prioritising measures against discrimination.

The structure of stage three was therefore based around the construction of a training pack (Vince and Kitusa, 1988) designed in relation to the development of managers. In order to test the effectiveness of the training materials the 10 most senior managers from the largest YTS in Avon (voluntarily) undertook the programme.

The pilot study

The training materials are referred to in this section as the 'development pack', which was initiated as a process of research/training. The training was designed to assist staff working on the YTS in their understanding of good practice on equal opportunity, particularly with regard to race and gender. It aimed to be both a staff resource (ie, producing useable data/sense-making) and at the same time to promote staff and organisational development. The individuals who participated in the pilot study were being assessed on the following:

- Their ability to understand how, in a practical way, equal opportunity issues affected themselves and their work on a day-to-day basis.

- Their ability to reflect on their work in order to achieve an understanding of individual responsibility within the policy of their scheme and of the MSC.

- The strategies that they implemented or plans they made to support the development of good practice.

The participants were asked to work through ten 'sections' covering key areas of equal opportunity policy and practice. These were:

Policy	Information
Terminology	Recruitment
Monitoring/evaluation	Positive action
Supervision	Management
Networking	Overall evaluation

Each participant received a copy of the development pack, and therefore had a description of each section; an outline of the understanding and level of competence required from each section; a description of the tasks that they were expected to work through; and an assessment sheet from which measurement of their progress and development could be made. At least half of the process took the form of self-directed learning. Each participant had a personal tutor to support and monitor them. They also had the opportunity to attend a series of workshops, one half-day for each section of the pack and a day each for induction into the process and evaluation of it.

The process occupied roughly 100 hours over a period of six months. Fifty hours of this were taken up by the taught part of the process:

Induction day	6 hours (one day)
The workshops	30 hours (five separate days)
Personal tutorial	8 hours (four by two hour sessions)
Evaluation day	6 hours (one day)

The remaining 50 hours (this figure was constructed as a guide to the minimum time necessary) were given to the self-directed part of the process. The structure of the process is represented in Table 4.

The workshops were delivered by myself and three other members of the support group (two black/one white). The tutorials were divided between the researcher and one other (black) member of the support group.

Table 4: The research/training process

Induction	
Workshop and tutorials 1 and 2	3 months
Individual and group evaluation	
Tutorials 3 and 4 to enable participants to fulfil tasks set over a longer period: eg, positive action strategies, monitoring data, etc	3-6 months

Some key points from the pilot study

Policy

The study initially highlighted the poor understanding participants had of what an equal opportunity policy is. The outcome of the pilot group's work on EO policy was a document which outlined their position in relation to practice as well as policy. In addition to a broad outline or statement, the group produced guidelines for monitoring training and trainee progress, which was a list of 'do's and don'ts' around induction, training agreements, training programmes, on and off the job trainer action, placement providers and the policy, grievance and disciplinary procedures. A good practice guide was also attached to this information which covered the issues of publicity, application forms, selection procedures, interviews and the use of tests.

One achievement was that policy stopped being a document in a filing cabinet that participants could not remember seeing, and started to become a developmental and working statement of desired change, containing specific actions to implement the policy. The group were also able to agree actions related to their own responsibility as managers. All participants in the pilot study were asked to produce policy documents. The standards varied considerably, but the process of having to write a policy both pressured individuals to extend their understanding and offered tangible, written evidence of present standards. As a group, they were able to combine the work into a comprehensive policy document that fitted the needs of the scheme. Even though all the participants were not directly responsible for the policy that finally emerged, they all contributed to the development of it, and therefore had some ownership of it.

Information

The effort individuals made to develop a resource bank of information also varied. Two or three participants in particular made contact with organisations that could provide them with relevant information and materials. The different levels of motivation among participants were indicated very clearly in this section. Some were able to be enthusiastic and active in relation to their own learning process, others found it a struggle to do anything other than the basic requirements of the exercise. This section, therefore, provided information about the relationship of individuals to the process they were in.

Language and terminology

The workshop provided the clearest starting point for the participants in terms of understanding the relationship between language and discrimination. The participants level of understanding was measured in relation to the words that they themselves found difficult to acknowledge as either discriminatory, stereotyped or carrying with them historically based prejudices. All participants were able to describe examples that they had encountered of the racist/sexist language of others. They used this information to begin to sort out possible future strategies. It was difficult to assess how comprehensively participants were making an effort to change aspects of their language. The section on language seemed particularly useful in highlighting individual defensiveness.

Recruitment

The pilot study asked participants to identify the potential pitfalls in recruitment practice, and to devise a model for recruitment practices within the organisation. All participants did this even though they might not be directly responsible for the recruitment of staff or trainees.

Monitoring

Participants determined the data that they needed for statistical monitoring and looked at the ways of putting developmental monitoring into practice. The defined areas for collecting statistical data were increased, and information technology was introduced to store and segment the information. One new area they included covered the number of black trainees that left the scheme during monthly periods. The information provided some surprises, including evidence that 56% of the scheme's intake of black young people left within the first 12 weeks of the two-year scheme. Such information was very useful because it enabled the managers to focus in on very specific tasks. The managers were also asked to create a model of the type of developmental monitoring needs relevant to a new YTS scheme.

Positive action

The development pack asked staff to devise action plans related to positive action on three levels:

- Individual action plans

- Action plans for any groups they work in

- Organisational action plans.

The pack stipulated that positive action plans needed to be realistic, practical, clear, comprehensive and possible. There were varying degrees of interpretation of what those words involved. The agreement between individual participants and the tutor was that plans needed to propose a practical starting point for action in their work. Working groups/teams needed to show plans that indicated a monitorable course of development. The important aspect of the study was to create an environment where planning was clearly linked to implementation and was not undertaken in a vacuum. Individuals needed to show planning to be practical, clear and assessable. The "specific incidents of racism and sexism" outlined in section six (Vince and Kitusa, 1988) were all based on situations that had been related to the researcher in stages one and two. Individual responses and solutions to these examples ranged considerably.

Supervision and management

The group of managers involved in the pilot study were only indirectly concerned with the issue of supervision; they all managed groups of supervisors. One focus of the work of the group was therefore about how to support and encourage their own staff to respond effectively to racism and sexism from their trainees, and to provide a clear equal opportunity content in the YTS training programmes they offered. Managers were required to demonstrate how they would support their staff to do this.

The approach of the study in terms of their role as senior managers, was to emphasise to them the idea that good practice on equal opportunity supports and enhances management practice. This proposition was not universally acceptable to the managers involved in the pilot study.

Networking

Participants were asked to develop support networks for themselves and their work around the issue of equal opportunities. The idea of this was that the managers would invite two or three people from within their locality to form an occasional support group, offering advice and external accountability for the development of their knowledge and practice on equal opportunities. Participants found this difficult. Those who did not form such informal groups were those who had had the least contact in the past with black people. Two individuals were able to develop their contacts and create forums for their continuing development. In one case, the individual approach taken by a white manager angered the black organisation he approached. The tasks outlined in this section were prone to avoidance. In some cases the last thing the managers wanted to do was to learn how to interact directly with members of the black community in their area.

Evaluation

The final section concerned ways in which the participants could look at what they had learned and developed through their involvement with the pilot study. This was included in the study to encourage a level of clarity from them about their own learning before the actual evaluation day. Participants did not necessarily make this connection.   Within tutorials, participants were encouraged to share what they felt they had learned, to consider what the process of learning was like for them, and to discuss any misgivings and difficulties they had.

The evaluation day was built around a number of questions:

- What did you feel was good about the development process?

- What was not so good?

- What do you feel you have learned?

- How would *you* have planned the process of staff/ organisational development in the scheme?

- How will you continue to develop what you started to learn through the development pack and the workshops you attended:

  a) personally?

  b) with those people for whom you are responsible as a manager? – which areas would you stress as being particularly important?

- What are you going to do about equal opportunity in the next three months?

The responses can be summarised as follows:

1. Participants felt good about the structure and the content of the process, looking at the issues specifically over a period of time (eg, "it forced me to focus very specifically on EO"; "I learned that EO means something to me"; "I was able to develop over a period of time").

Some participants did not like the 'confrontational' element of the programme and thought that it was too time consuming. Others resented the fact that they put more work into the process than their colleagues. Parts of the 'doing' of the tasks in the pack were 'very boring' to some, others 'didn't know when to stop' (eg, "being part of a process that others were committed to less than I was"; "I felt that I couldn't do anything right"; "It took up too much of my time").

2. There were a variety of things that the managers thought they had learned from the experience, for example:

- "a greater understanding of the legislation"
- "knowledge of where to get help and information"
- "the importance of commitment from above"
- "how to deal better with people making racist/sexist comments"
- "the meaning of positive action and its importance"
- "the distance we all have to go"
- "the scale of the problem"
- "EO is a complex issue, which needs to be considered on a feeling level as well as a factual level"
- "I was surprised by some of my own feelings on the issues".

3. The process of staff/organisational development within the scheme would have been developed differently by the participants in the following ways: eg, "Workshops would have been based within the colleges themselves and led by some of your team with support from senior college staff"; "top down, with the top directing firmly".

4. Continued development would occur for the individuals themselves through 'reflection' and 'discussion'; "by trying to find out about the state of EO policy within the County". For the people they managed, development would occur through "the development of a training programme for the rest of the staff delivered by us as a team"; "agenda items at meetings"; "running key person's meetings" (ie, each college had one person designated as responsible for EO); "using monitoring data to identify training needs"; "advise, suggest, direct, meet with others"; "regular meetings for policy development"; "awareness raising with college staff"; "checking recruitment and selection procedures".

5. Within the three months following the end of the pilot study participants were going to: "analyse data on trainees"; "ensure all my staff have and have read the policy statement and document"; "challenge staff who make unacceptable comments, statements".

Conclusions to the overall study

At the beginning of this chapter I said that one route towards acquiring the skills necessary to understand and implement change within an organisation can be gained through the development and implementation of equal opportunity policy and practice. I want to return to this idea, and look at the significance of this action research in the identification of strategies for both avoiding and encouraging change. The identification of managerial avoidance strategies are a particularly useful outcome of the action research because they illustrate some of the key difficulties of learning and change in relation to equality. The study itself was designed as one model of organisational change, and this overall process can be considered alongside the specific issues that individual managers and groups of managers found acceptable and unacceptable about moves towards equal opportunities within their organisations.

Avoidance strategies

In outlining the avoidance strategies that emerged within the three phases of the action research I have attempted to set out an appropriate map of the avoidance of change in organisations on equal opportunity policy and practice, and in more general terms on the relationship between equality and management learning. I call this process 'management by avoidance'. Management by avoidance occurs through the behaviour of individual managers and also at a group and organisational level. I highlight a range of processes underlying management by avoidance, particularly relating to change that is possible for individuals within an organisation, and to potential changes of organisational policy and practice (see Chapter 5).

Processes underlying management by avoidance

Denial of the problem: most of the managers involved did not deny the existence of racism and sexism in society or even within their organisation, but they frequently denied racism and sexism as an aspect of their own experience. Individuals in the action research found it very difficult to relate to equality. Racism and sexism were somebody else's problem, not theirs. "What can I do about it?" was the plea. Individual defence against equality opportunity was a strategic act, motivated by the need to avoid conflict.

Saying not doing: gaps between what was said and what was done emerged as strategies for development, were agreed and then not kept. The action research showed the power of 'intention' as an interim avoidance measure, and therefore the importance of integral procedures to evaluate intent.

Assumed not written: competence in terms of equal opportunity was often defined in terms of professional competence. Therefore, for example, personnel managers were competent on equal opportunity issues because they had been professionally trained to work with people. The need to have clear policy was avoided through the assumption that professional people already knew how to act. Organisations maintained that their more value-based policies were assumed into the organisation by professional standards and practices rather than built in through written policy. The outcome of this perspective was: that which could not be seen, could not be evaluated, would not be changed. In this way, organisations managed to avoid any direct accountability for the development of their policies in everyday practice.

Image not fact: organisations might produce publicity information with photographs of black trainees when there were no black trainees on the scheme. They avoided dealing with the issues in effective ways by becoming aware of how to deal with them in tokenistic ones.

Blaming the victim: where it was possible for individuals to acknowledge discrimination, it was not always clear to them who it belonged to and what it was. In terms of race, for example, the inability of black young people to 'get their act together' was an altogether more frequent interpretation than the bad practice of the organisation itself. The avoidance of action emerged from an individual's ability both to blame (and/or resent) another person in preference to seeing the faults in current practice. Avoidance was facilitated by the ease with which individuals accepted the myth that everybody is treated equally by the same organisational practice. Individual resentment gave rise to a consistent interpretation of positive action as 'reverse discrimination'.

Individuals therefore acquired a very active form of resentment, which was destructive of their willingness to act.

There was another form of blame, which was more organisational than individual. Whereas, individually, blaming the victim was about 'them', on an organisational level it was about what 'we' are supposed to do to accommodate 'them'. It was as if disadvantaged groups were seen as a demanding lot, and the existence of a code of practice for organisations gave rise to resentment about the fuss. Managers conveyed a grudging acknowledgement of the need to do certain things (eg, having a written policy). Actions undertaken from this emotional perspective had the effect of making the organisation a worse place for black people or women because policies were being implemented without any real knowledge of why they were needed. Managers were able to say "we did this and they are still not satisfied".

Fear, emotion and defensiveness: a key contribution to the avoidance of change by individuals involved in the study was their inability to effectively deal with their fears and emotions as an integral aspect of their work. Neither fears nor emotions were accepted as important aspects in an understanding of change. It is by no means a new idea to say that organisations suffer from the suppression of emotion and fears. The over-riding consequence of such suppression in the wider context of organisational development, is defensiveness. Some of the specific contributions the concept of defensiveness seems to make to the avoidance of change are as follows:

- an increased tendency to justify/rationalise;

- interpersonal hostility, mistrust, un-listening;

- increased dependency on hierarchy to establish boundaries;

- one-sided personal management styles;

- task-orientation and fear of process;

- increased distance from 'open' styles of policy and decision making;

- increased isolation through an increasingly individualised interpretation of responsibility;

- excessive competitiveness.

Values: any values that may have driven individuals and/or organisations towards equal opportunity policy become clichés, with no apparent relevance to the development needs of an organisation. Values become given, they are made to seem unchanging, whereas it may be that a shift in values is one of the key factors in the ability to organise towards change.

A rigid distinction between life and work: individuals have experiences outside their direct interaction with work which are equally a part of their value systems within work.

Hierarchical differences: the organisational structures represented in the study tended to be hierarchical. The visible power in the organisation therefore was invested in the senior manager(s). There were generally three different types of personality involved, those who were interested in and motivated towards equal opportunity sufficiently to think about it (even if they might reject aspects of EO at a later stage), those who were hostile to the issues from the beginning, and those who used their interest and hostility in political ways. These three different 'styles' demonstrated different management avoidances.

The (more or less) motivated managers were the easiest to work with (in terms of individual and organisational change) because they were open to learning something about equal opportunity. Personal avoidance strategies were mobilised in terms of very specific issues because this type of manager was prepared to say "no, that is going too far".

The (more or less) hostile managers were difficult to work with because their whole approach was about avoidance, and they were not interested in learning or change. The more their views were questioned, the more defensive they became. Their potential development seemed to depend on finding ways of directly challenging their more obvious avoidances.

The (more or less) politically astute managers were the most difficult to work with because they pretended that they had the motivation to learn and to change. Their main avoidance strategy was to agree to do the absolute minimum possible that would satisfy the consultant. Such individuals would carefully agree tasks and then deliberately interpret them in different ways, they would learn some of the language of equal opportunity to give the impression that they knew how to do the work, they would listen and then ignore, agree then forget, arrange to meet then cancel.

They were either dishonest, or they perceived a benefit to being ambiguous. Their learning was never certain, never clear. Their motivation to learn was bound up with the politics of the situation.

White, male power: managers had no consciousness of a collective white, male experience in terms of equality/inequality, just a collective experience based on the 'values in society'. The action research showed how the issue of power was continually avoided through the lack of recognition (knowledge/concern) of what dominant social values are, and how they are constructed and maintained.

The political definition of 'expert': the notion of expert was not simply a matter of the professional competence of an individual. It was also wrapped up with wider power issues within the organisation. Expert was not solely defined as the person who knows best (as a result of their training or experience) it was also to do with the person who fits best. In this way, organisations managed to control what constituted legitimate expertise, both internally and externally.

Important practices/low priorities: evaluation, monitoring, consultation, accountability, training were all put forward as key aspects of organisational change. They were perpetually avoided by organisations in the rush to undertake tasks and provide solutions to daily working crises.

Risk and uncertainty: the avoidance of risk and the seeming inability organisations showed to deal with the uncertainties inherent in the development of equal opportunity, mirrored a broader difficulty surrounding the need for control of change.

Tokenism and fear: where there was, for example, only one black trainee on the scheme, managers often acknowledged how hard she or he worked ("best one we've got"). Where there was more than one black trainee in the same scheme, managers acknowledged how "they tended to stick together". Sometimes such groups were seen as the cause of trouble. Most of the schemes that did have black trainees, only had one black trainee. Where more than token numbers of trainees were employed, managers' fear of groups of black trainees made them wary.

Delegation as avoidance: delegation was used as a way of marginalising equal opportunity. The responsibility for development was often passed down from (often male) senior managers to an individual (often a woman) lower in the hierarchy, with enthusiasm but little influence. This minimised the impact of suggestions related to change of practice and allowed senior staff to escape from being tied up with what they saw as 'secondary' issues. It was often the task that was being delegated not the power.

Making a difference: having outlined some of the processes involved in the avoidance of change, I now want to identify three areas that were accepted as useful, legitimate or at least clear in terms of change. In other words, the ideas or interventions that at the time seemed to make a difference.

Equal opportunity as an everyday issue: the most important realisation for some individuals involved in the action research was on the need for action at everyday levels of their work. Equal opportunity was thereby seen less as an externalised policy, and more as an integral aspect of work. Some managers were able to think of actions (and procedures for implementing them) quite quickly once they had understood the various ways in which equal opportunity issues affected and impinged on their own work. Similarly, once managers were aware of the expectations their organisational policies placed on them, they could carry a clearer picture of personal responsibility. Written guidelines were favoured as an aid to the changes that they might be expected to implement.

Awareness of emotional dynamics: it was possible for managers to accept that their emotions played a more significant part in the implementation of their work than they had previously acknowledged. In some cases, managers learned to work with more than defensive responses. With less defensiveness there was an increase in the ability to question established practice, or to listen more effectively to different perspectives on the nature and implementation of good practice.

Building a developmental approach: some managers were able to accept the need for more effective evaluation, monitoring and training. The emphasis on implementing policy (rather than simply having it) encouraged a more developmental approach simply because much more information was being generated and used within schemes. Policy was seen less as a set of general rules and more as an ever-developing range of guidelines for action, that could change according to the changing needs of the organisation on equal opportunity issues.

One consistent difficulty the organisations and individuals within this study have had with the implementation of change in relation to equal opportunity has been that defensiveness and avoidance strategies are more prevalent than action. The pilot study showed that, even in an organisation that had 'invited' change, the barriers to change posed by levels of avoidance created an uphill struggle for everybody involved. Despite this, the research described here suggests that it is important to try to work with and beyond these avoidance strategies. Paradoxically, change initiatives might productively begin from an exploration of what is avoided. The experience of the action research described in this chapter suggests that this will include at least the following fifteen items:

1   The mechanisms of problem denial.

2   The differences between intent and action (saying and doing).

3   The patterns of blame.

4   The patterns of defensiveness (fear).

5   Methods for the suppression of values, or values that are used to suppress.

6   Methods for the negation of emotion and experience.

7   Levels of interest or hostility towards problem-posing forms of learning and/or development

8   The various methods of political control – interpersonal and hierarchical.

9   Patterns of white, male power.

10 The levels of dependency on: professionalism, task-orientation, previous practice.

11 Methods for the minimalisation of evaluation.

12 Methods for the exclusion of clear accountability and consultation.

13   Methods for re-enforcing certainty within the organisation.

14   Methods for sustaining organisational isolation.

15   Methods for the continual suppression of power issues.

five

Management by avoidance

In the previous chapter I introduced the idea of management by avoidance. Management by avoidance refers to processes that are a part of the avoidance of change in organisations around equal opportunity policy and practice, and in more general terms around the relationship between equality and management learning. My initial work in this area led me to conclude that organisations contain a set of value driven avoidance strategies, or everyday defences, that emerge out of the climate created in organisations by white, male power. These included strategies for: (i) denying difference; (ii) suppressing and hiding from emotion; (iii) over-emphasising professionalism; and (iv) limiting processes of learning and evaluation. I suggested therefore, that one starting point for simultaneous learning about equality and management would be an exploration of what is avoided.

In this chapter I continue to think about the nature of management by avoidance by exploring how middle and senior managers in three local authorities comprehended and implemented equal opportunities within their everyday management practice. The action research was conducted with individual (mostly white, male) managers in local government and it sought to identify and develop their understanding of equal opportunity policy and practice as well as researching it. The research attempts to build on, develop and add to the ideas contained in the last chapter. As with Chapter 4, I highlight different avoidance strategies and shows how these limit individuals' perceptions of management as well as their management practice. This limited perception of the relations between equality and management supports and perpetuates a limited perception of change.

Background information on the action research

Local authorities are under a legal obligation to promote equal opportunity. The two major Acts of parliament that spell this out are the 1975 Sex Discrimination Act and the 1976 Race Relations Act. The specific nature of the obligation is that they should:

> ... make appropriate arrangements with a view to securing that their various functions are carried out with due regard to the need:
>
> (i) to eliminate unlawful discrimination
>
> (ii) to promote equality of opportunity and good relations between persons of different racial groups. (Section 71: 1977 Race Relations Act, Home Office)

At the time that this action research was undertaken (within the three year period, 1986-89) all of the local authorities involved had well developed equal opportunity policies. For many managers, however, these policies were little more than words on paper. Part of the reason for this was the problem that individual (particularly white, male) managers had in understanding how to implement equal opportunities in their daily practice (Jones, 1988). The action research was an attempt to investigate aspects of the nature of this problem and, where possible, point towards strategies for change. The interventional component of the action research was based on the assumption that if managers were to be effective in relation to the law, then they would need to know how to break free from the self-imposed constraints of their defences and avoidance strategies. They might therefore be able to develop management styles which were better suited to increasingly diverse organisations.

I imagined that a coherent picture of key perspectives and practices held by white, male managers on equal opportunity would provide information relevant to more general processes of change. I hoped to investigate and to work with white, male managers in public service bureaucracies, in order to understand the various key elements that were used to contain or control changes around equal opportunity policy and practice. This would include both individual avoidance strategies and structural barriers to change, created by and constructed through the implementation of white, male power.

As I explained Chapter 1, when developing this action research I was not interested in being an external observer of change processes within organisations. The reflections and analysis in this chapter emerge from a series of management training events. These were designed to identify and work with the barriers that local authority managers often placed in the way of change, both in terms of their understanding of equal opportunities and in relation to their own management styles and practices.

Three local authorities participated in these events (referred to as A, B and C). The overall theme in all organisations was to investigate the barriers to and possibilities for learning and change relating to equality. In this sense therefore, the action research explored the integration between good practice on equal opportunities and good management practice.

Information on the specific events within each authority

Authority A – Theme: women and men working together

Two management training events were run with senior managers (first to fourth tier, group sizes 16 and 18 managers) from two separate departments. The emphasis of the training in each department was in two specific areas. First, the relationship between men and women working together within the senior management structures of the organisation (ie, "we will have to learn how to talk about our differences and work together", senior female manager). Second, the changes needed in management practice and service delivery for a more effective implementation of the organisation's equal opportunity policy (ie, "It is essential that we should meet our obligations and responsibilities in this area as it is a primary objective of the administration we serve", male departmental director).

The specific areas covered in terms of the action research element of the work were:

- the issues for women and men about working together;

- the different ways of working each would like to see the other develop;

- ways of moving forward together – possibilities or barriers.

Authority B – Theme: the management of change: a course for white male managers

Three events were run with middle and senior white male managers from different departments within the same authority (12 in each group; 36 managers in all). The events fitted into the overall strategy of the authority to provide separate training for black managers, women managers and white, male managers and then to bring the management issues for these three groups together. Although Authority B had had an Equal Opportunity Policy for over 10 years, the Training Section identified a very low level of understanding of how to implement the policy within day-to-day management practice.

The specific areas covered in terms of the action research element of the work were:

- What did the authority's Equal Opportunity Policy (EOP) mean to white, male managers?

- The effect of EO issues on white, male managers.

- The understanding white, male managers had of the key concepts of equal opportunity in practice.

- The ability or inability of white, male managers to understand and implement change through a greater understanding of the EOP.

Authority C – Theme: managing equal opportunity (male chief and assistant chief officers)

Two events were run with the most senior male managers within the organisation (Groups of 12; 24 managers in total). The Training Section and the EO Unit in cooperation with the Chief Officer's Group set up the event. The perspective of the Training Section/EOU was to get "senior male managers to take the responsibility for change within their own work and departments" (principal women's adviser). The management perspective was to increase the potential for "service-centred achievements" on equal opportunity (Chief Executive).

The specific areas covered in terms of the action research element of the work were:

• The meaning of the authority's EOP to senior white, male managers.

• The fears, defences and avoidance strategies of senior white, male managers.

• The effectiveness of senior, white, male managers at managing equal opportunities in practice.

• The ability of senior, white, male managers to take responsibility for change.

A summary of the number of white, male managers involved in the training events of the action research is given in Table 5.

Table 5: Summary of the number of white, male managers involved in the training events of the action research

Authority A	34 managers	21 white, male
Authority B	36 managers	36 white, male
Authority C	24 managers	22 white, male
Total		79 white, male

The motivation behind these events emerged from thinking on the nature and impact of white, male power in organisations. In the following section I explain some of my thinking about this, and then discuss the results of the action research in relation to it. I highlight the barriers and possibilities for learning and change that emerged out of responses to equality policy and practice in organisations.

Patriarchy and white, male power in management practice

One of the underlying theoretical influences behind the action research outlined in this chapter is the idea that management practice in local government is constructed through patriarchal practices and the power structures of masculinity. Hearn and Parkin (1987) see patriarchy as a major element in the construction of management: "The development of the modern profession of management and its associating and legitimating theory and thinking represents a development of patriarchal authority" (Hearn and Parkin, 1987, p 18).

One ideology which underlies patriarchal management practice is masculinity. Brittan and Maynard (1984) have identified five elements of masculinity as an ideology. These are:

- *chauvinism*, expressed through structural and institutional forms which gives men the right to dominate women;

- *politics*, the domination of women emerges from the domination of men by other men – men have power over both property and persons;

- *competitiveness*, men prove themselves through dominating others;

- *culture*, the identification of the intellect and rationality with the male in history;

- *objectification.*

The fifth element is called 'the objectification process' by Brittan and Maynard and it is one to which the other four all relate. They use this phase to mean that the power of masculinity emerges from the primacy of technique and rationality as power in society. The objectification of nature through rationality lays the basis for the objectification of all social and personal relationships:

> ... all racist/sexist practice involves a power relationship in which the subjectivity of personal experience is intertwined with the objectivity of collective and political relationship. (Brittan and Maynard, 1984, p 209)

Masculinity has been explored particularly in terms of gender relations, or how it has determined the relationship between men and women. It has been seen as a 'fragile' concept because it is constructed in "the mother present, father absent family" and expressed in "the most dangerous things we live with" like pornography (Cockburn, 1988, p 316). Connell (1983) offers a different perspective on masculinity yet reaches a similar conclusion:

> I disagree profoundly with the idea that masculinity is an impoverished character structure. It is a richness, a plenitude. The trouble is that the specific richness of hegemonic masculinity is oppressive, being founded on and enforcing the subordination of women. (Connell, 1983, p 22)

In a later book, Connell (1987) outlines three separate structural levels of relationship between women and men: *labour* (eg, the organisation of housework; the division between paid and unpaid; discrimination in jobs; unequal wages), *power* (eg, the hierarchies of the state and of private sector institutions; interpersonal violence) and *desire* (eg, the production of hetero- and homosexuality and the relationship between them; the antagonisms of gender, women hatred, men hatred, self-hatred; trust, distrust, jealousy; the emotional relationships involved in rearing children). Connell believes that the institutions in which these structures are based each have their own regimes for monitoring and progressing male authority.

This domination is visible in the need that emerges in powerful groups to control potential changes that appear as threats to their stability and power base. Powerful groupings gradually integrate the content of external criticism as a new part of the existing regime. Watson (1990) talks about this in terms of the organisation of the state as a 'fraternal' discourse:

> In response to conflict and resistance men have been able to consolidate, or at least defend, their power, and regroup as a fraternity, specifically through discourses which deny the relevance of gender. (Watson, 1990, p 231)

This capacity to "regroup as a fraternity" has been influential as a defence against management learning and organisational change. Feminist analysis in the field of social policy has discussed how the interests of women have become constituted in terms of differences between men, reinforcing the notion of the public political domain as a masculine one (Pateman, 1985). What used to be seen in feminist analysis solely as state 'patriarchy' (ie, the defence and creation of men's interests), can also be seen as state fraternity, the assumption by the state of a masculine subject.

In organisations, fraternal power finds expression particularly through a manipulation of the language of participation and equality in particular. Most of the men in organisations with a sense of the political realities that surround them support the development of equal opportunity. Equality is an issue that has to be taken seriously by white men so that we can be the guardians of the changes and differences made by such policy. To put it another way, it has become important for white men to control the pace and effects of change in relation to equality through the very processes of equal opportunity.

For example, Siim (1988) argues that in Scandinavia the increased participation of women within the welfare state, has been part of a political process which occurred mainly under male leadership. As the management and finance of the welfare state in Scandinavia has become increasingly influenced by private sector practices, this power hierarchy has been reinforced, because private sector structures at that time tended to be more hierarchical and less participatory than those that evolved within the welfare state. Siim's conclusion is that women were made the objects of politics before they were able to mobilise themselves, whereas for men it was the other way round. Feminist state theorists argue for the need to make the political dimension part of everyday life: "The essential feature of the democratic revision of the political is that it is no longer conceived as separate from everyday life" (Pateman, 1985).

These theorists argue that changes of power relations need to occur in both public and private arenas in a way that means women can participate in political life as social and political agents rather than as recipients of prescribed political development. In public sector organisations, fraternal power is perpetuated where difference between people is played down. Managers see their staff as people, rather than white staff, black staff, male staff, female staff. This denial emphasises the oppositional nature of the struggle for equality, because a lack of acknowledgement of the existence of difference encourages a lack of belief and interest in the problems that occur as a result of difference.

In the fraternal organisation, management fears about the undesirability of certain types of change may have a greater impact than management strategies to encourage change. The fraternal organisation is a potentially hostile place for all. Managers who might want to work towards equality have to contend with the dangers of stepping out of line. Anyone who is attempting to develop equal opportunity policy or practice is in danger of being excluded, because the stability and self-containment of the fraternal organisation depends on actively mapping out the boundaries both for and through its participants (ie, conforming to established sexual/racial power hierarchies). To question the boundaries endangers individuals with various mechanisms of expulsion/exclusion.

In the fraternal organisation a lot more energy is expended on talking about equality than doing things about it. It is important to maintain the gap between saying and doing, because control of change is made possible by learning the language of the opposing forces, but ignoring the implications of this for practice. This is an active process because it is driven by conscious and deliberate avoidance and defensiveness around actual practice (eg, by moving the issue to the bottom of an agenda, and then managing the time so that it won't be discussed). In this context, the more interaction that occurs around oppositional forces, the more the ability of the system to subsume acceptable parts of that opposition into itself becomes reinforced.

Defensiveness within the fraternal organisation emerges from forms of denial (this is not an issue for me therefore it is not important); of silence (this may be an issue but if I keep quiet about it, it may go away); of confusion (is this really an issue, I'm not sure, I'll wait for someone to tell me what the issue is and what to do about it); and of the manipulation of language (this is the issue, I know all about it, no need for me to do anything other than what I'm doing). Each of these strategies allows for a different positioning of people in opposition, both outside and within the organisation.

One question addressed by this action research is, what specific practices or strategies might constitute the expression of these regimes in public service bureaucracies. To look at the thinking behind this question in more detail requires an analysis of the nature of white, male power.

Issues of power

It is possible to identify three related perspectives on power that constitute a general picture of power in organisations: discursive power, disciplinary power and episodes of power. I briefly discuss these, and then bring together a range of perspectives on power as a framework which can be used to highlight the nature of white, male power in organisations.

Organisations are environments where both language and meaning are refined, as forms for the expression and control of the work carried out. Organisational members can benefit from this distinctive language because it makes it easier to control the work, the skills that surround the work, and the distinctive nature of the work. However, organisational members also have to struggle with this same distinctive language as a limitation and restriction on their own ability to work, or as a form of control of their behaviour. Such struggles themselves are part of the creation, maintenance and development of a consistent discourse, or framework of meaning, which makes an organisation what it is.

Discourse is created in the interaction between various phenomena: the social and cultural factors that determine the construction of meaning, the factors that constitute institutional knowledge, and the various systems within which behaviour is defined. Fraser (1989) outlines a model which provides a more detailed breakdown of the nature of discursive power. Her model has various parts:

- The officially recognised idioms (ie, ways of talking about needs, rights and interests).

- The vocabularies available (eg, feminist, therapeutic, religious, etc).

- The paradigms of articulation that are accepted as authoritative.

- The narrative conventions available for constructing the individual and collective stories that constitute people's social identities.

- The modes of subjectification: or the ways in which various discourses position the people to whom they are addressed as, for example, 'normal' or 'deviant'.

The model provides an explanation of patterns of interpretation and communication as elements of the construction of power within social systems. Discursive power is created and maintained through the combination of some or all of these elements. Discourse can be seen as an expression of the relationship between language (in a very broad sense) and power.

The second generalisation about power which I highlight concerns the effects of the 'discipline' of organisation on human behaviour. Foucault (1979) explores the ways in which institutions create routines as methods of discipline and control. He outlines changes within penal systems, from the discipline implicit in sovereign power (the punishment could be inflicted on the actual body of the victim) to the discipline implicit in social power (the punishment is inflicted on the individual through being subject to a constructed routine). People were not solely subjected to power but became the subjects of a power that sought:

> ... to regulate, to legislate, to tell the right from wrong, the norm from deviance, the ought from the is. It wanted to impose one ubiquitous pattern of normality and eliminate everything and anybody which the pattern could not fit. (Bauman, 1982)

Disciplinary power is such that it creates an environment within which both punishments and rewards can be situated, and in which the behaviour of individuals and groups can be readily assessed. Through the encouragement of comparison between one individual or group and another, and through a continuous assessment of each individual or group against each other, discipline is exercised as a 'normalising' judgement (Sheridan, 1980).

Disciplinary power can be seen to create and promote normalising forces within an organisation. These forces become part of the human perception of how to behave, they become reinforced and developed through subsequent behaviour. Disciplinary power manifests itself less as tangible authority and more as processes of habituation or self-regulation to which people inevitably become committed.

The self-regulating effects of disciplinary power contribute to the structural development of an organisation. People within organisations are subject to the discipline that is our work, to forms of discipline in relation to the work, to our own experience of discipline (both actual and imagined) that is a constraint on doing our work. In addition, we standardise and routinise our own work, we discipline ourselves emotionally and rationally, through guilt about work we are not doing, by making comparisons with others, or by using a standard management approach to all situations rather than a variety of approaches for different situations.

All these practices are forms of disciplinary power, ways of 'normalising' a situation or environment. Although hierarchical power provides certain privileges and opportunities to some and not others, the powerful and the powerless in organisations can be seen as both having a role to play in the creation and perpetuation of processes of subjugation both for themselves and others.

Clegg (1989) acknowledges the paradoxical nature of organisations both as the site of people's entrapment within webs of their own creation, and the site of people's capacity to break free from them. He argues:

> ... against the reduction of power to either axis of the debate over structure and agency. It is neither the intentions of subjects ... nor the determination of structures which explain power.   Instead, power is best approached through a view of more or less complex organised agents engaged in more or less complex organised games. (Clegg, 1989, p 20)

Much of the everyday expression of power occurs in identifiable and changing episodes between people. These episodes are useful in identifying the various ways in which power is expressed in specific organisational contexts. They are articulated as a part of the reproduction of existing structures of power through everyday relations.

Perspectives on power

In order to construct a more specific framework for considering white, male power I have identified a range of perspectives. Lukes (1974) maintains that there are three different debates on power and that each debate adds an extra dimension to an analysis of it.

He finds the characteristics of the first dimension in the work of Robert Dahl, who conceptualises power "as the capacity of one actor to do something affecting another actor which changes the possible pattern of specified future events" (quoted in Lukes, 1974). Power therefore is a behavioural phenomenon, synonymous with influence or control.

A critique of the behavioural nature of this perspective of power, found in the work of Bachrach and Baratz, leads Lukes into a second dimension of power. This dimension acknowledges that power is being exercised not only when one actor affects another, but through the capacity to create parameters that limit another person's ability to act. In other words, power is exercised through an ability to control what is and is not practised:

> All forms of political organisation have a bias in favour of the exploitation of some kinds of conflicts and the suppression of others, because organisation is the mobilisation of bias. Some issues are organised into politics while others are organised out. (Schattschneider, quoted in Lukes, 1974, p 16)

Power in the two-dimensional view is the control over the agenda of possible action to ensure the exclusion of contentious issues. Lukes develops this view to the extent that power is not present just in the individual capacity to control the parameters of action but in the historical context of the form of organisation in which those individuals are situated. That is to say in circumstances directly encountered from the past, in socially structured, culturally patterned behaviour, and in the practices of institutions. At the third dimension of power, Lukes extends the definition beyond actual or observable conflict to acknowledge how such forces shape perceptions, cognitions and preferences in a way that encourages the acceptance of existing order. People are therefore, in a most complex way, inextricably bound up in a web of interests whether they are powerful or powerless. Such interests place limitations on their ability to act:

> People's wants may themselves be a product of a system which works against their interests and, in such cases relates the latter to what they would want and prefer, were they able to make the choice. (Lukes, 1974, p 32)

Giddens (1984) re-asserts a two-dimensional view of power whereby individuals can act or not, depending on their capacity to make a difference. He also acknowledges a need to recognise the circumstances of social constraint where people have no choice. Having no choice, therefore, does not mean that it is not possible to act, rather, that action is subject to the "dialectic of control in social systems". Thus:

> Power within social systems which enjoy some continuity over space and time presumes regularised relations of autonomy and dependence between actors or collectives in contexts of social interaction. But, all forms of dependence offer some resources whereby those who are subordinate can influence the activities of their superiors. (Giddens, 1984, p 12)

Giddens' disagreement with the emphasis on the socio-historical perception of power preferred by Lukes stems from a need in his own work to avoid concentrating on one or other side between the experience of individual actors and the influence of society. He is concerned with the study of social practices and the ways in which social actors continually recreate those practices. An important aspect to this is that these practices "are not brought into being by social actors but continually recreated by them via the very means whereby they express themselves as actors." (p 13). Therefore, within and through what we do, we reproduce the conditions that make actions possible. Another way to express this might be that "everyone in his or her own way is a victim and supporter of the system" (Havel, 1985, p 20). In thinking about the workings of power in organisations it is useful to acknowledge that there is a relationship between actors and actions that is at the same time, about both power and powerlessness:

> ... power is employed and exercised through a net-like organisation. And not only do individuals circulate between its threads; they are always in the position of undergoing and exercising this power. (Foucault, 1979)

I think that any attempt to pin down or define the notion of power in organisations would necessarily have its limitations. Power cannot be seen simply as an individual's ability to affect another, nor can it be described solely in terms of enabling a system to work in favour of specific values. In order to provide an idea of the concept of power I highlight various definitions, some conflicting, some connected, which together provide a picture of the issues involved when talking about power in organisations.

1. *Power as authority:* one actor has or is given the 'right' to affect another (Parsons in Lukes, 1986).

2. *Power as the realisation of individual will:* actions are undertaken in such a way that the probability of the individual being able to realise their 'will' is increased (Weber in Lukes, 1986).

3. *Power as legitimacy:* groups derive their own legitimacy from the very act of organising. Individuals have power legitimated within that context, as representatives. When the group disappears the power of the representative vanishes (see Lukes, 1986).

4. *Power as subjugation* (or *subject*-ion): people are subjects in a double sense, subject to others 'by control and dependence' and tied to their "own identity by consciousness and self knowledge" (Foucault, 1979). Such dependency takes the form of continuous processes that govern and dictate our behaviours, processes of 'normalisation'. This resonates with Gramsci's (1971) exploration of the relationship between conflict and consent, that power shapes people's definition of themselves, their needs and how to meet them ('latent conflict').

5. *Power as the mobilisation of bias:* the ability to create the conditions under which individual or collective values can be imposed and, in addition, to control the parameters of any future agendas (Bachrach and Baratz, in Lukes, 1974).

6. *Power as varying relations of control within social systems:* the resources exist within social systems for an influence that is two-way, despite and because of any hierarchical relationship. People therefore continually move in and out of situations of autonomy and dependence on an inter-personal level (Giddens, 1984).

7. *Power as prescription over interests:* what a person wants may in itself be a product of a system that works against their

interests, that is, a "false or manipulated consensus" (Lukes, 1974).

8. *Power as a "regime of truth"*: (Foucault, 1981). The truth of what is right as defined by the political, social and moral parameters within our society constitutes a regime which is limiting of itself and of the changing nature of truth. People's own experience, should it conflict with this truth, is seen as invalid. Therefore, the capacity to challenge the regime is itself limited, because the regime is within and outside all people. What varies, is the individual or collective ability to re-enforce or reject the regime through their own experience, the ability to "speak truth to power" (Havel, 1985).

The definitions of power that I have outlined form a framework within which it is possible to study certain aspects of power. This framework can be used to analyse and discuss the nature of white male power in organisations.

White male power

I have provided a framework composed of eight interlinked perspectives on power. I now want to give these definitions a practical context by using them to speculate on how white, middle-class men use each of these types of power to perpetuate our ability to control and to organise. The link between perspectives on power and their expression through the experience of white, middle-class men is relevant here for two reasons. First, I am a white, middle-class man myself, and will be speaking in part from my own experience. Second, most of the managers involved in the action research were white, middle-class men, and the study was designed to capture and to explore their experience.

Authority

I think that one of the things white, middle-class men are taught is to believe that we are right. We are told that we are responsible for ensuring that we should protect and provide for our own and that it is 'up to us'. We are led to believe that the world will fall apart unless we hold ourselves together. We are told that it is essential for us to believe in our own rightness and our own rights.

We have not, as men, been able to learn that we do not have to be right. Because we believe we have the right to control, and that we are the ones who can do it right we have defined authority in our own individual terms, ignoring any accountability to a wider set of values. Our society, through the system of education within which we all participate, encourages us to recreate the world in our own image. It has given white men the right to be powerful over others without teaching us how to be powerful with them. We tend towards seeing life as the exercise of power, not as learning how to exercise power.

The realisation of will

In addition to being taught that we are right and that we have more rights (eg, more right to work than a woman because we are meant to be the family provider), we are also encouraged to be competitive, individualistic, rational and emotionless. These are the tools we are encouraged to use in our interactions with the world. These are the mechanisms we use to increase the probability of us being able to get what we want from the world.

Legitimacy

The process of planning, developing and running organisations has so often been undertaken by white, middle-class men. As a result of this the value systems that underlie organisations are white male. Because organisations often reflect and develop from a base of white, male values, the actions of individual white men are given more legitimacy within organisations and groups. In having greater legitimacy we have greater opportunity.

Subjugation

As white men we are subject to the belief that we should be right, competitive, individual, rational and emotionless. We occasionally realise, in a variety of ways, that these characteristics can be damaging both to ourselves and others; however, they are what is expected of us. Our consciousness and knowledge of ourselves is such that we feel dependent on them, and would have to struggle enormously to let them go. We are the subjects of our own socialisation and this gives us shackles as well as freedoms. Our power therefore is not only in our greater potential to be able to act in a world that is predominantly defined by us, but also within our capacity to be defensive about what we know, or vaguely sense, to be wrong about it. Such defensiveness is powerful because it gives us the incentive not to act.

The mobilisation of bias

We have, as white men, been responsible for creating organisations that perpetuate racism and sexism, simply because we have mobilised our own assumptions without making them accountable to any wider framework of experience. We have not been able to make a connection between organising for our own advantage and organising to the disadvantage of others. We have assumed that anybody can be serviced equally by our organisations just because they exist.

Variable relations of control

The resources exist in any system for us as white, middle-class men to be both the victim and the beneficiary. We have not been able to understand and use our experiences as the victims of white male power to enable the system to change. While we as white men have vested interests in maintaining existing values, we should be able to acknowledge that we too are oppressed by forms of organisation that derive from white, male power, just as we would through any underlying discourse of organisation.

Interests

What we do in an organisation as white, middle-class men, is conditioned by a limited framework of interests. That is to say, our own interests. This framework, covering issues of class, philosophy, morality, organisation, places limitations on us even though they have emerged from what can be generally described as a white, male value system. It is not in my interest, for example, to be paid to work 35 hours a week and actually to work 60, to be expected to put my work before my family, to cancel my holiday in order to finish outstanding work. Managers acquiesce to such demands only because they believe that it is in their interests to do so.

The regime of truth

The regime that we impose on the world as white, middle-class men is that our values are the right values. If black people or women can accept these values, then they too can participate inside the boundaries of what we have called truth. We have ensured that our values exist within all people to some degree, and in doing this we have deliberately minimised the possibility of a change occurring that we do not control. We can speak our truth, but because we believe it to be the truth, we find it difficult to listen to what is true for others.

Given the above, I would suggest that, at present, our power as white, middle-class men in organisations has the following aspects:

- We are powerful simply because we are white men. The forms of organisation we predominantly deal with emerge from white male values, and because of this we begin with a considerable advantage.

- As white men we have had the power to develop the policies and practices of organisations. We are consequently responsible for dealing with the limitations and anomalies of those policies and practices through sharing power.

- We have the power to be enabling and supportive of the development of diverse values but we use that power to be defensive, dismissive and blocking. We let our fears get the better of our intelligence.

- We have justified our power to implement our fears by refusing to see any difference between people. In saying that we treat everyone equally we have defined the needs of others through our own needs.

- We have increased our power by maintaining that we are powerless to affect change. Through inaction we have maintained our power while pretending a sympathy for change.

- We have suppressed and ignored the development of effective forms of evaluation, consultation, accountability and management learning. We have done this because we have a greater investment in non-change than in change.

- We want to be told by others how to change, and through wanting to be told by someone else we reinforce our own lack of responsibility and commitment for different approaches.

If (as white, middle-class men) we are taking change seriously, then this is the type of change we have to deal with. Discussion about how to restructure the department, looking at the effectiveness of our team, working out the finer points of leadership style, none of these can effectively change anything unless these power issues are perceived, acknowledged and worked on as an integral part of change. Redressing inequalities present as a result of power in public service bureaucracies may well be central to the capacity of such organisations to both change relations and to relate to change.

Although I have deliberately framed these aspects of organisational behaviour in specific terms (white, male power), I do not think that such patterns are exclusively white and male. Rather, I think that they express something of the nature of the white, male discourse as organisational and personal power. For men in organisations it seems important to be aware of the various ways that we are caught in this power and powerlessness of our own creation. In the following discussion therefore, I consider the question: what is it we should be doing?

First it seems necessary to understand what it means to be positioned in this way in relation to power and powerlessness. One step is to develop a political sense of ourselves in organisations, not just a sense of how to manipulate organisational politics. It seems important to stop divorcing what we are from how we act. The strategies we develop to do this need to be done for our own good, and not in the paternalistic belief that we are doing someone else a favour.

It also seems important for us to acknowledge the emotional nature of work. Rather than being afraid of the consequences of emotion, we increasingly need to find ways of integrating the rational, emotional and political aspects of ourselves. We will need to be aware of how we project our needs and unwanted emotions onto others. We need to unlearn how to be responsible *for* others and instead learn how to act responsibly *with* others.

As white, middle-class men we often allow ourselves to think that our education and the struggle to attain professional qualifications gives us the necessary experience to do our work. The right qualifications for a job are not necessarily contained in our educational and professional qualifications, and we might need to acknowledge that in many situations our skills, knowledge, perceptions and experiences fall short. It is also necessary for us to acknowledge that the work we undertake in public service bureaucracies is not solely about the performance of tasks. If change is to happen, we need to become conscious both of the processes at work behind those tasks and especially of the underlying power relations that have conditioned the development of such processes.

At present we have not been able to understand the differences between people. It suits our ends as white men to say that 'basically, underneath, all people are the same'. It now seems necessary to get behind such justifications, so that we can relate to people whose experiences and lives are different from our own. Organisations change much more slowly than the needs they deal with. As white men we have to learn how to be more open to change, in our own styles of working and in our understanding of the appropriateness of organisational practice.

Analysis and discussion

So far in this chapter I have provided information on an action research process undertaken within three local authorities. This was followed by a conceptual discussion of power and particularly the nature of white, male power in organisations. Although this discussion may have been more appropriate in Part One, it provides an important frame for the more specific consideration of avoidance strategies that follows. Avoidance strategies have been a key everyday aspect of the discourse of white, male power within local authorities.

The focus of the action research was on responses from local authority senior managers responsible for ensuring the implementation of equal opportunities within their organisations. Using a series of training events, the project questioned how (particularly white, male) managers might integrate the principles and practices of equal opportunities into their daily work. The action research identified a range of defensive reactions from individual white, male managers to equality of opportunity which place limitations on the management of staff, on overall management practice, on service delivery, and on the management of change.

Two levels of analysis, representing two different aspects of learning and change were addressed in the action research:

- *Content:* what are the barriers to change and the possibilities for change arising out of the experience of white, male managers?

- *Process:* what will an effective process for approaching equality and change with individuals need to include?

Barriers to change

Denial of difference: most of the managers involved showed little or no acknowledgement that the differences between men and women, black and white, make any real difference in organisations in relation to, for example, management practice or the development of policy. Views were expressed in general terms: "we should be working together on this" or "we all have an equal capacity to get on and/or change the organisation". Managers lacked a specific understanding of how to work with the differences between female and male, black and white staff and/or service recipients. Managers were detached from the relations between equality and management as an everyday and integral aspect of planning and delivery. The denial of difference reinforces the manager's incapacity to deal effectively with problems that arise as a result of difference. It therefore reinforces difficulties with learning and change. The denial becomes a strategy for the prevention of change.

The need for change to be 'controlled': equality was seen as both a good and a bad thing at the same time. It was good because most managers agreed that racism and sexism are issues that need to be addressed by the organisation. It was bad because they perceived a danger of it 'going too far' or getting out of control, that is as soon as it started to affect the individual directly. Managers professed a need for changes to be 'measured', 'rational', 'reasonable' or 'gradual', in other words, 'controllable'. Also, changes that look like going out of control become issues that have been taken over by 'feminists', the 'loony-left', or people who 'use their colour to get ahead'. The white male manager's uncertainty about his own ground gave rise to suspicions about the desirability of change. In this way, a manager's suspicions become a manager's strategies.

Fear of not belonging: white, male managers often thought of their organisations as a hostile environment where managers are expected (or allow themselves) to over-work; where goal posts are continually being moved (or restructured); and where there is often little acknowledgement or reward. Such a culture gives rise to fears of 'stepping out of line'. Uncertainty about work and the anxieties generated from work promoted defensive responses, representative of a fear of not belonging or of rocking the boat. One of the major fears about belonging was related to advancement and career prospects; the gatekeepers of career prospects are often other white, male managers. The equal opportunity policy was seen, in some cases, as the instrument for blocking the promotion of white, male managers.

Factors that encourage and maintain inaction: the action research showed that there was a large gap between what a manager says and what a manager does. Managers were generally unskilled at translating the language of equality into actual practice. They therefore thought of change in a very generalised way. This stemmed partly from a lack of support from other managers within the organisation and, to a larger extent, from an individual lack of incentive. It was very easy for managers to find reasons not to do anything to encourage equality. Justifications for inaction (or non-management) came in all shapes and sizes: "Not enough time"; "Don't know how"; "It's discrimination the other way"; "Not enough interest", etc. Whatever their form, all justifications contribute to maintaining the gap between what the manager says and does.

White, male management styles as the norm: despite comprehensive equal opportunity policies, all of the authorities in the sample were run (and therefore developed) by a large majority of white, male managers. If managers are unskilled in terms of how to integrate equal opportunity policy into their daily practice then, even in local government organisations that have had policies for a number of years, the management style which predominates will reflect white male values. As a result, managers are caught in a process which restricts their concept of the need to change and disempowers their ability to effect change.

Defensiveness: the action research made it possible to identify different aspects of defensiveness in white, male managers. There were three consistent groupings:

- *Overt defensiveness:* for example "Is equality really at the heart of this policy I wonder"; "It is a fashionable issue"; "Service provision is not connected to equal opportunity"; "The commitment is not in all directorates"; "Is it cost-effective?"

- *Blaming defensiveness:* for example "I am uncomfortable with the lack of awareness of staff generally"; "The realities of EO are not known or understood by members"; "There is a low level of acceptance by our chief officer"; "We have poor equal opportunity role models".

- *Inaction (avoidance):* for example "It's a long learning curve, some managers don't have time to manage change"; "Education on a corporate level will have to continue for some time"; "We are getting there slowly"; "We need time and resources"; "We do not have the power in agenda setting"; "Access to power will be difficult for obstructed groups".

Each of these defences requires a different approach in relation to change. Whereas it would be possible to assess and encourage change in the overtly defensive manager simply in terms of language, it would be pointless to do this with a manager who consciously hides, for example, their own racism/sexism by blaming someone else. The individual styles of managers can fit particularly well into one of these categories or combine elements of all three. Each defensive response represents a different barrier to change. In Authority C the sample comprised managers from the top two tiers of the organisation. The defensiveness of the more senior managers was usually less overt. The most common element of this was a command of the language of equal opportunities coupled with a lack of skill in turning language into practice.

Patterns of blame: Managers had an unclear sense about their own responsibility to implement change on the issues of equal opportunity. Some form of blame or self-justification is common: blaming those people who suffer discrimination; more senior managers; less senior managers; the bureaucracy; lack of time;

lack of resources; lack of staff, etc. Blaming was a very characteristic emotional response in situations where managers wanted to slow down the pace of change. Management decision making is radically effected by this type of denial.

Abnegation of power: another barrier (although less so for first-tier officers) was the contradictory relationship of managers to the issue of their own power to effect change. On the one hand, managers professed limited individual power in the organisation, on the other they talked of inviting 'them' to 'our' meeting. Many managers had no clear concept of what constituted their power other than in hierarchical terms. Few managers had a sense of their power being entrenched in the unspoken values that drive the organisation. This was one reason why they found it difficult to perceive any real meaning to the prejudice and discrimination in their own and other people's work.

Individualism and professionalism: managers tended towards an individualistic perception of themselves as managers, that is they did not see themselves, for example, as belonging to the group 'white male managers'. This meant that they developed strategies that reinforced their individual competence or rightness. Many of the managers in the sample placed undue weight on the idea that they were solely responsible for the completion of their own management tasks. Also, there was a lack of sensitivity and skill when it came to working in groups. This meant that white, male managers needed strategies that seemed to them to reinforce their individual competence or rightness. For example: an autocratic approach, where good discipline formed the basis of good management, a paternalistic approach, where management was supported by encouragement ("helping 'them' to achieve"), an avoiding-my-authority approach, where managers find ways of ignoring anything uncontrollable or contentious.

It was not just individualism that created a barrier to change but also professionalism. The support that some managers gave each other was of a professional nature. Professionalism enables managers to support each other through exclusive language, standard practices, clearly mapped qualifications, and the security of acknowledged expertise. Professionalism gives white male managers a form of collectivity that militates against change, particularly on issues like equality.

Positive action is seen as discriminatory: the idea that a manager might act solely to redress the imbalances caused by institutional forms of discrimination was seen as 'going too far the other way'. With no clear understanding of the relationship between equal opportunity and their own work, positive action made little sense. In addition, a lack of skill in terms of specific action meant that managers became detached from important mechanisms for their own learning and change. When the concept of positive action is understood it can provide the key that managers need to understanding how to implement policy.

A set of specific avoidance strategies: avoidance strategy, in its many forms, can be the most common element in a manager's relation to equal opportunities. The action research pointed out a variety of forms of avoidance all of which showed how simple it is to develop and impose barriers to change:

Common avoidance strategies used by senior managers:

- labelling anyone raising the issues as a troublemaker (and publicise the label widely);

- denying that the issues are a justifiable part of organisational effectiveness;

- using their hierarchical position in ways that hinder the development of equality;

- being 'unavailable' to the people whose responsibility it is to develop equality;

- denying other managers down the line any support on equality;

- using a lack of resources as an excuse to place quality at a low priority.

More generally applicable avoidance strategies:

- not challenging the established order even when they know it is wrong;

- avoiding potentially difficult situations (conflict);

- taking no practical responsibility for equality;

- avoiding using procedures designed with equality in mind, eg, job specification forms;

- avoiding other 'cultures' in the authority;

- not giving equality any time (keeping it on the bottom of agendas);

- avoiding any discussion of the issues, eg, by not turning up to meetings or by making a joke of the issues;

- avoiding challenging staff on racist/sexist comments;

- keeping unnecessary bureaucracy in the way of implementing the policy;

- being deliberately slow on the issues;

- avoiding any form of evaluation;

- saying they are committed, but not doing anything;

- not showing what they really feel about issues.

The above lists illustrate how easy it is to prevent change. Countering avoidance strategies is not so easy and ultimately has to be the responsibility of managers themselves. The advantage to managers in challenging avoidance strategies within their own practice and the practice of others is that to do so increases their own effectiveness as managers.

What makes change possible?

In addition to demonstrating the extent and range of avoidance strategies, the action research showed that there were managers in each organisation who were attempting to promote change. There were a number of issues that assisted in the promotion of change within the three organisations.

Challenging key perceptions: the key perceptions that can be challenged are:

- that equal opportunity policy has nothing really to do with the everyday work of managers;

- that managers can treat everyone equally;

- that the style of management managers inherit just by being a part of the organisation is the most effective one;

- that white male managers can speak for everybody's experience of the organisation or the service, not just their own;

- that, where possible, conflict on equal opportunities issues should be avoided;

- that positive action is reverse discrimination.

Developing a management style that relates to equality: managers need to understand that equal opportunities is an issue that could enhance their management effectiveness rather than undermine it. So, for example, it is very easy for an experienced manager to acknowledge that a poor listener is a poor manager, it is very hard to get that same (white male) manager to acknowledge that he does not listen to his black or women staff. Managers need to use the equality issues that perpetually occur in their work to explore and redefine their own management practice.

Challenge avoidance strategies: despite any general and increased understanding of equal opportunity the white, male managers involved in the action research were not going to, and did not, change overnight. If change is to occur then it is necessary to move from the more general areas of possible change outlined above to the specific avoidance strategies characteristic of individual and/or groups of managers.

From defensiveness towards action: managers exhibit a range of different types of behaviour that move from defensive towards more non-defensive and active positions in relation to equalities issues. These are shown in Table 6.

Defensive managerial behaviour in relation to equalities usually fell into the first three of these categories, and occasionally into the last. The other two perspectives (the confidence to be wrong and the will to act) are the most helpful in terms of change, although it is important to acknowledge that the power issues are involved throughout all of the levels described. For example, a white male manager might be congratulated for having the confidence to be wrong, whereas a woman manager (as a result of underlying organisational discourses) might be punished or put down. Organisations like local government are already becoming receptive to the men who challenge on equal opportunity. There is a danger that this particular struggle will itself become a way of reinforcing white male power.

Table 6: Aspects of the behaviour of white, male managers
towards equalities

Behaviour	Types of response
Verbal defensiveness	I don't have a problem; what is the fuss about?
Silent defensiveness	I may have a problem, but I don't know what to do and I don't like to admit it.
Open confusion	I know there's a problem, I don't know what to do and I don't like to admit it.
The confidence to be wrong	I know there's a problem, I need to know more. I can struggle openly with it because that is how I can learn.
The will to act	I know there is a problem, I want to do something about it.
The danger of being 'right-on'	I know there is a problem, I know all about what I need to do to 'combat' it.

Developing practical and specific work-related actions: there was a tendency amongst managers to be general or vague about actions. It is necessary to think strategically about equality as an integral part of the work if changes are to occur. The recognition of individual defences and avoidance strategies is a starting point, consistent monitoring of the development of specific actions within the work is one strategy for making these individual changes stick.

The process of change: the process of action research described in this chapter was perpetually incomplete. It would not be possible for me to maintain that the data provided a consistent view, framework or formula for approaching ways of integrating management and equality. It did however, present a starting position, based on assumptions about white, male power and experience.

Early data in the research showed the importance of being able to work with an all white, male group. It meant that white, male managers had to be responsible for challenging each other. In the mixed training (Authority A), it was too often the women managers who, through stating their own experiences, provided answers for the men.   It was pointed out that white, male managers already seem to get a lot of the resources for management training, so where single sex training was done, similar resources were negotiated for black and/or women managers.   Additionally, the white male managers needed to be accountable to other managers for the outcomes of their work. This was achieved in this action research by bringing different groups together (Authority B) and through monitoring of post-event performance by specialist officers (Authority C).

The most comprehensive overall approach (Authority C) had the following elements:

- A range of existing reports and policy documents relating to equal opportunities was provided for background information and study.

- Interviews were conducted with the Chief Executive and three other Chief Officers where they were asked what they expected the training to achieve. This provided an idea of the type of attitudes and understanding senior managers already had.

- Close contact and review was maintained with the internal EOU. The training could be tailored to their current strategies for change. The EOU helped to develop case study material for the event, which was compiled from real examples of discrimination within the organisation.   When managers worked on these cases they had a practical relevance to the authority.   One to one follow-up of all participants was undertaken within three weeks of the end of the event by EOU members, leading to a review process for both short- and long-term development.

I think that there may be two contradictory answers to the question I posed at the beginning of this section, about an 'effective' process for encouraging managers to change in terms of their understanding and practice of equality. First, there is no such thing as an effective process for change. I cannot imagine any process of change fulfilling this claim since the very notion supports an idea of change as a rational and planned exercise, which (as I discovered over the course of the research in this chapter and in Chapter 4) it is not. The second answer is that the outline I have given for the way that change was approached in Authority C offers a temporary model that both encouraged and supported possibilities for change.

In this chapter I have explored the nature of white male power, which is one aspect of the workings of power in local government. The identification of the various practices and inactions that form the day-to-day expression of white male power needs to be acknowledged for significant changes to occur. An understanding of the workings of power in practice will enable more widespread ownership of the fraternal nature of local government management and provide a clear pointer to what equality means on a day-to-day basis for managers within their work. Understanding issues of power and equality will familiarise managers with processes that enhance their ability to relate to and promote change throughout their work. This will not happen while the emphasis in management practice is on defensiveness and avoidance of change, on controlling change rather than participating in it.

six

Everyday relations and the construction of inequality

In this chapter I discuss the management of equality in terms of relations between staff within local government. I try to focus on the effects that processes of promoting, avoiding or defending against equality have on the construction and implementation of equality policy and practice in an organisation. The theoretical framework that guided my shaping of this chapter emerged from the ideas and thoughts that I set out in the first Part of this book, and from my reflections on the experiences I had during the interventions I described in Chapters 4 and 5. I have identified a need to think about and act on organisational learning and change from a position that concentrates more on relations than on problems. In particular I point towards approaches to learning and change that take into account emotion, power and paradox. The introductory section of this chapter briefly restates some of my thoughts and then links them to the context of the struggle towards equality in local government.

I have explained that mainstream models of 'resistance' to change in organisations have often been based on the idea that resistance is a problem to be solved through appropriate diagnosis followed by an appropriate readjustment or strategy. The underlying assumption of such approaches is that there will be an appropriate strategy to fit an identifiable problem of resistance. This assumption is most unhelpful when studying equality because it emphasises the rational and managerial aspects of resistance, rarely looking at the underlying emotional context of the organisation or at the complexity of power relations in the organisation.

Nord and Jermier (1994) criticise managerialist perspectives for defining resistance as something to be 'overcome' because it may threaten managerial objectives. They suggest that the rational orientation of managers, and their belief in progress, makes them unprepared to work with behaviours "that emanate from passions, aggressive impulses, and archetypal and instinctual characteristics" (Nord and Jermier, 1994, p 402). They also suggest that managerialist perspectives have an outmoded view of power. Managers hold onto notions of "sovereign power" (Clegg, 1989), seeing power as located in human agents who control resources. This way of defining power encourages a notion of resistance which relates to actions against the expressed wishes of managers. If, as Clegg suggests, power is more decentralised, more web-like, more 'capillary', then resistance can also be expected to be a decentralised process. The challenge for explorations of avoidance in organisations is therefore to identify 'characteristic emotional climates' (Hearn and Parkin, 1987) alongside complex power relations.

The complex relations between resistance and power have been particularly explored and documented by Labour Process theorists (see Jermier, Knights and Nord, 1994) who are concerned to take account of the meanings that those who 'resist' give to their own practices. This leads them to focus on the interconnections between resistance and subjectivity, and on concepts of social identity. For Clegg (1994a), subjectivity is formed around the will to resist, and without such resistance organisational power relations are likely to be accommodated. In practice, this process is often paradoxical. Collinson (1994), in a case study concerning organisational commitment to, and governance by, equal opportunity legislation, suggests that "the rights inscribed in this governance can function both as powers that subjugate and as points for the articulation of resistance". It will not be sufficient for the study of management by avoidance to rely on the notion that "power evokes resistance" because some forms of organisation, through the very process of organising, also limit the potential of resistance to become active. A further challenge for explorations of avoidance in organisations is to bring such paradoxes of resistance and accommodation to light.

Emotional reactions to change often seem to be denied, minimised in importance and kept covert. This makes the identification of 'characteristic emotional climates' more difficult. Psychoanalytic approaches to organisation, which emphasise emotional and unconscious processes at work (Hirschhorn, 1990; Kets de Vries, 1991; Hoggett, 1992; Diamond, 1993; Hirschhorn and Barnett, 1993) offer various insights. I have noted how emotional complexity is dismissed from organisations through being labelled 'irrational', and that the paradoxical and contradictory is deemed irrelevant. I also explained how organisational structures emerge from defences against emotion, making it difficult for organisational members to express feelings within the organisation. Both of these mean that managers invariably find emotions and feelings difficult to articulate. In summary, I show that organisations give little space or opportunity for organisational members to access and understand their own and others' conscious and unconscious feelings about organisational life generally, and organisational change in particular. I argue that these processes can be seen as key mechanisms in the construction and implementation of management by avoidance. An important assumption in the study of avoidance is that individual feelings and actions are not only created in the context of the individual's bounded notion of the self and other. They are created through peoples' projections onto each other and the ensuing confusion of identity and role.

In my own thinking and practice I want to bring a perspective on the psychodynamics of organisational life together with a perspective on power in organisations, in order to delve more deeply into the everyday relations between the people within the organisation who are continually making and remaking organisational responses to equality. This chapter therefore attempts to explore how inequality is recreated through organisational relations.

Equality and local government

In the past 20 years, attempts by UK local government to implement equality policy has made it one of the key sites where the possibilities for and resistance to organisational change has been contested. One reason why local government has remained a key site for contesting organisational changes around equality stems from the particular requirements placed on local government by the law. The 1976 Race Relations Act (section 71) for example, emphasises the responsibility of local authorities to *implement* policy. During the 1980s the legislation, combined with a range of other inter-personal, social and political issues, prompted many authorities to declare themselves as equal opportunity employers, and in some cases to develop initiatives designed to promote greater equality internally within the workforce and externally in service delivery.

This has given rise to a body of literature that has reviewed the successes and failures of equality policy in changing both the internal workings and the external services of local government as an organisation (Ben Tovim et al, 1986; Stone, 1988; Jones, 1988; Ball and Solomos, 1990; Cockburn, 1991; Braham et al, 1992; Martin, 1994). Looking back from the vantage point of the mid-1990s, there seems to have been five main strands to local authority initiatives on equalities:

- The development of equal opportunity employment practices: including recruitment, interviewing, induction, monitoring.

- The development of guidelines for behaviour and practice.

- Specific policies and codes (eg, sexual harassment).

- Training, both in terms of individual awareness and organisational development.

- A wide range of authority specific internal and external initiatives and positive action programmes.

In addition to my own work on avoidance strategies, a number of barriers to the development of equality have been expressed in the literature on local government and local governance. Smith et al (1993), for example, provide a comprehensive summary. Their three key barriers are:

- Lack of clarity in terms of policy, practice and procedures which stem from the gap between intention and outcome. This gap consistently undermines the trust necessary for change.

- The inability of authorities to develop shared meaning. Managers and staff tend to prefer prioritising agreement rather than working through differences. The effects of this are that they do not learn how to work with and through difference, thereby limiting participation from disadvantaged groups. This creates and is sustained by an organisational dynamic.

• Exclusion at the start – or the tendency to make strategic plans without the involvement or early consultation of target groups.

Local government has not been effective in developing the relational aspects of equalities in organisations. Several studies looking at race in local government point towards the need for an analysis that gets beneath the formal, rationalistic and bureaucratic context of the organisation and into its appreciative context (Young, 1990; Gibbon, 1992). Young (1990) emphasises that the outcomes of changes brought about through equality initiatives are often indeterminate and contingent on a complex interplay of thought and language, process and power. The predominant characteristic of this interplay is ambiguity, especially around language and power. Other writers (Jewson and Mason, 1986) point to "a systematic pattern of muddle and deception" which is an intrinsic feature of the social relations constituting equal opportunities.

Similarly, studies of women's equality in local government have occasionally pointed towards those 'undiscussable' things that give rise to "a kind of in-built resistance to change created by traditional power relationships which must work against equal opportunity initiatives regardless of their structure, levels of resources or policy orientation" (Stone, 1988, p 11). These studies tend to emphasise that it is the underlying or emotional aspects of equal opportunity policy, for example "treachery, betrayal and bad faith" (Jewson and Mason, 1986), that might emerge in the process of implementation, which needs attention if change is to happen.

The gap between stated policy and actual practice has not arisen as a result of the inability of local government to develop specific mechanisms for improving certain aspects of equality policy, since many have done so, particularly in terms of recruitment and employment practices and sometimes in relation to the implications for service delivery. The key difficulty has been the management of equality as an everyday aspect of relations between staff within the organisation, and how the links between people and between groups create and recreate emotional relations and power relations, which are then avoided.

In the previous two chapters in this Part of the book I looked at different organisational responses to the practice of equality, and identified the various strategies managers use to avoid having to work with equality in the context of their day-to-day practice as managers. Managerial avoidance strategies pointed to those parts of an organisation's everyday life from which social power relations are both constructed and enacted. In this sense therefore, identifying avoidance strategies seems pivotal to understanding both how change is resisted and how it is made possible. Using this previous work, together with other experiences relating to the ways in which organisations manage equality (Diamante and Giglio, 1994), it is possible to propose five different types of organisational response to equality in terms of managerial commitment to equality, leadership values and responses to change initiatives (see Table 7).

In the last 20 years, most local government organisations have managed to move beyond the delusional and static types. Most authorities have equal opportunity policies and have made commitments to action in a variety of areas. Some authorities relate to equal opportunity as parodic organisations, they imitate the policy of other authorities without knowing why and without the benefit of processes that give rise to internal learning and change. In the parodic organisation action is often initiated but rarely followed through. What has been achieved is usually a result of fulfilling only the basic requirements of the law and the basic demands of 'difficult' staff. Parodic organisations often seem to have a covert system of punishment for staff who raise equality issues.

Table 7: How five different types of organisation manage equality

	Delusional organisation	Static organisation	Parodic organisation	Active/avoiding organisation	Learning organisation
Managerial commitment	No awareness of differences in the workplace. No commitment to action on equality.	Words not action. Policy statements exist but there is no commitment to action.	Commitment to short-term events. Imitates other organisations' policy without knowing why.	Confused commitment – manifested in both approaching and avoiding equality at the same time.	Communities of commitment. Long-term commitment to improving business by exploring relations among a diverse employee base.
Leadership values	The need for equality is irrelevant.	Avoid all but the legal requirements of equality.	Equality relates to image. The organisation does the minimum to keep people quiet both internally and externally.	It is desirable to work towards equality but "we don't want to open a can of worms".	The negotiation of equalities rights and outcomes underpins leadership within the organisation.
Response to change initiatives	There is no need to change and it would be a waste of money that could be better spent elsewhere.	Set up equality initiatives that focus only on employment practice (often in an inexperienced and overworked personnel or HR section).	Has basic policy and employment practices. Sets up a short course for middle/senior managers with the aim of "cascading down information" which is never done.	Coherent policy. incoherent approach to strategy and an inability by senior managers to act on and operationalise decisions on equality. Responses are solely rational.	Strategic decision making linked to an acceptance of the emotion, power and paradox of policy development in a diverse workforce.

The type that I wish to emphasise in particular is the active/avoiding organisation. Local authorities struggle with equality as active/avoiding organisations, where managers want to address issues of equality, yet at the same time are hesitant and defensive about doing so. In contrast to the parodic organisation, the active/avoiding authority responds from a genuine desire for `'fairness'. This sense of fairness is paradoxical: it is created from a motivation towards change and yet opposed by a fear of too much change. It is in the context of working in and with this paradox – what Diamante and Giglio (1994) refer to as "a permanent state of confusion" – that the present study is set.

A case example in local government

The studies of equality and local government organisation I identify above point towards a need for the complexity of emotional relations to be identified. This involves attempts to highlight what seems 'undiscussable' or highly defended. In addition, it is important to move beyond a managerial or rational perspective on resistance, to include both characteristic emotional climates and complex power relations in organisations. An analysis of underlying emotional and power dynamics seeks to reveal the paradoxical nature of equality in practice in terms of both individual and organisational relations. The identification of such paradoxes makes it possible to reveal links between avoidance at an inter-personal level, and avoidance of equality within the organisation as a whole.

The emphasis of the example I refer to in this chapter was on recording the thoughts and feelings of those people in an active/avoiding local authority who work within the confusion and uncertainty created by struggles towards equality, particularly in relation to gender. I was invited to work with a small group of council staff who all subscribed to the notion that good management practice is defined and promoted through good practice on equality. The organisation concerned is viewed exclusively through the eyes of the staff who are responsible (in either their specialist or generalist role) for trying to manage and work with the avoidance strategies of senior managers. In this way, the example attempts to highlight a particular perspective on the daily struggle with promoting and defending against equality.

I asked to work solely with individuals who are responsible for the development of equality as a part of their job in the council, or with individuals whose values mean that equality is an important part of their understanding of their role as managers and/or council staff. The participants involved, ranged from senior or middle management to secretarial staff. All 12 participants were white women.

I involved these people in the following procedure:

• Each individual participant kept a diary for at least 10 working days. The emphasis of the diary was to record everyday individual experience (both emotional and intellectual) of equality and inequality. (12 members of staff kept diaries.)

• Participants were invited to meet collectively in an inquiry group. The emphasis of the day was the collection and review of data in various areas. These were: the issues that emerged from the experience of diary keeping, stories of inequality in the council, constructing a stereotype of a resistant manager, and proposing strategies for future action. (8 members of staff attended the day.)

• Participants were asked to read through my first level analysis of the diaries and to comment on my analysis and interpretations. They also reviewed and commented on my first draft after editing and writing up the tapes from the inquiry group experience.

The thinking behind this process was generally influenced by my notions of research as learning. More specifically, I was attempting to bring to light everyday experience through the reflective diaries, and then in the inquiry group to encourage participants to reflect on their reflections. In addition, stories, stereotypes and strategies provided a sense of a community of staff all working on equality. In addition to the inevitable anger that arose there was also an opportunity for playfulness. It was very easy and amusing to stereotype a "manager who is resistant to equality", and participants competed with each other with their stories: "you think that was bad, have I ever told you about the time I ...". I was concerned to work with and from the bias in the group towards equality and thereby to highlight equality from the perspective of people who, through role or choice, continually work in the context of managerial defences and avoidance strategies.

Reflections on the experience

At the beginning of this chapter I referred to the conceptual framework within which this exploration of the relations involved in the construction of equality is set. I emphasised three different areas in which an analysis of management by avoidance can be situated. Writing on equality in local government highlights the importance of including an analysis of the *emotional* influences on resistance to equality. The importance of emotion also occurs in the literature on resistance to change, especially the writing that is critical of rational, managerialist perspectives. In addition, this literature outlines the importance of a conceptualisation of *power* as a pervasive and complex phenomenon that can be perceived through transactions in particular (Martin, 1994). Psychodynamic perspectives on resistance and defences in organisations show that peoples' experience and relations around equality presents them with *paradoxes* (or 'paradoxical tensions') that can either reinforce their 'stuckness' or unlock possibilities for change. Taken together, these three underlying processes provide a way of reflecting on the experiences within this example.

Emotion

There were two particular aspects to the emotional experience of women in the active/avoiding organisation. First, they seemed to have to manage more than their own emotions. Second, they worked with a series of perceived threats.

Managing emotions: the women involved in this inquiry had very strong emotional reactions to equality on a day-to-day basis (Table 8). This strength of their emotion arose in part from their own positions – they each felt very strongly about the organisation's responsibility to progress policies and practices relating to equality – and partly from the ways in which they were positioned by others. It is not easy to say which comes first, the position or the positioning, but the consequence is that these women had to manage more than their own emotions.

Table 8: Emotions evoked by equality in an active/avoiding organisation

Feelings expressed	Examples from diaries
Angry	"I am undermined and disregarded"; "they said they hadn't received the report. I knew that they had".
Murderous	"I'll kill him"; "how dare he".
Betrayed	"That was treachery from other women".
Desperate	"It is hard to breathe let alone try to stay positive".
Frustrated	"Banging my head against a wall"; "another half-hour of argument".
Disrespected	"No respect for so-called non-professional staff".
Regretful	"I should have done it but I didn't, and I could have done it better than the one who did".
Powerless	"I really should be more assertive"; "the person is higher than myself, and I did not therefore feel that I could question the request".
Embarrassed	"My manager embarrassed me in front of a group, why didn't he say something was wrong when I first submitted the report to him?"
Lonely	"There was no one there to represent me, my document, or with any real understanding of equal opportunity".
Hopeless	"This organisation drives me to drink"; "I give up".
Guilty	"I should have handled it better"; "I feel unhappy that I allowed it to happen".
Set up	"I step in too easily into this role".
Overburdened	"I try to do too much".
Patronised	"I should mind your own business if I were you love".

In addition to managing the interface between the active/avoiding nature of their organisation and their own anger about the slow progress of equality, they were attempting to manage, respond to, ignore and deflect, the expressed and repressed anger of others for whom equality is a threat. This makes the position of 'the equal opportunity manager' both a demanding and a dangerous role. One of the skills that looked increasingly necessary to this particular group of women managers was their ability to manage the projections of other, less equality oriented male and female staff. The danger faced by managers and staff who want to progress equality was the continual internalisation of the hostile emotions of others.

Management by avoidance, on an emotional level, seems to be built out of a powerful managerial ambivalence towards, and denial of, feelings about equal opportunity. This ambivalence was well known to the women in this particular case, and seemed to them like an unstated organisational value. It is not surprising, therefore, to discover that murderous, desperate or hopeless feelings are an aspect of everyday working experience for women who actively work towards organisational change. This process is a key 'transaction' of power in the organisation whereby power is exercised through interactions that lead to the internalisation of emotions by those organisational members who are seeking to promote rather than avoid change.

The frustration felt by staff emerged and was compounded through the gradual collection of small instances where equality in the authority had been badly managed or flouted. Two of the 'stories' provide good examples:

Outrageous statements

The thing that makes me feel boiling-bloody mad is that one of our Directors, the one who is responsible for EO, allows someone directly below him to come out with outrageous statements. He just lets him get off the hook. What he says then to someone else once the one who makes the outrageous statements goes out the door: the director will ring someone up and say "can't we get him trained, can't we do something with him". He's clearly aware that this bloke is well off the mark, but he's not willing at the time to say now hang on a minute. And, he always off-loads and tries to get it dealt with, but in a way that is totally inappropriate, and there's probably never a time when this man has been confronted by his senior officer.

Well it is rather funny isn't it?

Shortly after I started this job, and started doing training I received anonymously in the post a questionnaire, supposedly a jokey thing, aimed at finding out about somebody's ethnic background. It included questions like "if you are West Indian, what colour are the dice swinging in your car?"; and, "have you any idea who your father is?" and all sorts of questions about Afro-Caribbean stereotypes and the more offensive ones at that. It was totally anonymous and I was totally shocked and upset by it. I decided that I would go and tell my Director about it, not because anything could be done about it because there was no way of tracing who had sent it to me, but in order to let him know that this sort of stuff was coming in and that I was angry and upset. So I went and showed it to him. I said that this came in the post this morning I would like you to have a look at it. And he looked at it and his first response was "well it is rather funny isn't it", and his second was that there was nothing he could do about it.

One of the strongest themes in the stories that the inquiry group told was the inertia at senior managerial levels on everyday occurrences of discrimination. These experiences link to the literature which acknowledges 'undiscussable' (Stone, 1988) aspects of equality "created by traditional power relationships". Senior managers were seen as not knowing how to act. If a manager is "clearly aware" that a subordinate staff member is "well off the mark" but cannot manage the confrontation involved in giving feedback to this person on their behaviour, then the senior manager's authority and effectiveness, is inevitably undermined. Taking opportunities like this, rather than missing them, was seen to be a vital mechanism for learning and change.

An unending series of incidents like the two stories above combine into patterns that engender anger and hopelessness. Strategies that seem appropriate to counteract such behaviour become hard-edged, almost vengeful. In order to discourage such inaction the inquiry group wanted a clearly stated commitment to equality from the Chief Executive and the Leader of the Council. For them this meant saying that "we will not tolerate the type of behaviour we have highlighted; that we expect every member of Council staff to take it seriously; that we will take action against people. If we had that type of statement from the top then that would provide a context from which we could do many other things". "Disciplinary action against a senior officer would serve as an example to others".

Feeling threatened: in an organisation caught in the confusion between the desire to be active and to avoid, the process of communication that is used to conduct relations between people who support equality and those who do not could be termed cynical and sarcastic non-communication. This way of communicating was a defence against threats to respective positions that had become habitual. It was sustained through an ever-present, mostly covert, inter-personal hostility.

Individuals used phrases like 'doing down' or 'scratching away' to represent this hostility. It was as if the frustration of action and inaction combined had created a volcano waiting to explode. The 'scratching away' was a way of letting some of the heat and air out, without causing a major eruption. The effect however, was the limiting of communication within the authority. Interaction between people with different perspectives on equality in the Council has become locked into sarcastic retorts and cynical asides. Such behaviour will eventually institutionalise the inability of either side to hear and work with what is being said.

Threats might be felt, perceived and acted on by everyone in the organisation. The staff who sought changes in the organisation's response to equality felt cynical and sarcastic about the senior managers' ability to change, and they experienced the senior managers as cynical and sarcastic towards equality. Interaction was often mediated through cynicism and sarcasm. In the active/avoiding organisation many different people are likely to feel threatened by equality for one reason or another, which means that listening, communication and trust become a major struggle.

This sense of threat and lack of trust was a powerful emotional backdrop within the authority, built from a myriad of broken promises, backstabbings, paternalism, harassments and losses of face. It was very pervasive. Several times, before, during and after the diaries were being completed, some of the participating staff needed to be reassured that individual diaries would never be seen by anyone other than me, and certainly not by anyone else in the council. I had stated very clearly at the beginning that the diaries were confidential and that I would be the only other person to read them. I realised that it was hard for them to trust me too.

Anxiety is enhanced by carrying, yet not being able to express, strong feelings. Fear and doubt are created, through this process, in those who want to change, and a culture of mistrust emerges and prevails, keeping the organisation's practices unchallenged. Working within such an organisation seemed to have brought the women involved to an entrenched point in their experience, feeling that they should not be the ones to change. For example:

> For a typical manager to become untypical he or she has to feel less threatened. I'm blowed if I am going to be the one to let them feel less threatened. You either have to make them feel less threatened or you have to make them see that the threat is not important, that it doesn't matter. I'm talking about the basic threat to their jobs. If more women are going to get top jobs then less men are going to get top jobs. It is that sort of threat that I can imagine is real and a huge barrier to progress.

Anxiety was not only perpetuated through individual and organisational responses to equality, it was also perpetuated through individual and organisational responses to impending external change. "The underlying anxiety for many people, particularly the main wage earners in the family, is local government reorganisation. I have to look to my position now so that when I'm competing for a job I will have a good chance of getting it".

Power

Power in an active/avoiding organisation is constructed out of various implicit and explicit processes. There exists a range of avoidance strategies, key episodes of power, which are characteristic of the everyday strategic nature of equality in action. Underlying this were some more general disciplinary practices.

Avoidance strategies: it was possible to identify a number of explicit avoidance strategies used by managers to undermine or disregard the implementation of equality policy. In this particular authority the group pointed to 10 avoidance strategies (these contrast and intersect with the avoidance strategies I have already identified in Chapters 4 and 5).

- Power play: "everything he asks for is urgent which makes me wonder why he has left it to the last minute, thus making it urgent. This portrays to me a man who is trying to be important".

- Agenda slippage: "controversial agenda items become the victim of lack of time. This is not an accident".

- Disrupting work schedules: "why is it that our own work schedules are frequently interrupted by senior managers".

- Keeping the focus on the task: "somehow this makes insensitivity okay".

- Training replaces managerial action: "I think that the equality training replaces managerial direction or action to establish what the organisation's expectations on staff are, instead of reinforcing it".

- Saying not doing: "He didn't want to do anything but register with me that things were going wrong and that he was opposed to doing anything about it".

- Agreeing not doing: "I would rather be told that I can't have what I want than them saying I can and then doing nothing".

- Taking responsibility or not taking responsibility depending on which is appropriate: "I am not given the opportunity to implement ideas despite strategic responsibilities. My manager takes responsibility for everything, and decides on strategy himself. He takes others' ideas and makes them into his contribution".

- Double binds: "He asked for a document from me that cannot be written until he gives me the information necessary to write what he wants".

- Road blocks: "In order to progress I have to by-pass the normal channels".

In addition to identifying these avoidance strategies the inquiry group constructed a stereotype of a "manager with no time for equal opportunities". They were asked to brainstorm what such a manager would say having heard their thoughts and feelings about equality. The whole list was compiled very quickly and their comments identified three general categories of managerial response:

The manger who is against, and will challenge or defend: I don't know why we are doing this for women when there are all these unemployed men around; you are a very unrepresentative group; EO costs too much; if it comes down to equality or jobs which would you choose?; show me the figures to prove it; I know lots of women are very happy working in this county; my wife's a working woman so I understand your problems; etc.

The manager that recommends circumspection and fair play: if you've got a policy then all problems will be ironed out in time; I am all for pushing things forward but we have to do it in such a way that it will gain support; why don't you concentrate on things that we can actually achieve?; you can't beat people over the head with it, you will have to do it by persuasion; this isn't going to happen overnight you know; if we do this we will only alienate the people we are trying to involve; there will be a backlash; this report says too much. It will give ammunition to our enemies, it will tell them what we actually do so that they can object to it; you have to persuade rather than coerce.

The manager who would do something if he or she could only have it explained: I'd do more about it if I knew what you meant; can you explain yourself a bit more clearly?; why haven't they come forward to complain?; why haven't you come to me with this before?; well surely it doesn't apply to this department?

The strategic nature of equality in action: the reflections contained in the diaries summarise something of the everyday strategic nature of equality in action, and especially something of the power relations present between staff. Take the following example: "The Director informed me that we already have a policy, and I have just spent 4 weeks writing one, no one outside that department seems to know about this. Why did he wait?"

Why did he wait? The answer to such a question is impossible to discover, but the almost endless possible interpretations (he had more important issues to deal with; he wanted to frustrate my work; he is involved in inter-departmental one-upmanship that I know nothing about; his hidden agenda is to stall equal opportunities whenever possible; he is a busy man and he forgot; etc) testify to the complexity of each interaction that involves power and equality.

There are key moments in organisational life when it is possible to identify how power and equality relate. One such episode is when a female member of staff gets locked into a fight with her male boss. The fight somehow seems to reflect and act out the wider struggles over equality in the organisation. She brings her anger to the engagement, he brings his defensiveness. This pairing is characteristic of organisational 'stuckness' on equality and of a broader, more organisationally related paradoxical tension. Such relations are both an indication of what appears to managers to be the safest style of leadership around equal opportunities (manipulate–forget–avoid) and a fundamental obscuring of the potential for a form of leadership based on negotiated experience and inevitable difference.

Managers who do have a perspective on equality are frequency positioned as having a problem. The positioning of staff responsible for developing equality within an active/avoiding organisation is likely to be undertaken as an inter-personal expression of power differences. This may be an important dynamic for undermining and controlling the progress of equality. For example, one of the managers in the study had had a rough ride in a meeting and was feeling upset. After the meeting, her departmental director saw that she was upset, "he asked me if I was okay and then told me that I wasn't and I should go home". In this instance, an act of seeming concern or support towards the individual was used to position her as unable to cope. On reflection the manager thought that her director may have felt, at the same time, both sympathetic towards her emotion and angry with her because of it.

The rational boundaries of change: the members of the inquiry group discussed strategies that were based primarily on emotional responses. They had a good understanding of the link between strategy and emotion, and of the underlying dynamics of threat and competition that drive the organisation. Yet, in their everyday work, they could rarely find ways of communicating this link.

The exercise which asked the focus group to describe or 'stereotype' the verbal responses of a manager with no time for equal opportunities was completed very quickly. This suggested a familiarity with such responses. One feature that stands out of the stereotypes (some of which are highlighted above) is that the statements are mainly rational. The message that the inquiry group members had internalised moved between "You are wrong" and "If you would only tell me what to do I would do it". The emotional reality of negotiations over equality did not emerge in the exercise.

My own interpretation about this is that emotion is dangerous for both 'sides', those for and against equality, and rationality becomes a defence against the complex and anxiety-provoking human issues present in any interaction to do with discrimination and inequality. It seems that access to "characteristic emotional climates" (Hearn and Parkin, 1987) are not just missing from interaction, but are refused on an organisational level. This collusion over rationality between different groups points towards the nature of relations between resistance and power within this organisation. Power is enacted as a self-disciplining force created through and bounded by rationality.

Set against the internalised perception that rational forces are the key to successful negotiation and change, are the feelings that were expressed by the participants around strategy. The five elements of strategy that the focus group developed were all driven by emotions: the desire to force the Chief Executive to see how shocking it all is; the pleasure of seeing a senior manager sacked as an example to the rest; the determination to enforce not facilitate the policy; the anger behind the wish to take them away and train them (even though the participants had already identified training as ineffective); the conviction that "I'm not going to be the one" to make them feel less threatened; and the fear of the threat to the self and of unemployment. There was a feeling that, if only it was possible to work with and through such emotions then avoidance would be minimised.

Paradox

It was possible to identify four paradoxes that seemed characteristic of the emotional climate underlying management in this active/avoiding organisation.

First, a key dynamic of equality in the organisation was the difference between what was said will be done and what was done. This perpetuated a paradoxical tension between the desire to do something that seems fair and just, while being in a state of willing ignorance or "skilled incompetence" (Argyris, 1990) of what fair and just actions might involve. This mixture of doing and not doing is linked to 'image' both for the individual manager (who does not want to be seen to be personally sexist, racist, or against equality) and for the organisation itself (that needs to have any 'state of confusion' covered up and to present itself as in control of the equality policy).

Second, equal opportunity training in the organisation was seen as a mechanism of control. Training was an attempt to control the managers who were most hostile towards equality, and who were trained to "make them more aware". Equal Opportunity training was controlling of the staff who were most supportive towards equality because they returned from training more open to the frustrations of the acting/avoiding double bind. Training was seen to be a need even when it was clear that it met few needs. Members of the inquiry group felt that training suppressed the emotional content of equal opportunity and constituted both an ineffective method of development for staff as well as an ineffective method for controlling staff. The paradoxical tension of training existed because courses consisted of those people who were frustrated *within* the experience of training (ie, they had been sent on the course and disagreed with the need for equality policy and practice) and those people who were frustrated *after* the experience (ie, they learned something within the course that they could not implement in the organisation).

Third, 'needling' (the outcome of sarcasm and cynicism around equality, see above) between staff was a very common form of communication. Needling was at the same time both a manageable way to express emotion indirectly (as well as to score points over people) and an impossible medium for the development of a dialogue. Needling was a powerful expression of the competitive nature of relations within the organisation. Communication within the authority was seen as 'fatally flawed'. This was due to a paradoxical tension concerning trust, that "I trust him and don't trust him". It seemed that it was never really possible in the organisation to know whether those who might be for you, might also be against you. For example, "I have a boss who does understand equal opportunity, but somehow he can't hear what I'm saying. It feels like talking a different language, the put downs and the underminings are not clear and treachery is always a possibility".

Thus, 'needling' created a paradoxical tension whereby it represented a manageable way of communicating around equality without too much emotion, on the other hand needling was an impossible way of communicating anything positive, or of releasing the actual emotions driving it. The intensity of the maliciousness behind the needling evolved with the intensity of threat experienced. "If it is outside of their idea about what women are, or should be, then the provocation becomes greater and more pointed".

Finally, the notion of leadership in the organisation is based on the responsibility of senior managers to lead the implementation of equality policy, and yet they were often positioned by the participants as unqualified emotionally and relationally to do this. Participant responses suggested that the safest style of leadership was seen to be avoidance, whereas a more effective form of leadership around equal opportunity might emerge from clarity of role, clarity of authority and dialogue. The authority was stuck in a culture of inter-personal relating based on competition ("there's a lot of back-stabbing going on, both ways"). The enforcement and enacting of hierarchical distinctions between people at different levels without clear lines of responsibility meant that competitiveness was a rampant force in the organisation. Competition was an underlying dynamic of inter-personal behaviour both for men and women. Women may be competitive but "they do it less secretly and more vindictively"; male competitiveness was viewed as "quite scheming"; and also "the women who have got anything out of it really have to fight for it". Men's "skulduggery" in securing their own positions featured; it was suggested that women may be better at stabbing themselves in the back than men. For example "I won't apply for that job, I'm not really good enough for it".

In general, both those who wanted to promote equality and those who wanted to avoid it were caught in a paradox of knowing what was needed but not being able to implement it, of being both active and avoiding. Attempts to promote or resist the implementation of equal opportunity policy can become very circular and demoralising.

Ways of emerging from the active/avoiding double bind

As I explained in Chapter 3, the fact that such paradoxes can be recognised and held, points towards the possibilities for both learning and change. In terms of double-loop learning and change – which addresses significant shifts in organisational members' understanding of the dimensions of their organisation and its work – change is seen to be the outcome of the conflict between 'established' and 'alternative' frameworks. Change occurs not from compromise towards one or other side, but from "the development of a new perspective that transcends either the original one or its proposed alternative" (Bartunek and Reid, 1992, p 117). One way out of the active/avoiding double bind involves working with the generative consequences of interaction between the different parts of the paradox.

One method or process that has been used to address paradoxical tensions has been to work through metaphorical representations of different positions (Broussine and Vince, 1995). When something is defined metaphorically this is not just an invitation to *think* about it in a certain way, it is also an invitation to *interact* in terms of certain implied assumptions (Schon, 1979). Metaphors express particular concerns and interests in ways that make claims on the nature of the target of those concerns and interests (Danziger, 1990). This is one definition of the 'generative' properties of metaphor, that they promote engagement and (through such engagement) change.

The notion of metaphor as an invitation to interact is based on a definition which acknowledges more than a similarity between two apparently distinct subjects. Metaphors also make possible both the identification of links between sub-systems and the creation of new connections. Thus, two different sub-groups or hierarchical levels of an organisation with distinct metaphors describing the same thing may generate new connections or new ways of seeing an issue. Such connections can be particularly powerful in facilitating an organisation's capacity to change (Barrett and Cooperrider, 1990).

The power of metaphors also stems from their ability to retain and represent the emotions as well as the rational perspectives that are a part of conflicts (Vince, 1995c; Broussine and Vince, 1995). They "provide vivid, memorable and emotion-arousing representations of preconceived experience" (Ortony, 1979). Averill (1990) asserts that emotional aspects of experience that are difficult to contain often become the subject of metaphor. She highlights six different areas in which this occurs, identifying six "major metaphors of emotion" (Averill, 1990, p 112). Another perspective is that emotions are the 'target' of metaphor (Sarbin, 1986) in the sense that such metaphors are seeking to explain emotion. This emotion is not solely related to the individual but to the organisation as well. This is why Burke (1992) asserts that metaphors are "windows into the soul of the social system".

In organisations where direct emotions are often suppressed and avoided, individual and organisational defences against emotion become very powerful. Metaphors can provide an opportunity for managers to look indirectly at emotional and unconscious forces at work. Unconscious defences are very immediate and powerful. It is rather like looking directly into the eyes of Medusa: the fear of emotion can turn managers to stone. Metaphors serve a reflecting or suspending function, allowing the manager to look indirectly at powerful emotions (through her or his shield) without being turned to stone.

The generative properties of metaphor assist both individuals and organisational groupings to align their emotional states with their task needs (Krantz, 1990a). Krantz argues that this allows organisational members to undertake their work roles more "deeply and passionately", and offers access to the emotional relatedness that is evoked by interaction within an organisation. "The compelling aspect of metaphor is not therefore the mental image itself but the way in which the image reaches into the subjective terrain of unconscious experience" (Krantz, 1990a). Engagement with the generative properties of metaphor may provide one way out of the acting/avoiding double bind, and also ensure that emotional and political perspectives on equality do not become lost in rational approaches driven solely by task-based and strategic imperatives.

Metaphor is an invitation to interact in terms of certain implied assumptions (Schon, 1979). In this action research for example, the collectivity of local authority staff involved was defined through an assumption that good practice on equality might support, perpetuate and educate managers about good management practice. Both I and they assumed that it might be possible to learn about and change an organisation through the struggle *towards* equality rather than struggling and defending *against* equality. Such a perspective allows, in organisations, a shift away from feeling that initiatives on equality are bothersome and conflictual, towards a conceptualisation of equality that fits with the idea that organisations are places where learning and change is possible.

My experience of this action research also revealed to me however, that the connection between equality and management does not make sense to everyone. It seems to me that there will always be managers within organisations who feel no desire to make use of this metaphor, to hold such a connection, let alone to explore its relevance to change. I do not think that the underlying assumption that we used in this action research to define our collective perspective would necessarily create the conditions for moving from an active/avoiding organisation towards a learning organisation. In the long term, such movement may depend more on the ability of managers to work with and through emotions and power relations evoked by a much wider range of issues. One limitation of this action research was not undertaking a similar study of the emotions and relations of those managers who are ambivalent about equalities in the organisation. Information in this area may have done much to identify a starting point for dialogue.

In the introductory thinking that is a part of this chapter, and in the case example, I tried to explore the dynamics of emotional and political processes that maintain this particular authority as an active/avoiding organisation. The active/avoiding double bind is especially disruptive of the communication, partnership, collaboration and dialogue necessary for strategic decision making. Staff who desire changes in organisational responses to equality are as caught up in this double-bind as their senior managers, who they experience as resistant to change. Routes out of this circularity have been proposed in the past few years, particularly under the organisational imperative to 'value diversity'. In the next chapter, I explore these various approaches further by looking at the link between equality and organisational approaches to the management of change.

seven

Equalities and organisational change

Introduction

In the previous three chapters of this book I have reflected on some of my past experiences and ideas about how equality in organisations and organisational learning and change combine. In the final chapter of this Part I think more generally about the current relationship between equalities and organisational change. I look in particular at a range of writing, thinking and practice in the area of 'managing diversity'. I take a critical view of this literature in two different senses: I offer a critique of the literature on diversity, particularly in terms of its individualism. I then try to develop a more 'critical' approach to equalities and the management of change, in the sense of looking at the wider social and political issues involved.

In the section of this chapter covering alternative approaches to equalities and the management of change I have highlighted a range of different attempts to grapple with the relations between equality and organisational change, providing brief case examples of each approach described. My aim in this chapter is to move towards a set of themes emerging from different ways of working with equality that can influence management thinking and action.

Managing diversity

In this section I review and discuss some of the literature that has emerged, first in the USA and now in the UK, under the heading of managing diversity.   This body of knowledge has developed rapidly, and for two key reasons. First, in response to data which revealed how the composition of the North American workforce is and will continue to change between now and the end of the century (Hudson Institute, 1987: quoted in McKendall, 1994). The Hudson Institute report *Workforce 2000* has forecast that from 1985 until the year 2000, black people and women will constitute 85% of the growth in America's workforce. Similar changes are imagined for the UK (Kandola and Fullerton, 1994). This data has encouraged both academics and practitioners to argue 'the business case' for diversity (Cox and Blake, 1991; Ross and Schneider, 1992).

The second reason for the growth in managing diversity has been reaction and opposition to the affirmative action legislation and positive action policies introduced in the 1970s and 1980s. As Gordon (1992, p 25) has said, "affirmative action supporters needn't be paranoid these days to figure out that someone is out to get them". Managing diversity is part of the new-right thinking that began with the Reagan Government and continued through the Bush Administration. In its clearest form, this thinking brands affirmative action as "the cult of ethnicity" which "exaggerates differences, intensifies resentments and antagonisms, drives even deeper the awful wedges between races and nationalities" (Schlesinger, 1991: quoted in Gordon, 1992). In the business world, diversity has tended to replace rather than supplement affirmative action programmes. According to Lowery (1995, p 150), this is because "corporate executives found diversity a lot easier to swallow than affirmative action, and much easier to sell to a predominantly white workforce".

These two reasons go some way to explaining the underlying philosophy of managing diversity. In part it is the response of the right-wing to the evils of 'political correctness'. In part it is a response to the changing faces and voices of the future workforce. These two reasons connect in the "overarching principle of all actions in a diversity-orientated organisation" (Kandola and Fullerton, 1994, p 160), a focus on the individual, not on the group.

The management of diversity implies "respect for employees as individual actors rather than toward treatment of employees as members of groups with easily categorised differences" (Ellis and Sonnenfeld, 1994, p 99). This theme is repeated again and again in the literature. "The diversity of individual's frameworks of understanding is the key potential source of innovation" (Herriot and Pemberton, 1995, p 18). Jamieson and O'Mara (1991, p 9) suggest a need to transform "the workplace to one in which people are valued as individuals ... to individualise the way we manage". Garfield (1994, p 9) proposes that "we are as diverse as we are numerous, each of us can be considered a segment of one". Ross and Schneider (1992, p 52) think that "every individual is by definition unique. The focus is not on equalising the differences between groups, but on responding to individual needs and aspirations". Finally, "people are individuals and they have to be managed as individuals" (Gordon, 1992, p 24).

Bold claims have been made about the organisational imperative for managing diversity. For example:

> The diversity challenge is probably the biggest
> human resource challenge of this century as it
> permeates every facet of the organisation's
> internal functioning and external marketplace.
> (Griggs and Louw, 1995, p 25)

The general aim of the diversity movement is to control and connect two areas of organisational life: the management of the people that constitute its workforce (often referred to as human 'resources', 'assets' or 'investments') and the maximisation of profit. A strong emphasis has been placed on the competitive advantages of managing diversity in organisations. Maddock (1995) sees equality measures as a business necessity. Stringer (1995, p 48) advocates a focus on creating "more effective relationships so that everyone in the workplace can be at their most productive". Cox and Blake (1991) suggest that there are cost advantages and resource acquisition advantages; markets are broadened, the organisation becomes more fluid, creativity is improved, and problem solving is more effective because it is undertaken from a heterogeneous position. Jamieson and O'Mara (1991, p 9) also make an explicit link between "human resource management" and competitive advantage. They want to transform "the workplace to one in which people are valued as individuals, their diverse viewpoints are supported, potential is fully used, quality of life and lifestyles are high, and performance is at its competitive best".

Ross and Schneider (1992) outline "the business case" for managing diversity. They suggest that the management of change is made easier by attracting people with new and different ways of thinking. They make a link between diversity and quality (see also Dobbs, 1994b), and suggest that a diverse organisation is better at anticipating the changing needs of customers, better at recruiting, promoting and retaining the best people. Overall they proposed that the increased motivation in the workforce that accrues from diversity means increased productivity.

In practice, the underlying characteristics of the diversity movement mix a variety of perspectives on the nature of diversity with approaches to the management of change. Cox (1991) identifies five elements of diversity and how to achieve them. These are outlined in Table 9.

Table 9: Elements of diversity and how to achieve them

Elements	Tools
Pluralism: getting different perspectives	Training programmes using varied inputs to solving problems
Structural integration into the organisation in all job roles	Education, affirmative action, career development, new reward systems and packages
Absence of prejudice and discrimination	Focus groups, awareness training, internal research, monitoring practices and policies
Identification with the organisation	The consequence of all the other interventions described
Low levels of inter-group conflict	Evidence of promotion rates, conflict resolution training

Source: Cox (1991)

In the UK, similar models have arisen. Kandola and Fullerton (1994) propose seven aspects to diversity in organisations, connecting with characteristics outlined by other authors:

Clarity and ownership of core values: where diversity exists there must also be 'core similarity' (ie, agreement on core values) to prevent cliques and in/out groups. This is also referred to in the literature as 'ownership' or the 'willing support' from the majority of people within the organisation. "There is nothing lukewarm about ownership. It implies full and active commitment" (Ross and Schneider, 1992, p 125). The 'signs' of ownership include: changes in the internal language, managers question their own assumptions, people are prepared to challenge discriminatory behaviour, managers are able to discuss appointments objectively, and they actively support policy proposals.

Fairness: auditing all processes within the organisation in terms of their 'objectivity and fairness'. "If organizations can ensure that they are able to treat individuals fairly, and they are able to respond flexibly to individual needs, they do not need to worry about groups. Equal opportunity should look after itself" (Ross and Schneider, 1992, p 51).

Teamwork: the value of teamwork and open ways of working promotes a 'skilled workforce'. (See also Katzenbach and Smith, 1993.)

Management capability: "the emphasis should be on the managing, not the diversity" (Kandola and Fullerton, 1994, p 156). Herriot and Pemberton (1995) advocate 'principled leadership' as a key implementational factor in the management of diversity.

Flexibility: in working patterns and all policies, practices and procedures. "If an employee wants to work between 4pm and 11pm, and this does not interfere with colleagues or customers, then those are the hours those employees should work" (Kandola and Fullerton, 1994, p 158).

Individual focus: treat people as individuals rather than as members of groups with easily categorised differences (see above).

A culture that empowers: organisations will "ensure that all employees have an understanding of how the organisation operates, what it values and how it expects its employees to behave" (Kandola and Fullerton, 1994, p 163). In addition, diversity writers advocate a diverse culture one which is "responsive to different needs" as opposed to "mono-culture" (Ross and Schneider, 1992, p 53).

These characteristics are set alongside generalised approaches to organisational change. For example, Herriot and Pemberton

(1995) refer to Hammond and Holton (1991) who have identified four "conditions for successful business change". These are: top-down support; the identification and reward of required behaviours; the identification of resources; and the building of ownership. In terms of the relationship between diversity and change, Thomas (1994) identifies the following process: top management expresses a commitment to diversity, the organisation undertakes a formal audit of company culture, training is provided. Cox and Blake's (1991) suggestions for change involve:

- Leadership: top management is active, their support is crucial, they provide role models.

- Training: is a crucial first step, though limited as a change tool if used in isolation.

- Research: information is sought about current perspectives which makes it possible to identify issues and make decisions about areas of change.

- Analysis and change of culture: the organisation undertakes a full cultural audit.

- Follow-up: the organisation creates ways of motivating change, evaluating the results, institutionalising the changes.

Intervention initiatives have usually included one or more of the following categories (Ellis and Sonnenfeld, 1994): multi-cultural workshops; multi-cultural core groups (which meet monthly "to confront stereotypes and bias"); female and minority support groups and networks; advisory councils to upper management; managerial reward systems (based on the ability to promote women and minorities); mentoring programmes; and corporate communications that are designed to publicise cultural pluralism.

In order to ground some of this information about diversity, I will give a brief example of a diversity initiative in local government.

The City Government of San Diego's diversity process (see Dobbs, 1994a)

The first part of the City of San Diego's diversity process was to adopt a team approach to the development of an implementation strategy. The team included both representatives from different departments and external consultants who had been selected on a national basis. The team began by making contact with key personnel (existing personnel with specialist functions relating to equality, union representatives, key managers) and internal and external stakeholders. At the same time the team developed a coherent philosophy and image to promote the organisation's diversity initiative. The next part of the process was a data collection and feedback exercise. A random selection of employees were interviewed to discover their key areas of concern (which in this case was career development, communication, and promotion).

The data were used by the diversity team to plan an implementation strategy. This included: setting up diverse interview panels as standard; introducing their diversity model as underpinning all management training; making as many presentations for information and awareness as possible; running educational sessions; setting up task forces where necessary. The explicit values of the diversity programme were marketed internally throughout the organisation in a variety of ways. In addition, the City Manager (Chief Executive) holds afternoon sessions every Friday to discuss diversity issues. These are open to all employees and they are set in the context of a comprehensive equal opportunities policy.

The deployment and institutionalisation of the diversity process is achieved through an annual expenditure of US$300,000. The most significant driving forces (in addition to this) have been identified as: leadership by the City Manager; clarity in the values underpinning the process; diagnostic activities; the participation of internal and external stakeholders; and open communication. The most significant restraining forces were: that the process was seen as a way of 'fixing' or getting back at the 'other' group. Also, people questioned whether the commitment and expense was necessary, why current practices needed changing at all, and expressed their fear of the impact of the process on the organisation.

What is wrong with managing diversity?

In the 1980s when I started interviewing and working with managers on the relationship between equal opportunities and management I quickly noticed one consistent justification for inaction: yes, of course racism and sexism exist, but ... we are all individuals, there is no difference underneath.   Looking at the literature on managing diversity I have been struck by the institutionalisation of this justification and by the creation of a paradox concerning change.   On the one hand the movement towards managing diversity can be seen as a dramatic shift of emphasis in workplace relations; on the other hand it can be seen as no change at all. The paradox of diversity is in the mixture of two messages, the notions of "letting go yet remaining in control" (Ross and Schneider, 1992, p 203).

If this paradox could be openly addressed within an organisation then it might be possible to imagine that what is currently silenced by diversity initiatives could be given voice. The movement towards workplace diversity does not attempt to hold this paradox of change. Instead, change is being implemented in organisations as a shift of 'culture', and is therefore becoming a strategy for managing the sense-making of employees, a strategy for "calculative compliance" (Willmott, 1993). In this setting,

> ... employee behaviour is ... congruent with realising the values of the corporation, but only in so far as it is calculated that material and/or symbolic advantage can be gained from managing the appearance of consent. (Willmott, 1993, p 537)

My view is that the diversity movement in organisations is often an attempt to take the politics out of intervention, to individualise social relations, and to create a compliant workforce. The inability of practitioners to bring an analysis of processes of power and relatedness to bear on these issues ultimately seems to be a mechanism for denial and a mechanism for control. The individualising nature of the diversity movement attempts to depoliticise and silence the radicalising impact of the collective experience of both marginality and difference. "To the extent that each system reinforces and reproduces the other, an analysis of organisations cannot exclude the importance of these significant elements of identity" (Nkomo, 1992, p 507).

Exponents of managing or valuing diversity consciously or inadvertently promote a fantasy that power differences and political dimensions of organisational life will matter less once the uniqueness of each individual employee is recognised, and once all employees have accepted the organisation's mission. This is true neither for the people working in organisations, nor for the organisations themselves. Individual managers for example, are locked into and help recreate the politics of their own behaviour in organisations. As Thomas (1994, p 62) points out: "Most middle managers have made a considerable investment, emotionally and otherwise, to arrive at their current points in their careers. Being too forthright and direct in the wrong crowd is a trait they abandoned long ago".

To illustrate this in organisational terms, I will refer once again to the City of San Diego's diversity process.

> The political environment with competing programmes and goals among managers poses a challenge to the integration of diversity and quality in government. Managers concerned with furthering their own program goals and the performance of their respective units often give low priority to co-operation and teamwork with other units and agencies, thus eliminating opportunities for cross agency quality and diversity interactions. Also in conflict are the needs of public interest groups and lobbyists and the competing demands on congress from their citizen constituents, resulting in conflicting policies that must be reconciled before they can be effectively implemented. (Dobbs 1994b, p 41)

Public service organisations are full of competing demands and conflicting policies that relate to and emerge from a wide variety of social and political interests. Similarly, individual interests are set within a social and political context.

Another key problem with diversity is diversity training. Ellis and Sonnenfeld (1994) have suggested that the benefits of diversity training are: the enhanced provision of voice; knowledge and facts balance myths and stereotypes; shifts in corporate philosophy; exposure to the issues is better than ignorance whatever the risks, it clarifies the challenge to the whole firm as a social community. They also point towards the pitfalls: often training can be little more than a 'one-shot information blizzard', the quality of trainers can be poor, programmes are often not tailored to meet specific organisational designs, and there has been insufficient monitoring and evaluation of programmes. They conclude that diversity programmes are: "positive in tone, yet often lack systemic, firm wide integration into other human resource policies and do not tap the passionate disagreement that often rages beneath a platitudinous facade" (Ellis and Sonnenfeld, 1994, 80). It seems that it is as difficult for diversity programmes to relate to the emotional level of experience in organisations as it is for them to include an analysis of power.

That diversity programmes are prone to unskilled intervention can be in little doubt. This is reflected in some of the writing about such training. Herriot and Pemberton (1995) lapse into mirroring the very stereotypes and assumptions that awareness training seeks to break down. In describing the process of diversity awareness training they explain how participants take on a role different to their own in order to act out their assumptions.

> In doing so they experience some of the discomfort of having these assumptions placed on them.... The white male can admit he doesn't like feeling he has to take a lead and would prefer to take a back seat. The black woman can admit she wants help in gaining the management skills which she sees her white boss use. (Herriot and Pemberton, 1995, pp 205-6)

While such perspectives prevail in the people who favour diversity training programmes, there seems little chance that they will have any impact on organisational power relations. It also seems unlikely that they would be designed to do so in the first place. More likely, their function is a means for taking employees "beyond blame, beyond guilt, beyond sermonising" (Gordon, 1992), in other words to detach employees from the actual political and emotional impact of marginality and exclusion. As a result, diversity has become a nebulous concept which has supplanted rather than supplemented specific employment goals (Lowery, 1995).

Supporters of the diversity movement make distinctions between their own approach and other organisational approaches to change. Gordon (1992, p 24) explains that managing diversity "is not about ethics or social responsibility or doing the right thing ... it is about human performance, it's about making a profit, it's about remaining competitive". Maddock (1995, p 20) stresses that equality measures are much more to do with business necessity than social justice. Both Kandola and Fullerton (1994) and Herriot and Pemberton (1995) discuss the overlap between the diversity-oriented organisation and the learning organisation. They work with this idea on the basis that "organising is the repeated occurrence of the knowledge process" (Herriot and Pemberton, 1995, p 151). What they omit is that it is also the repeated occurrence of the power process, since the construction of knowledge is itself a form in which power expresses itself (Clegg, 1994b).

My critique of the diversity movement focuses on the following issues:

- Diversity emphasises culture change, and therefore attempts to control employee sense-making through notions of employee empowerment. Willmott (1993) refers to this process as "calculative compliance".

- Diversity in organisations is often an attempt to take the politics out of change by individualising social power relations. The inability of diversity strategies and practitioners to bring an analysis of processes of power to bear on these issues makes diversity initiatives into mechanisms for denial and for control.

- Diversity deliberately avoids engaging with an emotional level of experience in organisations, preferring instead to emphasise a consistency between organisational mission and general human resource management.

- Diversity has tended to supplant rather than supplement specific employment and equal opportunity goals.

- Diversity is seen as a cure-all. There has been no attempt to bring the initiative together with other related approaches to organisational change.

In the next section of this chapter I pick up this last point and attempt to offer a broader perspective on managing diversity in the context of approaches to equality and organisational change.

Alternative approaches to equality and organisational change

In this section I identify three other areas of thinking that affect equality and the management of change. First, management in the context of policies for *social regulation*. Second, *management and organisational learning*, by which I mean both the broader, systemic issues involved in organising and the inter- and intra-personal aspects of development that can be a part of the concept of managing. Third, *critical management*, which refers to the wider social and political significance of attempts to relate equality and organisation design. A summary of the focus, orientation, methods and underlying philosophy involved in these four approaches is contained in Table 10.

Social regulation

Nanton (1995) argues for equal opportunities to be seen as a form of social regulation. He suggests that the erosion of responsibility for direct service delivery and the dramatic reduction in the finance available to UK local authorities has had a profound effect on the ability of local government to develop equal opportunity.

> Financial restraint on local council expenditure, along with the enhancement of market competition, appears to have increased tension between concerns of equality on the one hand, and those of economy, efficiency and effectiveness on the other. It is the latter concerns which have come to dominate the public sector ethos. (Nanton, 1995, p 205)

Equal opportunity has, therefore, lost considerable ground as a result of the widespread development of the contract culture in local government. However, Nanton also suggests that the contract culture has given rise to an increase in both external and internal processes of inspection and audit. He believes that, in the context of contract cultures, "if the links between equal opportunities and regulation can be established, this will go some way to reestablishing the legitimacy and importance of the equalities process" (Nanton, 1995, 209).

Table 10: Thinking about the equality and management of change

	Managing or valuing diversity	Management and social regulation	Management learning	Critical management
Focus	Individual: the diversity of individual frameworks of understanding is the key potential source of innovation.	The individual and the group: justice for aggrieved individuals and group-based justice.	Systematic thinking: our actions create the problems we experience.	Power relations: an understanding of power and its relevance to strategic change. Pluralism and the associated conflict of values.
Orientation	Competitive advantage. "A satisfying and productive environment in which organisational goals are met and surpassed".	Bureaucracy. "At the level of practice, EO policies in local government consist in fundamentally administrative or bureaucratic processes".	The primacy of the whole. Building 'Communities of commitment'.	The wider social and political significance of 'culture' programmes. 'Utilise opportunities for micro-emancipation'.
Methods	Strongly managed vision. Teamwork, flexibility, empowerment. Diversity awareness programmes. Auditing all processes in terms of their objectivity and fairness.	The common language of regulation provides scope for the transfer of skills and knowledge between equalities practitioners. Combines an externally imposed code with self-imposed definitions and guidelines.	Dialogue rather than discussion or debate. Practice Fields. 'Teams as a mirror of organisation. Process and content are inseparable'.	The struggle with 'silenced' questions. 'Individuals learn to struggle with the problematical experience and significance of indeterminacy'.
Underlying philosophy	*Managing + individual potential:* all employees are 'valued and optimised'. 'Principled leadership'. 'Fairness'.	*Managing + regulation:* combines deterrence and compliance, but sets greater store on compliance.	*Managing + learning:* 'The learning problem is prior to the managing problem'. 'Collaborative learning'. 'Double-loop learning'.	*Managing? + power:* The need to understand power and thereby the legitimacy of multiple interests. Self is a cultural creation. 'The autonomy of the individual is forged as s/he plays with the question of which standpoint s/he will consciously strive to enact'.

Practitioners of equality are seen to be in a similar position to practitioners of quality, both are required to make decisions about when to win *compliance* (ie, when to prevent problems through imposing standards, cajoling, negotiating, persuading, educating, monitoring) or when *deterrence* (ie, punishment through recourse to either external laws or self-regulatory processes) should be used.

Nanton points towards some of the difficulties with a social regulation approach. It could become bureaucratised and apply irrelevant standards to little effect. Regulation strategies often have difficulty keeping up with the rapid pace of change. Regulation can also lead to remoteness and detachment from the day-to-day experience of the communities a local authority serves. He places much importance on the "style and effectiveness of leadership" as a key factor in avoiding these problems.

The following case example describes a regulatory approach taken by the Ontario regional government in Canada, which attempted to promote change through a combination of the legal and the developmental.

Ontario, Canada's 'Employment Equity Act' (Ontario Management Board Secretariat, 1992a, 1992b and 1992c)

The previous Ontario State Government took an approach to diversity based on legislation which asked organisations to make 'reasonable progress' in their practices and planning. The Act set out a number of principles. First, to establish the right to work without having to face discriminatory barriers. Second, the workforce, at each level and in each job category, should reflect over time, the representation of designated groups within the community in which it was situated. Third, every employer was asked to make sure that its employment policies and practices were free of systemic and deliberate barriers. Fourth, employers were asked to establish and put in place both positive and supportive measures.

Organisations were expected to initiate four basic steps. (1) To inform employees about employment equity principles and process. (2) To undertake a workforce audit and create a 'workforce profile'. (3) To review workforce policies and practices and to identify discrimination 'barriers'. (This notion refers to "rules, practices or conditions that adversely affect members of a designated group more than other people".) (4) To develop a plan that makes 'reasonable progress'. Reasonable progress involves: actions to eliminate barriers, both positive and accommodative measures (positive action), supportive measures that are of benefit to all employees, anti-harassment and anti-discrimination policies, numerical goals and timeliness. Both employers and 'bargaining agents' (eg, the unions involved) were required to take joint responsibility for the implementation of their plan.

The Act required organisations to complete these four steps within a specified time period. (For the Ontario public sector 12 months; for broader public sector and private sector organisations with over 500 employees 18 months; for private sector organisations with between 100 and 499 employees 24 months; for private sector organisations with between 50 and 99 employees 36 months.)

The legislation was administered by the Employment Equity Commission who were responsible for information and materials, guidance, policy directives, public education, audits (with power to effect settlements or order compliance), public consultations, and the production of an annual report. A tribunal was set up to mediate, decide on complaints, resolve disagreement, hear appeals, and receive referrals from the Commission. Organisations were to receive a certificate to indicate that the employer had carried out the steps and processes required by the legislation and prepared the necessary reports.

Shortly after the Employment Equity Act came into effect, a new administration was elected in Ontario. One of their earliest decisions was to repeal this legislation.

There are two points to think through in relation to the Ontario approach to managing change. First, approaches based on legislation are overt (more honest) forms of 'calculative compliance', they deliberately set out the broad framework of competence that organisations are required to establish, as well as guidelines for the monitoring of progress. In this way they can clearly define both the boundaries of organisational design and development and the imperative to make change happen. Second, this approach highlights the political nature of organisational learning and change. The Ontario Employment Equity Act established 'equity' as a necessary aspect of organisational life. This would certainly have addressed many of the issues involved in the 'active/avoiding' organisation, and made individual avoidance strategies more difficult to maintain.

Management learning

If management is reframed as learning then "the learning problem is prior to the managing problem" (Burgoyne, 1994). The very process of managing becomes learning "in, for and on behalf of organizational processes". The development of equal opportunity policy and practice not only occurs to regulate fairness and justice, but also as a container for the evolution of individual and systemic knowledge which may form the basis for organisational change within that context. This knowledge can be used, developed, ignored, defended against and avoided. As I showed in Chapter 2, individuals and organisational groups tend to move in one of two directions with it, either towards some form of 'insight' which promotes change, or towards 'willing ignorance'.

Organisations can therefore be seen both as classrooms for managers' perpetual struggles with change, and as systems that can learn from the dynamic and generative processes formed from the continual interplay of their constituent parts. Although the diversity literature acknowledges links between itself and the "learning organisation" (Kandola and Fullerton, 1994; Herriot and Pemberton, 1995) it tends to emphasise a distinction between a focus on the individual (diversity) and the system (learning organisation). At a systemic level there is a useful body of knowledge and practice some of which can be used to link equality and organisational design. Notions of the learning organisation can also be utilised to broaden the framework organisations use to integrate equalities and organisational design. The advantage of an approach based on organisational learning is that designs grow gradually, and each organisation is likely to create a different configuration. This "encourages collaboration and team learning, promotes open dialogue and acknowledges the interdependence of individuals, the organization and the communities in which they reside. Learning is a continuous, strategically used process, integrated with and running parallel to work" (Marsick and Watkins, 1994, p 354).

The ideas behind management and organisational learning provide two specific insights that are useful to broadening thinking about equalities and organisational design. First, a very strong emphasis is placed on how people apply the new insights and methods they might receive through workplace development programmes. The literature on learning organisations introduces the notion of "practice fields" (Kofman and Senge, 1993) within which managers are given sufficient opportunity to experiment, reflect and practice newly evolving skills and ideas. This idea is a significant shift from the notion of providing 'training' for skills and awareness.

Second, dialogue is a key strategy in the learning organisation. Improving dialogue depends on finding effective ways to help individuals and systems clarify their assumptions and mental models. This process begins with the assumption that shared meaning is desirable and will be achieved, not by proclaiming a dominant voice (as in the case of discussion or debate) but by acknowledging the pluralistic voice within organisations. Learning organisations therefore "find a means to bring the cacophony of their many voices to the surface and then to agree collectively on an encompassing vision" (Marsick and Watkins, 1994, p 355). Theories of the learning organisation therefore encourage a focus on the communication processes underlying a diverse workforce. "The topic of diversity, by its very nature, requires dialogue among and between differences" (Lindsay 1994, p 21). Learning how to interact through dialogue, as opposed to debate or discussion, is a first step towards organising in relation to difference.

The following example, describes a recent action research project that sought to promote structural change in organisations through a focus on gender relations. The relationship between work and family was the theme for initiating improvements in organisational structure and culture.

The Ford Foundation: "Re-linking livelihood and work"

Action research undertaken for the Ford Foundation with three large private sector companies (Ford Foundation, forthcoming), looks at changes in organisational structure through a focus on 'work–family' relations and dynamics. The research team focus on and argue that a key impediment to organisational change in terms of 'equity' is a cultural *and* structural assumption about the separation of work and family. They identified that corporate notions of the 'ideal worker' were based on staff who were prepared to put their career first ('career primary'). They also identified corporate expectations that women staff would be 'family primary'.

The culture and structure of work–family relations in these firms contradicted the desire expressed by most staff (men and women) for both good careers and good family lives. The perception of staff was that their organisations discouraged the expression of family experience, thereby positioning family issues as 'undiscussable'. The researchers found that the organisations involved tended to avoid and control the extent of change by treating work–family relations as issues of personal choice. Staff felt that they had to sort out their own needs in a 'hidden' way, outside of work, which neither helped their ability to manage work or to manage family responsibilities. This was seen to have negative consequences for staff attachment to work, and was detrimental to the energy staff had for innovation and change.

The action researchers placed great emphasis on working within the companies at a systemic rather than an individual level. The culture and structure of the organisations involved in the action research encouraged their staff to act in self-limiting ways. Employees colluded in their own control by acting on the organisations' behalf in ways that undermined the integration of their family and work lives. This study highlights the relationship between culture, structure and compliance, and shows how organisations mobilise their power, getting staff to police themselves on the organisation's behalf. This self-limiting behaviour is achieved particularly through the individualisation of collective issues. An unforeseen consequence for the organisation of this dynamic is the limitation of employee freedom to be creative and innovative.

The action research asked the organisations involved to address the links between work and family as a way of progressing gender equity. The emphasis of this change was the reframing of work–family concerns as systemic rather than individual. They utilised the energy of staff to integrate good working lives with good family lives in such a way that it was applied to changes in the organisation of work.

For example, in one of the companies involved:

> ... management was trying to shift the structure to empowered work teams and this effort was not proceeding smoothly. Control dominated the culture: 'driving the business need' meant controlling where, how and when people worked. The culture was individualistic, one that people described as sink or swim. Although an array of work–family benefits were theoretically available, only a limited version of flexitime was actually

allowed. Managers were afraid, given the culture of control, that if other benefits were made available, productivity would fall. The costs to the site were considerable in terms of unplanned absences, lack of coverage, turnover, backlash against people who took the time they needed, and mistrust of an organisation that claimed it had benefits but made their use so difficult. This way of dealing with work–family issues created a closed loop that reinforced existing practices, stifled innovation, and bred distrust of the empowerment concept. When, on the basis of our work, management openly recognised these issues and extended the use of work–family benefits to all employees, teams came up with collective approaches to flexibility that had dramatic results. The site experienced a reported 30 per cent reduction in absenteeism, customer responsiveness was increased as times of coverage were extended, divisions between employees decreased since apparent favouritism was reduced, and self-managed teams that previously had little responsibility are now active participants not only in decisions about work schedules but in other business issues such as team selection and evaluation. In addition, working on the work–family issue gave managers insight into the negative consequences of the culture of control and why this site had been having so much difficulty in moving to empowered teams. (Ford Foundation, forthcoming, p 11: draft report)

In this way the action research initiative linked individual and organisational change, both cultural and structural. The project therefore highlights the linking of work and family as a 'strategic opportunity' that creates benefits for both the employees and the business.

The action research carried out for the Ford Foundation is interesting in two respects. First, the approach to organisational change recognised the need to identify an issue with which most organisational members could relate (both men and women) as a focus for structural change within the system as a whole. Work–family became a powerful metaphor for change that affected the individual and challenged the organisation on practical, everyday levels. Second, the methodology used for the action research was a deliberate model of strategic and developmental change, based on the reframing of management as a process of participative inquiry and learning, rather than as a process focused on managerial tasks.

Critical management

The term 'critical management' (Alvesson and Willmott, 1992) expresses a need to draw out the wider social and political significance of attempts to relate equality and organisational change. The term is being used here to express the political or power relations inherent in attempts to organise around concepts like diversity or equality. One of my main arguments is that an understanding of power is an essential aspect of strategic change in organisations. An understanding of power puts people in a better position to manage the change process. As Hardy (1994, p 207) explains, the formulation of strategic intent, the way in which the environment is perceived, the choice of a particular strategy, and the process whereby strategic intent is shared among organisational members all have political implications. An inability to appreciate the complexity of power in organisations emphasises our tendency to ignore the implications of using it, and thereby to deny our own political biases. This creates a false picture of the possibilities for organisational change, and supports the fantasy that initiatives like diversity can be detached from social and political relations. A more realistic view is that organisations are made up of, for example, "race relations played out in power struggles, which includes the realisation that race is not a stable category" (Nkomo, 1992, p 507). Alongside an increased awareness of power is the need to retain an understanding of the legitimacy of the multiple interests that exist in organisations (Hardy, 1994).

The second aspect of a critical perspective introduces an intrapersonal aspect to diversity, the recognition that a multitude of persons and voices exists not only in every organisation, but also in every one of us (Hazen, 1994, p 72). Hazen believes that we are able to become better organisational change agents as we become aware of, converse with and learn from the differences within us, the various facets of ourselves. Each of us can be viewed as a "pandemonium of images" (Hillman, 1983, p 66, quoted in Hazen, 1994). We each embody many discourses, perspectives, stances, feeling states and ways of knowing. Our individuation "is a process of differentiating, of differing, of recognising the many complexities, voices and persons that we are" (Hillman, 1983, p 66: quoted in Hazen, 1994).

One way of linking an intra-personal perspective to everyday organisational practice is to help organisational members to engage with processes of introspection and projection (Lindsay 1994). This recognises that individual learning will vary according to who the individual interacts with, and links to a complex notion of identity. It is no longer sufficient to suppose the existence of an individualised self with a true nature, which can be the source of personal, inter-personal and organisational purpose (Burgoyne, 1994). Identity and self-experience "is dynamic and complex, a matrix beyond representation" (Bollas, 1995, p 147), bound up in both fantasy and cultural meaning. Lindsay (1994) emphasises the importance of making sense of the internal aspects of self when she notes that the tendency to project onto others is both a function of group work and a fundamental basis of discrimination and inequality.

Another way of viewing intra- and inter-personal perspectives on equality and organisation is in terms of the relation between such dynamics and the broader political and power relations that organisations create. As I have demonstrated, one way of linking the personal and the political is through the identification of managerial avoidance strategies which defend against equality and change. Personal defences against equality stem from individual processes of denial, projection or reaction formation. However, these defences become social and habitual, contributing significantly towards the creation and perpetuation of organisational structure. The everyday avoidance strategies of managers are both shaped by and shape the organisation's response to equality.

The recent literature and initiatives on managing or valuing diversity have been inspired by the need for a response to the changing faces and voices of the future workforce. In some cases they also reflect a backlash against what has been termed 'political correctness', and a reaction against mechanisms for the monitoring of compliance to equal opportunity legislation and policy. Diversity has come to be accepted as a fact of the future workforce, and as such is a term that is likely to linger in management and organisational thinking and practice. This will be unfortunate if the approach remains focused on the individual level, and remains solely oriented towards competitive advantage.

In introducing a critical perspective on equality and diversity, I am trying to make sense of what needs to be involved in attempts at organisational change which take equality into account. In isolation, I do not believe that the emerging approach to managing or valuing diversity does this. A more critical approach expresses "the wider issues of inequality and power with which management and organizations are associated and within which they are located" (Grey, 1995), and therefore expresses more coherently the links between equality and organisational change.

Once these links have been made in theory, the question arises: how might they be expressed within the context of organisational change? More specifically, how could local government organisations adopt an approach to the management of change which is based on equalities? The answer to this second question is necessarily provisional since it seems unlikely that an easy answer will ever be available to the complex processes of organisational and social power relations that are enacted around equality. However, it is possible to find examples of ideas and approaches that can provide insights into the relationship between equality and organisational change.

Local authorities need to examine carefully how equality issues are kept alive at all the different levels of the organisation. This can be illustrated through another short case example.

The borough council

The borough council is (informally) structured in terms of the relations between four connected groupings. The first of these is the *community* that the borough serves. The community is represented by elected members as well as through the direct influences of community organisations, forums and ideas. The second grouping is the *Chief Officers' Management Team* (COMT) which is ultimately accountable for the management of the borough, and reflects the continued 'strong role for the centre' in local government. The third grouping involves a range of *self-managed teams*, which come and go according to policy and decision-making needs, and which form a loosely coupled network of groups whose general function can be seen as a reflection and (the recommendation of) action. The COMT usually has representation on these groups, which are made up of managers from all hierarchical levels of the organisation, but are also 'people who are known to deliver'. These teams cover general areas of policy like economic development, the voluntary sector, housing, service development. The grouping, or layer, of *organisation* is expressed through the day-to-day services within different departments.

Increasingly, all of these groupings are having to manage and relate to a range of internal and external stakeholders. The COMT is influenced more and more by a range of partnerships between other organisations within the locality (eg, with health trusts or specific local businesses). The self-managed teams are influenced by service review boards and by the implications of Compulsory Competitive Tendering (CCT). The departments are influenced, for example, through their direct contact with the local community, through the setting up of new projects, and through initiatives towards customer empowerment.

There are two key principles underlying the borough's approach to equality. First, the community that is served by this council is very diverse. The 1991 Census figures show that disadvantaged and vulnerable groups constitute the majority of people who live in the borough. This has given rise to a greater emphasis on developing equality in service delivery than on developing equality in employment.

> Councils ... become distant from their communities as the internal workings of the Council ... become the central focus of Council work. This process is often accelerated by the urgent need to respond to external financial and legislative pressures. As Councils move away from the community and turn internally upon themselves there is a danger that the Council loses touch with its own purpose: providing services for local residents. (Council Guidance document)

The Borough has written guidance for 'Strategic Equality Plans in Service Delivery' (STEPS) which is both a strategic model for reviewing mainstream services from an equalities perspective, and a staff development mechanism.

> The key features of this model are that there is senior officer commitment, front-line staff are involved in the process of review, an external input is made by equalities staff to support the review team and together they address access and service outcomes. It is through this process where front-line staff develop solutions that there is ownership for change. We have found this to be the best on the job training on equal opportunities. (Council Guidance document)

The second principle is based on an effort to ensure that equality remains on the agenda of all internal, task-based groups. The COMT has created a 'free standing' Equality Unit (not linked into a specific department) and the head of this unit is a full member of the COMT. Members of the Equality Unit (which has ten staff) are encouraged to be a part of any of the self-managed teams. The effect of this is to encourage the growth of networks within the organisation that are continually thinking about the relationship between equality and change, and also neighbourhood networks that can give voice to changing needs.

Inevitably, there are difficulties that are integral to this example: the full involvement of the head of the equalities unit on the COMT has only occurred as a result of long-term struggle. Communication processes in relation to equality within the organisation are inevitably 'hit and miss'. Power relations and internal politics are an ever present aspect of negotiations over equality. A 'culture of opposition' to equality and managerial avoidance strategies persists. However, the over-riding achievement of this organisation has been to develop equalities from a focus on service delivery issues, to ensure that a continuing discussion of equality issues is present within the day-to-day processes that constitute the organisation's design and purpose, and that all policy development groups are open to influence from staff who want to keep equalities issues alive in the organisation.

Conclusion: key shifts in equalities and the management of change

In this final section I describe some of the necessary shifts of emphasis in the relationship between equality and the management of change in local authorities. These can be summarised as:

- Moving from a 'culture of opposition' towards organisational learning.

- Moving from a focus primarily on employment practices and internal codes towards a focus on service delivery.

- Moving from an individualistic perspective towards an awareness of and action on social power relations.

From opposition to learning

There is usually a forceful 'culture of opposition' to equality within local government, even in organisations where there is a high commitment to its implementation. Councils easily become stuck in a repetitive cycle of action and avoidance as a result of the members' and managers' reluctance to face the emotional and political processes that give rise to managerial avoidance strategies against equality. Increasingly, managers are being asked to learn ways of working that are conducive to the increasing pace of change. Such learning can emerge from the powerful interplay between commitment and opposition, between action and avoidance that is characteristic of the dynamics of equality in organisations. There will inevitably be avoidance strategies in response to attempted developments in equality. The question arises: what can be done to ensure that managers are better equipped to work with both the dynamics of equality in the organisation and the management of change?

One answer to this question is that organisations need to find ways of acknowledging the defensiveness and mistrust that is created and perpetuated through debates over equality between different organisational groups. Trust is an increasingly important concept in relation to evolving organisational forms (Vince and Booth, 1996), yet trust in the context of equalities is both difficult to win and easily lost. As local government organisations move away from being deeply hierarchical and multi-level, towards being more network or partnership based, then the issue of trust becomes increasingly important. One communication process I have emphasised which attempts to address this issue is the notion of 'dialogue'. In the long term, local authorities need to make more use of, and continue to develop, what they already know about creating dialogues with external communities, with user groups and with partner organisations and groups. They need to bring the lessons learnt from such experiences back into the organisation in order to create more effective communication between diverse internal groups and perspectives. The dialogue begins from looking inside.

Despite the fragmentation of authorities into more or less autonomous or decentralised corporate groups (whether client or contractor), the structure of local government organisations in the UK has remained deeply hierarchical. There is a paradoxical tension around power and authority in local government and this is focused on the role of the centre. On the one hand centralised control looks increasingly redundant as devolved groups grow within specific areas of policy development and delivery. On the other hand, the political structure of local government has not been able to mirror these changes in ways that include more participatory and autonomous forms of local democracy and action.

Few authorities have risen to the political challenges of change that local government increasingly faces in a way that would assist in the development of equalities. At a time when strong community development and user involvement strategies are required to ensure the accountability of autonomous providers, both senior officer and elected members retain powerful central roles in both the development of services and the extent of community 'partnerships'. The opposition that exists towards equalities in authorities is reflected in and reinforced by a wider opposition, an unwillingness to learn from and with different and conflicting local communities.

From employment practice to service delivery

Local authorities will need to engage more explicitly with the differentials of power in communities created by social and institutional inequalities. In practice, this means changing the underlying assumption that equality initiatives are oriented towards doing something special for disadvantaged individuals or groups. In place of this perception, local authorities might learn how the work they do on equalities assists in the provision of services to *all* members of their community. This cannot be achieved where there continues to be an emphasis on employment practices to the exclusion of service delivery issues. Increasingly, an organisation's ability to evolve structures and designs that are productive in terms of internal and external equalities will depend on the ability of the authority to involve both the general community and specific user groups in the development of services that are relevant to diverse, conflicting and changing needs.

One of the key managerial insights necessary in relation to equality is in the continuing need to look for opportunities to change services, to develop new projects, to open up the organisation. This is about learning how to bring the 'other' in, about learning how to relate to the other. Managers can display considerable fear, cynicism and avoidance towards the involvement of communities and users in the changing nature of service delivery. External conflicts in a diverse community might be even more threatening, even less controllable than internal struggles for equality. Managers need to learn more about how to open up the organisation and that equality can be a decisive factor in an authority's drive for organisational learning and change.

From 'we are all individuals' to an awareness of social power relations

The movement towards the individualisation of organisational approaches to equality represented in the 'diversity' literature is an attempt to remove the politics from struggles over inequality and thereby to silence conflicts and differences between groups with differential positions of power in organisations. The development of action on equalities issues within local government will be limited if authorities are overly influenced by the theory and practice of 'managing diversity'.

As I stated at the beginning of this chapter, my aim has been to identify a set of themes emerging from different ways of working with equality that can influence management thinking and action. It seems particularly important to me that any processes for engaging with equalities in the future are not constrained by the move towards individualism represented in theories of diversity. I prefer to imagine that a variety of approaches can be utilised in any attempts at organisational change.

In the four chapters that constitute Part Two I have identified a range of issues concerning equalities and management learning in local government. These studies have been set within the general context of considerable change in local government, and within the specific context of continuous struggles with organisational responses to equality. In the final section and chapter of the book I develop perspectives emerging from organisational learning and critical management, as well as drawing some conclusions about managerial defences and avoidance strategies.

The power of managerial avoidance strategies and defensive routines to maintain the gap between intent and action has remained a consistent feature of equalities over the past 10 years. The paradox of equality in local government is the way in which authorities are both active and avoiding in their approach. They are therefore in a position to work with the paradoxical tension between their ambivalence towards and their enthusiasm for equality. This paradox is present for many individual managers, while for others it is clear that their ambivalence far outweighs their enthusiasm. The work that needs to be done in relation to this ambivalence may have no end. A starting point however, is to find ways of working with the issues highlighted in this chapter, and to realise the central part that equalities have to play in management learning and organisational change.

Part Three

Reflections: Two

I have become much more aware of the emotions present in moment to moment behaviour within both working groups and learning groups. I have also realised how few of these moments are explicitly reflected on and talked about in management learning.

The moment of beginning with a new group is a good example of this for me. When I *begin* to occupy the role of tutor or consultant to a group of managers, I often feel as though I am seen through a variety of conflicting emotions. I might be viewed with hope, as a person who can share his knowledge and expertise, a person with whom it will be possible to learn. At the same time I might be viewed with envy, as group members struggle with my actual or imagined power over the group, and frame it as helpful, judgemental or hostile. It is clear to me now that I can never begin to work with a group as someone free from a range of existing internal and social relations, constructed out of fantasies and projections belonging both to myself and to others, and from the perpetual interplay of power.

Such feelings seem to me to be what management learning is about, since they mirror the everyday dynamics of management interaction at an emotional level, set in a context of organisational power relations. These feelings are the starting point of my ability or inability to help to create an environment where management learning can take place. They are initially what prevents the learning group (myself included) from starting to have a creative dialogue, from beginning to interact together. Once we have acknowledged the emotions that surround and shape our interactions it becomes possible to imagine that learning about ideas and approaches can begin. In my experience I have found that this place may only be reached after a long time, or it may happen after a very short period together. I never really know which it is going to be.

I also have to be aware of when and where it is appropriate to interact with and through the emotions generated by processes of management learning. I was struck by a recent experience at an academic conference, where I talked around my ideas about emotional and relational aspects of management learning. Academic conferences, as well as being interesting in their potential for discussion and development of ideas, are essentially competitive experiences. For whatever reason there is often much nastiness dressed up in a mask of rationality. At the end of my talk I was asked about how I could present the importance of the emotional as well as the rational in such a rational way. The voice in my head said: "don't get drawn into having your emotions here, it is not a safe place". Having such clear boundaries seems very important.

Another aspect of my experience of learning groups is my increasing clarity about how bound up people are in processes whereby we try and get others to take responsibility for our wants. I sometimes find myself doing things and not really know why I am doing them. I notice managers taking on and acting out the needs and wishes of other managers. All of a sudden I might stop and think, why am I doing this?, how did I get into this position?, why aren't they doing this for themselves? It is not simply that I have been subjected to the wishes of another, it is that our relations have become the subject. Following on from this, it gets harder and harder for me to imagine a self that is separate from relations: "for any episode of self experience is dynamic and complex, a matrix beyond representation" (Bollas, 1995, p 147). I mention this because my experience of management education and development, and of organisational learning and change over the past few years is that many people want to deny the impact of the relatedness between the self and the other. They try to individualise everything. My experience of working on equality and management learning is the same.

I come across the attempt to individualise social relations with persistent regularity. Recently, for example, I received the following communication through the 'Diversity Forum' Internet discussion list. Keri in Australia wrote:

> Surely all individuals are unique, different and of worth. Isn't the purpose of effective diversity management to ensure that the value, rights and needs of each individual are properly recognised, developed and rewarded. While some individuals can be seen to 'belong' to a particular 'type' because of a particular characteristic (black, female, short, people with disabilities, born in the wrong suburb, eats the wrong food ... and so on ...), ultimately we must be concerned about removing barriers to the fullest development and expression of each individual. In short, all barriers to the full attainment of each individual's potential should be removed. Or is this too simplistic an approach?

So much of the established thinking about and practice of management education and development seems to me to be represented in Keri's communication. It imagines that I am me and you are you, and that our individual potential can be realised (if we can be open about ourselves). It is as if the boundaries between the self and the other are very clear. But they are not. At any given moment, I am not just myself, I am also your creation of me. The impact of this on my thinking about management learning is crucial. It leads me to think that intra-personal processes like projection and introjection are a vital aspect of the theory and practice of management learning. It also leads me to think that the social and political relations between the self and the other are perpetually an aspect of what constitutes self-experience. This explains something of my interest in the psychodynamics and politics of management learning and organisational change.

In response to Keri I wrote:

> I think it is too simplistic an approach from my perspective. I think that the desire to individualise is an attempt to obscure the effects of social power relations in organisations. I think that the perspective you put forward is fast becoming institutionalised, and is giving rise to a paradox concerning change. On the one hand the movement towards managing diversity can be seen as a dramatic shift of emphasis in workplace

relations, on the other hand it can be seen as reinforcing traditional power relations, and therefore is no change at all. My own view is that this attempt to individualise social relations, and the consequent inability to bring an analysis of processes of power to bear on these issues, can only ultimately be seen as both a mechanism for denial and a mechanism for control. The tendency towards individual potential seems to me to be an attempt to depoliticise and silence the radicalising impact of the collective experience of both marginality and difference.

I didn't hear back from Keri in Australia, but I did hear from Jennifer in the USA:

Thank you ten fold for your eloquent response! I have been engaged in this discussion/argument with my office's diversity team. They are all so eager to focus on the individuality of difference that in doing so they completely ignore power differences. Even 'diversity trainers' we've had have taken this approach. It is my opinion that focusing on individual differences while ignoring power differences is just another way – and a VERY effective way – of perpetuating the status quo while giving lip service to diversity. Whenever I bring up social power differences, the reactions are anything but pleasant. I just shared your comments with them and hope that your words may be more effective than mine have been. (PS Thanks for making my day. This work can be lonely, and it helps to hear your own thoughts from someone else. Then I don't feel so crazy.)

I was moved by this response because I associated both with this sense of feeling lonely and with being positioned as crazy. The desire in individuals and in organisations to rationalise away power relations is very strong.

Such rationalisation also affects our ability to see the links between intra- and inter-personal relations. For example, I notice how two group members communicate with and through the other, continually responding to each other in the complicated construction of their separate and mutual identities. They just cannot help it. I also know from my own experience how easy it is to get locked into such circular behaviour.

How good is the management learning I do if I don't work with emotions and power relations? I cannot find a place in my practice for being 'person-centred'. In a group someone said to me: 'tell me what you are feeling now'. I felt angry at the question, but then I think that is what it was designed to do, because the group member was too afraid of his anger to have it himself, and would rather that I had it for him. Sometimes, people imagine that they are being open and sharing when they ask such a question, but they are not. They are being controlling, it is an attack. My advice is: beware of people who soften their voice and say: 'how are *you* feeling?'

If I was asked to isolate one aspect of management learning that seems to me to be important then I would say: to increase managers' capacity to work with the processes, dynamics and relations of groups. There are certain experiences of group learning I have had that are unforgettable. I remember singing so loudly to that tape as I drove away from my first Leicester Conference, and even now, how-ever-many years later I can still conjure up the feelings of joy and empowerment, the quality of the moment I brought away with me. I had an intense sense of the emotional relatedness of people within organisation, the inter-connection of our sameness and difference continually creating, reinforcing and changing the organisation.

Given this experience of my first visit to the Leicester Conference it seems somewhat inevitable in retrospect that my second visit would end in more sombre mood. I still came away with a powerful sense of the relatedness of people in the creation of an organisation, but this time the feelings about the learning organisation I had been in were that it was driven by anger, competition and envy. The feelings that I brought away may have been more difficult to accept and integrate, but it seems to me that they were equally important in assisting in my learning about relatedness, and in disturbing the status quo enough for me to entertain change.

I can find many reflections on learning in groups, but one particularly comes to mind in this context. I had read Palmer's (1979) chapter and discovered his description of learning as the capacity to doubt even those things that seem unquestionably true. It is only through my participation in group learning that I have come to fully appreciate the impact and importance of this wonderful proposition. In the process of discovering something of my capacity to doubt I have learned how to learn. As I find myself increasingly doubtful in relation to my knowledge about the workings of equality and inequality in organisations, I also find myself increasingly connected to the study of it.

eight

Equality and management learning

In this book I have discussed my changing perspectives on equality and management learning over an extended period. My personal subject and the subject I am interested in are connected in my writing. I began with a sense of myself as a change agent, a person who held a planned strategy for change. I have moved into less certain territory, involving explorations of the shifting emotional and political aspects of everyday experience and thoughts about the paradoxical nature of organisational change.

I have been attempting to capture a change process over time, and through this to point towards some of the issues involved in management learning and organisational change. My engagement with others, and with my own sense of what the work is about, has involved me in continually revising my approach to management learning. In this final chapter of the book I draw conclusions from my experience of management learning in order to suggest issues and processes for action. My themes continue to be equality, organisational learning, management education and organisational change. I reflect on what can be done to support managers in working through defences and avoidance strategies, not solely in terms of equalities, but also in relation to other areas where learning and change is inhibited by difficulties with emotions, relations and power.

One idea that I try to communicate strongly in this book is that change involves shifts of habits and attachments, shifts in the dependency that we have in our established frameworks of meaning. I place a great deal of emphasis on the workings of anxiety, and in the potential of this emotion to (at the same time) both promote and discourage learning. The boundary or margin between taking the risk to act or find voice, and fleeing or fighting against action, retreating into silence or to dictated lines, is a key moment in management learning. One way to make such moments and processes available to managers involves emphasising an explicit link between equality and management learning. I have made this link by talking about the emotions involved in management by avoidance, the avoidance of power issues, and the avoidance of the dynamic processes underlying relations between the self and the other.

I have also attempted to acknowledge the complexity of working towards organisational learning and change. I use my own experience to illustrate the importance of not looking for solutions, but instead to look for ways of exploring and engaging with uncertainty and paradox, with the emotional and political in organisations. This experience can be seen as I move from the utilisation of a change process set up as a kind of correction centre (masquerading as a training event) towards an acknowledgement of change happening "in connection with others, through friendships and collaboration, ... as a result of uncertainty and risk, through organisational politics, and ... for reasons I cannot fathom". In Chapter 6 I talked about working with managers who also live with this type of paradox in their work. They live with a desire to punish the white, male managers around them as well as a desire to move collaboratively towards organisational learning and change. The starting point for them, and for me, was to become conscious of this paradox, conscious of the fact of being in a process of management learning.

Management learning and organisational change

I am interested in working with "the dispersed, multi-form and uncertain nature of management knowledge" (Burgoyne, 1994, p 40), and there are various areas in which I have attempted to develop my practice, based on this uncertainty. In summary they are:

- the relational aspects of learning and change;

- engagement with the self and the other;

- learning in groups;

- the paradox of 'managing' change.

The relational aspects of learning and change

Part of the task that is usually imagined by the management developer or change consultant is to work towards a starting point where the potential for organisational learning is increased. This can take time, and all such efforts may fall apart if the organisation concerned cannot find ways of opening itself up to the possibility of learning and change. Often, the starting point for intervention in organisations is not where it might at first seem. It is possible to undertake considerable work within an organisation before reaching a starting point for learning, and recognising it as such.

Most approaches to the diagnostic stage of intervention emphasise the identification of the 'current state' of the organisation, highlighting specific needs or problems, within the context of a 'desired state', the imagined change. The model allows for the unpredictability of the consequences of intervention by recognising the impact of feedback loops (of reflections in practice) on the imagined change. In this way, clarification of what the organisation wants to change is generated through the process of action towards change. The emphasis of diagnosis, despite allowing for some uncertainty, remains focused on the problem.

One of the ways in which I think this might be developed is to move away from an emphasis on problems towards an emphasis on relations. There are occasions when organisations can gradually become aware of the possibilities of learning as a result of the relationship they establish with a consultant. It seems that sometimes this requires almost no effort on the consultant's behalf since the organisation itself will have structured the possibility for different ways of learning into its everyday practices. More usually however, it can take a great deal of effort to negotiate, collaborate and communicate with organisational members in order to create the necessary emotional and organisational safety so that they feel they can trust the consultant with their learning (and so that I can trust them with mine).

I have found myself increasingly faced with a shift of emphasis away from diagnosis of existing organisational cultures or problems, towards the rather more arbitrary matter of relations. In essence, the question lying underneath an initial engagement with an organisational representative is: do we like each other enough to work together, to trust and to build the relationship? In other words, is it possible for us to make a commitment. Such trust can take time to evolve or it can be there in an instant, I just do not know at the start.

This experience of the need to build a relationship between the change consultant and the client organisation often seems to be a reflection of the dynamics inside the organisation. Inside organisations and between organisational actors, the question of communication becomes enmeshed in the complicated history of inter-personal competition and alliance that constitutes everyday relations within working groups. It is often the irrationality of relations rather than rationality towards tasks and problems that can drive individual actions and organisational groups. In my work with teams within organisations I have encountered feuds between individuals that go back many years, so far back that the initial reason for their mutual dislike has been forgotten by the parties involved. Their dislike of each other has become a habit, and has become a part of what guides their decision making. When these disputes are not worked through, such relations place an underlying restriction on the extent of strategic change.

As I have stated in Chapter 2, the development of managers' abilities to relate and communicate through processes of dialogue can provide access to the varied individual *and* social meanings within organisations: "the experience of the meaning embodied in a community of people" (Isaacs, 1993). Dialogue is therefore a process of communication that attempts to set individual managerial experience and action within the context of collective thought and shared assumptions, and the living social processes that sustain them. It is important to consider not just how managers (like those two whose dislike of each other has become a habit) relate, but what their relations represent in organisational terms. Many organisations have a stake in keeping their conflicts at an individual level, in allowing managers to act out tensions that stem from organisational issues.

One area for development in management learning concerns how practitioners create ways in which underlying dynamics can be worked through and understood in organisational terms. At present, we too often collude with ignoring these dynamics, either because of our own discomfort in working with them, or as a result of political pressures from the organisations we work in. The further development of dialogue as an organisational process is vital if managers are to move beyond existing, inhibitive rules about interaction and to work effectively within increasingly complex and uncertain forms of organisation.

Managers and management development practitioners would both benefit from an greater awareness of the living experience of thinking, not simply a reflection on it. Increasingly, we will be asking managers to hold their immediate emotional responses in *suspension*, in order to be able to feel them. Whether we are working managers or working with managers, the task is to find ways of holding our emotional responses long enough in order to know where they come from, be it our own stories or the organisation's stories. As practitioners we will be taking responsibility for more than an individualised attention to learning, we need to develop a collective approach, where individual and social experience both contribute to the continual evolution of the underlying structure through the very process of action. This will allow the learner to relate more effectively to ever shifting visions of the whole.

These issues beg the question, what kind of structures for individual and organisational learning and change can be developed that will create a bridge between a focus on the relational and the ability of individuals and organisations to realise their tasks? One way to build such a bridge is through an acceptance that management inquiry is integral to everyday management. The importance of the relationship between action and inquiry has been a well established part of the literature for many years (Argyris et al 1985; Torbert, 1991). Management inquiry is integral to the everyday process of management. The knowledge and experience that constructs an organisation is always provisional and subject to change. This means that the skills of discovery, analysis and sense-making, the ideas involved in research as learning, are consistently important in the ever present task of re-creating organisation through human interaction.

Current thinking about organisational structures suggests that modern organisations should be based around emerging organisational designs (networks as opposed to hierarchies) and that these require new conceptualisations of management. These include the more relationally-based skills of partnership, collaborative negotiation, ethical behaviour, team-building and community-building skills (Snow, Miles and Coleman, 1992). Many qualitative approaches to inquiry emphasise the development of collaborative, participative and action-based skills (Reason, 1988, 1994; Denzin and Lincoln, 1994; Torbert, 1991). The procedures underlying these types of inquiry, because they focus on the relationship between researcher and researched, are particularly well suited as a model of everyday management learning. Learning to inquire helps managers to a better understanding of the complicated emotional and political processes that surround them. In this sense therefore, change consultants working with organisations need to find ways of promoting not only the *learning* organisation, but also the *inquiring* organisation.

As an example I want to talk briefly about a County Council Management Programme, developed by myself and my colleague Mike Broussine. The original opportunity for this work emerged when the council approached the university where I was working with a view to setting up an in-house Master of Business Administration (MBA) programme. For various reasons this was not possible, and representatives of the Council and the Business School sat down to think of alternatives. Personally, I was pleased that the idea of an MBA could not be implemented. Although MBAs are the mainstream management qualification, the traditionally didactic style and approach characteristic of our MBA does not lend itself to working overtly with emotions and power relations.

We therefore took the opportunity to talk about an organisational change initiative based on management inquiry. The programme that subsequently evolved, provides both a qualification for individual managers (a Research Diploma leading to a Master of Philosophy Degree) at the same time as working within organisational, managerial and strategic needs as defined by senior council managers. The objectives of the programme are threefold: meeting the organisation's needs for well written internal research that can inform and underpin decision making, meeting individuals' needs for the development of management competence through personal research, and integrating these organisational and individual needs.

The programme introduces managers to action research and human inquiry methods and provides support for those managers to work together as a group of researchers on a policy issue that has been delegated from the Chief Officers Group. They have six months to complete their research as a group. They can then continue with research on an organisational issue of their own choice for their diploma. Within this type of programme we are attempting to achieve an integration of individual and organisational learning, to promote a view of research as learning, and to focus on and review emotional and political processes around specific policy areas.

Engagement with the self and the other

It seems to me that there is scope for the development of management learning not solely in terms of relations, but also in terms of relatedness. Relatedness refers to the complex relations between persons and groups that establish the underlying emotional structures of an organisation, creating the emotional climate within which individual and group emotions and relations are then situated.   Exploring these structures involves the development of an understanding of the ways in which the self is created through emotional relations with others. Working with these relations provides access to the underlying emotional dynamic of organisation.

One of the struggles involved in working with organisations on their learning and change is moving beyond the traditional expectations and instruments that dominate our own field of work.   Many practitioners of management development have relied too heavily on established management and organisational development instruments which can suppress as much of the potential learning process as they highlight. In the past it seemed reasonable to imagine that managers could be brought together in order to share individual feelings and perceptions in such a way that all present could reflect for themselves on their current and evolving knowledge and experience. All this required was taking the risk to be open. In this book I have placed much emphasis on moving beyond conceptualisations of the autonomy of individuals, towards working with the complex ways in which individuals are constructed by and within the very process of interaction with the other.

The current challenge in management learning involves finding ways of working with this complexity, with the relatedness between persons and groups that sets the underlying emotional structures of an organisation. One way of working with the emotional life of organisational groups has been through a contextualised group relations methodology (Gillette and

McCollum, 1990; Vince, 1995a) which emphasises the 'here and now' experience of managers in groups as an expression of the emotional possibilities and constraints within a given organisation.

This method evolved from the approach developed by the Tavistock Institute of Human Relations in London and particularly through their Leicester Conferences (see Miller, 1989). However, there are many organisations worldwide which have developed the model in their own terms, including the Grubb Institute, London (Armstrong, 1991), the AK Rice Institutes in the USA (Colman and Geller, 1985), and the Forum International de l'Innovation Sociale in Paris. The contextualised group relations approach allows managers to understand not just the self in relation to others in the organisation, but also the internalised 'organisation in the mind'. The organisation in the mind offers a powerful picture of what an organisation seems to be to individuals and groups of managers within their organisational roles, and in terms of the relationship between role and action.

One way of working with the organisation in the mind is to engage managers in processes for learning that are not just characteristic of their individual management styles, but are also an internalised reflection of the prescribed and preferred ways of working in the organisation as a whole. In this way, processes operating within a learning group of managers constitute a mirror of processes in the wider organisation. The emotions that emerge in the learning process are as difficult to accept, acknowledge and work with as the managing process. Psychodynamic approaches to group relations see such emotions as an integral part of doing the job of management, and provide a contained or well-bounded environment within which managers can learn how to work with and from emotional responses. The function of this particular method is both to support managers in being less of a captive to their own emotions, and to highlight the relatedness between individual feelings and the emotional character of the organisation.

All managers (management developers and change consultants) develop habits as a result of successful actions in the past. However, it is easy to become dependent on particular ways of working. Once a manager discovers one way of managing that works, they can quickly come to rely on always managing in that way. The manager becomes caught in processes of self-limitation which inhibit change and development. Through such dependency, individual managers limit both their ability to adapt to new situations and to bring creativity and innovation to old ones. In other words, self-limitation becomes the main sub-conscious task of the organisation or group.

The task in terms of management learning is to find ways to focus the attention of managers on what is happening around them, on the processes that continually shape a changing organisation. This may be achieved through designs oriented towards revealing the complexities and paradoxes of everyday human interaction (emotional, rational and political) within the organisation. Inevitably this challenges organisations to: fully legitimise learning and change, introduce managers to the group processes that underlie their work, reduce task obsessiveness, and stimulate different forms of communication and interaction between individuals and groups.

Learning in groups

One starting point for learning about groups and group processes is a person's own experience within a group both as a participant in, and an observer of, individual and group behaviour. The individual within the group can attempt to learn about their own prejudices and biases, to look at their defences and avoidance strategies, to recognise personal fears and anxieties, to review the impact of past history on the present, as these occur in each moment. In terms of the group as a whole: the group's preferred ways of working emerge through individual habits and patterns of behaviour and response, the rules the group create for and impose on itself emerge, and the designs that are specific to that group's defences against learning and change.

The most powerful learning about groups and group processes is likely to occur from experiencing and reflecting on the behaviour of the self and others within and between groups. Such experience relates particularly to feeling and understanding what is happening in the 'here and now' of different group settings. Interacting effectively and honestly with here and now feelings and experience is an essential part in developing an awareness of the conscious and unconscious processes that take place within and between groups. Learning occurs therefore from staying with what is actually happening in 'this' group, between the people who are together in the present. Observing and experiencing the here and now of groups makes it possible to reflect on the various processes present between people, and which are both consciously and unconsciously shaping the direction, the structure and the character of a group.

There are a number of issues for managers who are attempting to understand and learn about personal and organisational dynamics through groups and group processes. These include:

- *Attending to the group's process as well as the content of interactions within the group.* A group can be said to be more than the sum of its individual parts; in addition it has a dynamic created through relations.

- *Learning to take risks.* This implies both a willingness to move beyond anxiety and to engage in dialogue with others. The fear of taking risks is usually (although not always) worse than the outcome of the risk taken.

- *Developing an awareness of how to participate and interact with here and now behaviour and experience in the group, particularly at an emotional level.* The discovery and expression of 'authentic' feeling (as opposed to behaviour designed to avoid or deny feelings) allows the inter-personal dynamics of the group to become visible.

- *Acknowledging how issues of inter-personal, social and societal power affect and impact on the group.* There is often a high degree of defensiveness in groups on issues of power, both in terms of personal authority and social and cultural grouping.

These last two points seem to me to be particularly important for management learning. In our management development, management education or consultancy roles we use groups to create an appropriate container for learning. Whatever the shape of the containers we create for learning, be it didactic or experiential, emotional relations and power relations will have an impact on the process.

I have been particularly critical of 'facilitation' in this book, because I have come to realise, through my own changing picture of myself in that role, that those who do facilitation may have little or no sense of the emotional and power dynamics that are created around the role. In Chapter 2 I use the example of facilitating peoples' emotional responses as a reinforcement of the implicit power relations between tutor and student by making it seem as though only the student has emotions. I see this position as both defensive and unhelpful, rooted in a denial both of the facilitator's own emotions and of the power involved in taking up such a role. As practitioners of management learning, we will need to learn how to work more overtly with emotional and power relations, and with the connections between emotion and power.

At this point I would like to introduce a story about self-awareness which I think is important for anyone who wants to work with and in groups on learning and change. I find the story useful in reflecting on what people bring into groups, and for pointing towards the double-edged nature of facilitation. The story is by Margaret Atwood (1983), and it is called 'Making poison'.

> When I was five my brother and I made poison. We were living in a city then, but we probably would have made the poison anyway. We kept it in a paint can under somebody else's house and we put all the poisonous things into it that we could think of: toadstools, dead mice, mountain ash berries which may not have been poisonous but looked it, piss which we saved up in order to add it to the paint can. By the time the can was full everything in it was very poisonous.
>
> The problem was that having once made the poison we couldn't just leave it there. We had to do something with it. We didn't want to put it into anyone's food, but we wanted an object, a completion. There was no one we hated enough, that was the difficulty.
>
> I can't remember what we did with the poison in the end. Did we leave it under the corner of the house, which was made of wood and brownish yellow? Did we throw it at someone, some innocuous child? We wouldn't have dared an adult. Is this a true image I have, a small face streaming with tears and red berries, the sudden knowledge that the poison was really poisonous after all? Or did we throw it out, do I remember those red berries floating down a gutter, into a culvert, am I innocent?

> Why did we make the poison in the first place? I can remember the glee with which we stirred and added, the sense of magic and accomplishment. Making poison is as much fun as making a cake. People like to make poison. If you don't understand this you will never understand anything.

When people work with groups of managers as a facilitator or consultant they often seem to bring with them the idea that they are going to help those managers in some way, and this is frequently true. The motivation to facilitate can come from a conscious desire to offer support to others, to assist in their personal explorations, developments and change. This may not be the only motivation, however. What if part of the reason why people become 'facilitators' stems from a desire to position the learning group participants as the ones who need help? What if our motivation to be facilitators, our openness to working with the poisonous concoctions of others, is based on the fact that this is preferable to working on our own? When working in or with groups it is likely that a variety of feelings and positions will emerge as a result of interactions with others. It would be surprising if these were only based on the desire to care, support and nurture others and not also on the desire to compete with and undermine them.

Taking on board the complexities involved in the emotional and power relations that are an integral aspect of group learning means finding ways of working with groups that do not skate over or deny the manipulative starting points in our own practice. Yet, this also means providing learning environments that are well bounded and creative in their ability to bring to the surface and hold emotions and power relations, and that encourage groups to work with these issues towards their own understanding of the possibilities and difficulties of learning and change. Working through emotions and power relations inevitably provokes anxiety, and anxiety creates the possibility for either promoting or discouraging learning. Groups can develop the possibilities for promoting learning when they begin to address for themselves the uncertainty, conflict and anxiety in here and now experience.

I think that the simultaneously simple and complicated task faced by those who are responsible for the learning of others in groups is to find ways of making a group aware of itself as a learning group (Kasl et al, 1993). This is not as easy as it sounds. It is likely to involve: facing individual and group habits and dependencies, working through the anxiety of immanent learning, having clear boundaries around structures and roles, acknowledging the emotions and power relations present, and it requires an ability to hold uncertainty and paradox.

The paradox of 'managing' change

There is a paradoxical tension at the heart of attempts to manage change. One side of this paradox is that most managers, management developers and consultants recognise change as an uncertain, continual and integral aspect of organisation. The other side of the paradox is that we also continue to act on change in terms of the identification of specific problems and the implementation of solutions, as if we were certain that these can be worked with. This tension is intriguing, because it means that attempts to manage change are often themselves made from a confused starting point. Attempts to manage change primarily happen in a transitional space, an in-between state that is both creative and confusing. This space provides the impetus for us as practitioners to imagine new ways of working, at the same time as touching on our anxieties about letting go of old ways.

As managers, management developers and consultants, we work in ways that attempt to reassure the anxieties present both in our own organising and in the organisations with whom we are working. We behave as though these complex problems can be solved, because that is what we want to believe and what those we work with want to hear. Anxiety also emerges around the fear that if we do not present and implement a rational and incremental proposal then we will not get repeat business. Another way of expressing the paradoxical tension we are caught in as practitioners of change management is that our current frameworks do not help us to work with anxiety, paradox and uncertainty because they were mostly designed to relieve anxiety, unravel paradoxes and re-establish certainty.

Generally, neither working groups of managers, nor learning groups, like to dwell for long on the anxieties and confusions, the dynamic and uncertain nature of the change processes they are experiencing. It seems preferable to imagine ways of fixing the problems, helping rational managers to find and implement rational solutions. My argument is that some client organisations and some practitioners of management education, management development and consultancy want to engage with a different complexity in organisational change. This involves a belief that many of the challenges to managing and organising are best faced not by finding solutions, but by finding different ways of engaging with situations and people, by being open to the paradoxes inherent in all attempts to change.

From this perspective, 'effective' managers are not those who have the most knowledge, but are those who value and implement a spirit of inquiry. The process of organising is viewed not as a choice between (for example) hierarchy and networks, but as a developing appreciation of organisational members' roles in relation to others. The success of intervention in the change process need not be seen in terms of its effectiveness in obtaining solutions or the desired outcomes. Perhaps the success of interventions is more visible in terms of the emotional insights and engagement individuals develop, which help them to remain involved in the political processes of effecting change from within the organisation.

It seems to me that the major outcomes from processes of management learning are often powerful emotional insights that have some practical (perhaps short term, perhaps long term) relevance for the individuals, groups or organisations that experience them. These insights however, still have to be put into action. Within organisations this is often anxiety about engaging with a political process involving the exercise of internal and external power. The relationship between learning and action often depends on the ability of participants in learning groups to hold onto creative emotions despite the political pressures of their everyday organisational experience. In the face of this pressure, some managers will retain their emotional insights only briefly as they are quickly swamped by the effects of the organisations they have returned to. Others may find that they have greater resilience and may hold emotional insights for considerably longer, possibly for years, because the experience has been fundamental in some difficult to define but none the less tangible way. The challenge for managers is how they contain or hold these emotional insights so that they have practical relevance to their engagement with other organisational members and within the organisational structure. The impact of insight is change.

So far in this final chapter I have considered what is still to be learned about management learning. In the next section I return to the specific issue of equality and equalities, and think about how to engage with this aspect of organisational life.

From active/avoiding organisations to critical management learning

As a white, middle class man I am not writing about equality in order to propose some imagined solidarity with women and black people. Any such connections are made and broken through engagement in practice, and through our continuing negotiations over difference. I am writing about equality because it is an area of inquiry and action that brings to the surface many of the issues that seem to me to be important in management learning. These include: power in organisations, emotions and relations in organisations, and the ways in which management education, management development and consultancy are practised. I am proposing that management learning needs to be critical in the sense of exploring the wider emotional and political significance of its own processes and practices. Engaging with equality in organisations makes this possible. I also see this as one way in which organisations can relate to learning and change.

Equality in organisations is a continuing political process, shaped and reshaped in terms of power relations. In this political environment there exist both askable and silenced questions about equality (Nkomo, 1992), and legitimate and marginalised voices. As a result, equality can also be seen as a powerful metaphor for exploring the relational and paradoxical nature of management learning and organisational change. In local authorities, management by avoidance has brought to light organisational and managerial processes that show how legitimate voices remain legitimate, and how marginalised voices remain marginalised. The work that I have undertaken around equalities in organisations has attempted to highlight the connections between emotional relations and power relations in particular. Managers who have conflicting views of how moves towards equality within an organisation might be implemented often find themselves caught up in emotional relations with others that help to perpetuate the existing power relations.

In Chapter 7 I proposed three particular areas where organisations and organisational groups need to become conscious of their learning. These are:

- Moving from a 'culture of opposition' towards organisational learning.

- Moving from a focus primarily on employment practices and internal codes towards a focus on service delivery.

- Moving from an individualistic perspective towards an awareness of and action on social power relations.

At the heart of the change is the effort towards some form of 'critical' organisational learning. As in Chapter 7, I am using the word critical to express something about power, something about the political nature of management:

> Political means not issues of organisational politics but (or and) all of the wider issues of inequality and power with which management and organisations are associated and within which they are located. (Grey, 1995)

I think that the emphasis of change in terms of equalities in organisations has shifted in the past 10 years. Initially, attempts to implement equal opportunities were based on the fulfilment of legal requirements and on a broad notion of 'fairness' which sought to humanise the workplace. Inevitably, it was discovered that the idea of fairness was often synonymous with blaming the victims of discrimination for making such a fuss, employing more men in low-grade administrative posts, and reinforcing the status quo.

In response to the resolute lack of change in equal opportunities, a broader, regulatory approach emerged, mixing processes of positive action and monitoring of action in order to try and ensure as much compliance as politically possible to a set of policies. This did have the effect of humanising the organisation, in the sense that the human conflicts and hostilities intensified, and different political positions became clearer. These conflicts emerged both overtly – expressed in particular in reactions against the equal opportunities 'thought-police', the 'loony-left' or the 'politically correct' – and covertly – as senior managers learned the language of anti-discrimination and developed various avoidance strategies to minimise the impact of positive action.

More recently, with the evolution of 'managing diversity' a different type of humanising is being attempted. Equalities no longer means equal opportunities, bound up in ungovernable organisational codes, rather it involves the recognition of the 'uniqueness' of every individual. This is a return to fairness, where all employees are 'valued and optimised' within a strongly managed 'vision' of a diverse workforce all of whom have a stake in creating the competitive advantage necessary for organisational survival. This could become a particularly cynical vision of fairness, based on the manipulation of peoples' fears of unemployment and wrapped up in the collective imperative towards competitive advantage. The learning in this approach is about learning how to meet and surpass organisational goals.

There are, however, different visions of equalities and the management of change that can be expressed through a critical approach to management learning. In order to review what critical might mean in practice I want to return to Table 7 (p 162) which summarises how different 'types' of organisation manage equality, and Table 10 (p 193), which summarises different ideas behind equality and the management of change. I reproduce the two right hand columns of each of these two Tables as Table 11, in order to help explain my thinking about the relationship between equalities, power and learning in organisations.

In many organisations that are currently involved in local governance, there is an ongoing paradoxical tension between action and avoidance in relation to equalities. In addition, some managers within organisations find themselves struggling both to cope with the paradox of action/avoidance and to find ways of moving in the direction of an organisational notion of learning and change. Groups of people who are willing to imagine the improbable but strategically important notion of a variety of commitments to equalities will provide increasing possibilities for change. The success of strategic groups, working internally and externally, will depend on the ability of such groups to frame themselves in terms of learning. A different form of policy may well emerge from deliberate practice fields, where worm-cans can be opened based on the desire to *inquire* into change. A different form of policy will certainly emerge from an imperative towards dialogue, which will assist with the inclusion of power relations in attempts to learn and change.   In addition to the connection between equalities and learning (Table 11), there is the connection between learning and a critical form of management (Table 12).

Table 11: Active/avoiding and learning organisations

	Active/avoiding organisation	Learning organisation
Managerial commitment	Confused commitment – manifested in both approaching and avoiding equality at the same time	Communities of commitment. Long-term commitment to improving business by exploring relations among a diverse employee base.
Leadership values	It is desirable to work towards equality but 'we don't want to open a can of worms'	The negotiation of equalities rights and outcomes underpins leadership within the organisation.
Response to change initiatives	Coherent policy. Incoherent approach to strategy and an inability by senior managers to act on and operationalise decisions on equality. Responses are solely rational.	Strategic decision making linked to an acceptance of the emotion, power and paradox of policy development in a diverse workforce.

Table 12: Management learning and critical management

	Management learning	Critical management
Focus	Systemic thinking: our actions create the problems we experience	Power relations: an understanding of power and its relevance to strategic change. Pluralism and the associated conflict of values.
Orientation	The primacy of the whole. Building 'Communities of commitment'.	The wider social and political significance of 'culture' programmes. 'Utilise opportunities for micro-emancipation'.
Methods	Dialogue rather than discussion or debate. Practice Fields. Teams as a mirror of organisation. Process and content are inseparable.	Critical self-reflection. 'Individuals learn to struggle with the problematical experience and significance of indeterminacy'.

I am using the word 'systemic' here in the sense that Senge (1990) uses it, to say that each part of a system has an influence on the rest, "an influence that is usually hidden from view" (Senge, 1990, p 12). Problems within a system are not caused by something outside of itself, but rather created by actions and inter-actions from within. Systemic thinking (which I think of as distinct from systems theory) provides some but not all of the possibilities for thought and action in organisations in relation to equality and management learning. The learning problem may well be prior to the managing problem (Burgoyne, 1994), but a critical stance involves reflecting back on the attempts to enhance control that may also be an aspect of management learning. In addition to processes of reflexivity and dialogue, a critical management learning will acknowledge a plurality of voices, within the self, within groups and within organisations. Equalities will continue to be a site, a subject, an issue where social power relations are contested and can be analysed, where conflict assists organisational members in finding temporary positions.

I think that there are different conflicts and possibilities today to the ones that organisations faced when they were struggling with the implementation of equal opportunity policies in the mid-1980s. Then, it seemed to be enough to try to create a guiding framework for individual and organisational action. Today such a project is a small part of the work to be done on equalities and management learning. Increasingly, a commitment to equalities and management learning involves:

- *Developing an understanding of the way emotions and politics relate to define organisationally specific avoidance strategies.* Insights into complicated and often paradoxical inter-personal and inter-group relations provide one key to learning and change. Managers with different perspectives towards the value of organisational action on equalities easily get themselves locked into circular, reactive and reductive relations, based on an inability to feel their own emotions, to contain the emotions of others, or to see the emotional character of their organisation. The fear and inability to relate at an emotional level deters action on equalities, and supports the evolution of avoidance strategies.

- *Recognising that inter-personal and organisational avoidance strategies are episodes of power, that reflect key moments in the possible management of change.* Avoidance strategies are designed both consciously and unconsciously to deny, delay or destroy attempts to make change happen. They exist alongside attempts to change in organisations as a mechanism to stop things 'going too far'. Avoidance strategies also often provide managers with a provisional outcome, a temporary release from the pressure to act in an area of organisational life that never seems to be able to be completed. It becomes easier to avoid than to act, yet avoidance is often responded to with pressure for action. The active/avoiding organisation is a powerful representation of the difficulty that organisations have with promoting learning and change.

- *Building processes for the development of dialogue and cultivating opportunities for group learning.* Dialogue is a key process for breaking down the avoidance strategies that characterise an organisation. It is also a process that allows and encourages both a perspective on power and the holding of emotions to be an integral part of interaction. Maintaining opportunities for group learning within and outside the organisation provides ever-changing, experiential knowledge about different ways of expressing and articulating the continuing desire for equality.

I think that managers, management educators, management developers and organisational change consultants all need to approach the issues raised by equality and management learning if we want organisations where learning and change is a legitimate aspect of everyday action.

References

Alderfer, C.P. (1990) 'Staff authority and leadership in experiential groups', in J. Gillette and McCollam (eds) *Groups in context*, Reading, Mass.: Addison-Wesley.

Alvesson, M. and Willmott, H. (1992) *Critical management studies*, London: Sage.

Argyris, C. (1982) *Reasoning, learning and action*, San Francisco: Jossey-Bass.

Argyris, C. (1989) 'Strategy implementation: an experience in learning', *Organisational Dynamics*, vol 18, no 2, pp 5-15.

Argyris, C. (1990) *Overcoming organizational defences*, New York: Prentice-Hall.

Argyris, C. (1994) 'Good communication that blocks learning', *Harvard Business Review*, vol 72, no 4, pp 77-85.

Argyris, C. and Schon, D. (1978) *Organizational learning*, San Francisco: Jossey-Bass.

Argyris, C., Putnam, R. and Smith, D.M. (1985) *Action science*, San Francisco: Jossey-Bass.

Armstrong, D. (1991) *The 'institution in the mind'*, London: The Grubb Institute.

Atwood, M. (1983) *Murder in the dark*, Toronto: Couch House Press.

Averill, J.R. (1990) 'Inner feelings, works of the flesh, the beast within, diseases of the mind, driving force, and putting on a show: six metaphors of emotion and their theoretical extensions', in D.E. Leary (ed) *Metaphors in the history of psychology*, Cambridge, Cambridge University Press.

Avon Accredited Training Centre (1985) *Equal Opportunity and the Youth Training Scheme. Exploring attitudes and practices in Avon: an initial report*, AATC Research Report, March.

Avon Accredited Training Centre (1987) *A guide to developing equal opportunity policies and practices within Youth Training Schemes*, AATC Research Report, September.

Ball, W. and Solomos, J. (1990) *Race and local politics*, London: Macmillan.

Barrett, F.J. and Cooperrider, D.L. (1990) 'Generative metaphor intervention: a new approach for working with systems divided by conflict and caught in defensive perception', *Journal of Applied Behavioral Science*, vol 26, no 2, pp 219-39.

Bartunek, J.M. and Reid, R.D. (1992) 'The role of conflict in a second order change attempt', in D.M. Kolb and J.M. Bartunek (eds) *Hidden conflict in organisations*, London: Sage.

Bateson, G. (1973) *Steps to an ecology of mind*, St Albans: Paladin.

Bauman, Z. (1982) *Memories of class: the pre-history and after-life of class*, London, Routledge and Kegan Paul.

Bennett, R. (1991) 'What is management research?', in C.N. Smith and P. Dainty *The management research handbook*, London: Routledge.

Benson, J.K. (1982) 'A framework for policy analysis', in D. Rogers and D. Whetten, *Interorganisational coordination: theory, research and implementation*, Iowa State University Press.

Ben Tovim, G., Gabriel, J., Law, I. and Stredder, K. (1986) *The local politics of race*, London: Macmillan.

Berg, D.N. and Smith, K.K. (1988) *The self in social inquiry*, Newbury Park: Sage.

Berg, D.N. and Smith, K.K. (1990) 'Paradox and groups', in J. Gillette and M. McCollom (eds) *Groups in context*, Reading, Mass.: Addison-Wesley.

Bhavnani, R. (1984) *Terminology: the colour blind cover up, or the pink man's burden*, Bristol CRE, Paper for Employment Working Group.

Bollas, C. (1995) *Cracking up*, London: Routledge.

Braham, P., Rattansi, A. and Skellington, R. (1992) *Racism and anti-racism: inequalities, opportunities and policies*, London: Sage.

Brittan, A. and Maynard, M. (1984) *Sexism, racism and oppression*, Oxford: Basil Blackwell.

Broussine, M. and Vince, R. (1995) 'Working with metaphor towards organizational change', in C. Oswick and D. Grant (eds) *Organization development: metaphorical explorations*, London: Pitman.

Brown, S. and McIntyre, D. (1981) 'An action-research approach to innovation in centralised education systems', *European Journal of Science and Education*, vol 3, no 3, pp 243–58.

Burgoyne, J.G. (1994) 'Managing by learning', *Management Learning*, vol 25, no 1, pp 35-55.

Burke, W.W. (1992) 'Metaphors to consult by', *Group and Organisation Management*, vol 17, no 3, pp 255-59.

Burnes, B. (1992) *Managing change*, London: Pitman.

Burrell, G. and Morgan, G. (1979) *Sociological paradigms and organisational analysis*, London: Heinemann.

Chatwin, B. (1989) *What am I doing here?*, London, Jonathan Cape.

Chisholm, R.F. and Elden, M. (1993) 'Features of emerging action research', *Human Relations*, vol 46, no 2, pp 290-96.

Claxton, G. (1984) *Live and learn*, London, Harper and Row.

Clegg, S. (1989) *Frameworks of power*, London, Sage.

Clegg, S. (1994a) 'Power relations and the constitution of the resistant subject', in J.M. Jermier, D. Knights and W.R. Nord, *Resistance and power in organisations*, London: Routledge.

Clegg, S. (1994b) 'Weber and Foucault: social theory for the study of organisations', *Organisation*, vol 1, no 1, pp 149-78.

Cockburn, C. (1988) 'Masculinity, the left and feminism', in R. Chapman and J. Rutherford (eds) *Male order: unwrapping masculinity*, London: Lawrence and Wishart.

Cockburn, C. (1991) *In the way of women: men's resistance to sex equality in organisations*, London: Macmillan.

Collinson, D. (1994) 'Strategies of resistance: power, knowledge and subjectivity in the workplace', in J.M. Jermier, D. Knights and W.R. Nord, *Resistance and power in organisations*, London: Routledge.

Colman, A.D. and Geller, M.H. (1985) *Group relations reader 2*, Washington, AK Rice Institute.

Commission for Racial Equality (1984) *Racial equality and the Youth Training Scheme*, CRE Publication.

Connell, R.W. (1983) *Which way is up?: essays on class, sex and culture*, London: Allen and Unwin.

Connell, R.W. (1987) *Gender and power*, Cambridge: Polity Press.

Conner, D.R. (1993) 'Managing change: a business imperative', *Business Quarterly*, vol 58, no 1, pp 88-92.

Cooper, C.L. and Mangham, I.L. (eds) (1971) *T Groups: a survey of research*, Chichester: John Wiley.

Cox, T. (1991) 'The multi-cultural organization', *Academy of Management Executive*, vol 5, no 2, pp 34–47.

Cox, T. and Blake, S. (1991) 'Managing cultural diversity: implications for organizational competitiveness', *Academy of Management Executive*, vol 5, no 3, pp 45-56.

Cunningham, I. (1994) *The wisdom of strategic learning*, London, McGraw-Hill.

Dainty, P. (1991) 'Meaningful management research', in C.N. Smith and P. Dainty, *The management research handbook*, London: Routledge.

Danziger, K. (1990) 'Generative metaphor and the history of psychological discourse', in D.E. Leary (ed) *Metaphors in the history of psychology*, Cambridge: Cambridge University Press.

Dawson, P. (1994) *Organizational change: a processual approach*, London: Paul Chapman.

Dawson, S. (1992) *Analysing organizations* (2nd edn), London: Macmillan.

de Mare, P., Piper, R. and Thompson, S. (1991) *Koinonia: from hate, through dialogue, to culture in the large group*, London: Karnac Books.

Denzin, N.K. (1994) 'The art and politics of interpretation', in N.K. Denzin and Y.S. Lincoln (eds) *The handbook of qualitative research*, London: Sage.

Denzin, N.K. and Lincoln, Y.S. (eds) (1994) *The handbook of qualitative research*, London: Sage.

De Sousa, E. (1987) 'Racism in the YTS', *Critical Social Policy*, vol 20, pp 66-73.

Diamante, T. and Giglio, L. (1994) 'Managing a diverse workforce: training as a cultural intervention strategy', *Leadership and Organisation Development Journal*, vol 15, no 2, pp 13-17.

Diamond, M.A. (1990) 'Psychoanalytic phenomenology and organisational analysis', *Public Administration Quarterly*, vol 14, no 1, pp 32-42.

Diamond, M.A. (1993) *The unconscious life of organisations*, Westport Connecticut: Quorum Books.

Dobbs, M.F. (1994a) 'San Diego's diversity commitment', *Public Manager*, vol 23, no 1, pp 59-62.

Dobbs, M.F. (1994b) 'Managing diversity: a unique quality opportunity', *Public Manager*, vol 23, no 3, pp 39-42.

Dodgson, M. (1993) 'Organizational learning: a review of some literatures', *Organization Studies*, vol 14, no 3, pp 375-94.

Easterby-Smith, M., Thorpe, R. and Lowe, A. (1991) *Management research: an introduction*, London: Sage.

Elden, M. and Chisholm, R.F. (1993) 'Emerging varieties of action research', *Human Relations*, vol 46, vol 2, pp 121-42.

Ellis, C. and Sonnenfeld, J.A. (1994) 'Diverse approaches to managing diversity', *Human Resources Management*, vol 33, no 1, pp 79-109.

Engelstad, P.H. and Gustavsen, B. (1993) 'Swedish network development for implementing National Work Reform Strategy', *Human Relations*, vol 46, no 2, pp 219-48.

Fenton, S., Davis, T., Means, R. and Burton, P. (1984) *Ethnic minorities and the Youth Training Scheme*, Research and Development Report 20, Sheffield: Manpower Services Commission.

Fineman, S. (ed) (1993) *Emotion in organisations*, London: Sage.

Fiol, C.M. and Lyles, M.A. (1985) 'Organizational learning', *Academy of Management Review*, vol 10, pp 803-13.

Flax, J. (1993) *Disputed subjects: essays on psychoanalysis, politics and philosophy*, London: Routledge.

Ford Foundation (forthcoming) *Re-linking life and work* (authors' pre-publication draft).

Foucault, M. (1979) *Discipline and punish: the birth of the prison*, Harmondsworth: Penguin.

Foucault, M. (1981) *The history of sexuality: volume one, An introduction*, Harmondsworth: Penguin.

Fraser, N. (1989) *Unruly practices: power, discourse and gender in contemporary social theory*, Cambridge: Polity Press.

Freire, P. (1972) *Pedagogy of the oppressed*, Harmondsworth: Penguin.

Freire, P. and Shor, I. (1987) *A pedagogy for liberation: dialogues on transforming education*, London: Macmillan.

Fritz, K. (1982) 'Because I speak cockney they think I'm stupid: an application of Paulo Freire's concepts to community work with women', Newcastle: Association of Community Workers.

Garfield, C. (1994) 'Embracing diversity', *Executive Excellence*, vol 11, no 10, pp 8-9.

Garvin, D.A. (1993) 'Building a learning organization', *Harvard Business Review*, vol 71, no 4, pp 78-91.

Gergen, K.J. (1992) Organisation theory in the postmodern era', in M. Reed and M. Hughes (eds) *Rethinking organisation*, London: Sage.

Gibbon, P. (1992) 'Equal opportunity policy and race equality', in P. Braham, A. Rattansi, and R. Skellington (eds) *Racism and anti-racism: inequalities, opportunities and policies*, London: Sage.

Giddens, A. (1976) *New rules of sociological method*, Cambridge: Polity Press.

Giddens, A. (1984) *The constitution of society*, Cambridge: Polity Press.

Giddens, A. (1991) *Modernity and self identity: self and society in the late modern age*, Cambridge: Polity Press.

Giddens, A. (1993) *New rules of sociological method* (2nd edn), Cambridge: Polity Press.

Gill, J. and Johnson, P. (1991) *Research methods for managers*, London: Paul Chapman Publishing.

Gillette, J. and McCollum, M. (1990) *Groups in context: a new perspective on group dynamics*, Reading, Mass: Addison-Wesley.

Glaser, D.G. and Strauss, A.L. (1967) *The discovery of grounded theory: strategies for qualitative research*, New York: Aldine.

Goodman, P. (1982) *Change in organizations*, San Francisco: Jossey-Bass.

Gordon, J. (1992) 'Rethinking diversity', *Training*, January, pp 23-30.

Gramsci, A. (1971) *Selections from prison notebooks*, London: Lawrence and Wishart.

Grey, C. (1995) 'What is critical management?', a posting to the critical-management list on Thursday 9 November, 2:12pm, archived at: http://www.mailbase.ac.uk/lists-a-e/critical-management.

Griffin, C. (1986) 'Qualitative methods and female experience', in S. Wilkinson (ed) *Feminist social psychology*, Milton Keynes: Open University Press.

Griggs, L.B. and Louw, L.L. (1995) *Valuing diversity: new tools for a new reality*, New York: McGraw-Hill.

Guba, E.G. and Lincoln, Y.S. (1990) 'Can there be a Human Science?', *Person-Centred Review*, vol 5, no 2, pp 130-54.

Gurnah, A. (1984) 'The politics of racism awareness training', *Critical Social Policy*, vol 11, pp 6-20.

Hall, B. (1975) 'Participatory research: an approach for change', *Convergence*, vol 8, no 2.

Hammersley, M. (ed) (1993) *Social research*, London: Sage.

Hammond, V. and Holton, V. (1991) *Towards a balanced workforce?*, Berkhampstead: Ashridge Management Research Group.

Handy, C. (1985) *Understanding organisations* (3rd edn), Harmondsworth: Penguin.

Hardy, C. (1994) 'Power and politics in organisations', in C. Hardy (ed) *Managing strategic action*, London: Sage.

Hassard, J.S. (1991) 'Ethnomethodology and organisation: an introduction', in C.N. Smith and P. Dainty (eds) *The management research handbook*, London: Routledge.

Havel, V. (1985) *The power of the powerless*, (ed J. Keane), London: Hutchinson.

Hawkins, P. (1991) 'The spiritual dimension of the learning organization', *Management Education and Development*, vol 22, no 3, pp 172-87.

Hawkins, P. (1994) 'Organizational learning: taking stock and facing the challenge', *Management Learning*, vol 25, no 1, pp 71-82.

Hazen, M.A. (1994) 'Multiplicity and change in persons and organizations', *Journal of Organizational Change Management*, vol 7, no 6, pp 72-81.

Hearn, J. and Parkin, W. (1987) *Sex at work*, Brighton: Wheatsheaf.

Heron, J. (1981) 'Philosophical basis for a new paradigm', in P. Reason and J. Rowan (eds) *Human inquiry: a sourcebook of new paradigm research*, Chichester: John Wiley.

Herriot, P. and Pemberton, C. (1995) *Competitive advantage through diversity*, London: Sage.

Hirschhorn, L. (1990) *The workplace within: psychodynamics of organisational life*, Cambridge Mass.: MIT Press.

Hirschhorn, L. and Barnett, C.K. (1993) *The psychodynamics of organisations*, Philadelphia: Temple University Press.

Hoggett, P. (1992) *Partisans in an uncertain world: the psychoanalysis of engagement*, London: Free Association Books.

Home Office (1977) *Racial discrimination: a guide to the Race Relations Act 1976*, London: HMSO.

hooks, b. (1991) *Yearning: race, gender and cultural politics*, London: Turnaround Books.

Illich, I. (1971) *Deschooling society*, London: Calder and Boyars.

Isaacs, W.N. (1993) 'Taking flight: dialogue, collective thinking, and organisational learning', *Organisational Dynamics*, vol 22, no 2, pp 24-39.

Jamieson, D. and O'Mara, J. (1991) *Managing workforce 2000: gaining the diversity advantage*, San Francisco: Jossey-Bass.

Jaques, E. (1955) 'Social systems as a defence against persecutory and depressive anxiety', in M. Klien et al (eds) *New directions in psychoanalysis*, London: Tavistock.

Jaques, E. (1990) 'On the dynamics of social structure', in E. Trist and H. Murray (eds) *The social engagement of social science, vol 1.*, London: Free Association Books.

Jermier, J.M., Knights, D. and Nord, W.R. (1994) *Resistance and power in organisations*, London: Routledge.

Jewson, N. and Mason, D. (1986) 'The theory and practice of equal opportunity policies: liberal and radical approaches', *Sociological Review*, vol 34, no 2.

Johnson, G. (1987) *Strategic change and the management process*, Oxford: Blackwell.

Jones, P. (1988) 'Policy and praxis: local government, a case for treatment', in A. Coyle and J. Skinner (eds) *Women and work: positive action for change*, London: Macmillan.

Kandola, R. and Fullerton, J. (1994) *Managing the mosaic: diversity in action*, London: Institute of Personnel and Development.

Kasl, E., Dechant, K. and Marsick, V. (1993) 'Living the Learning: internalising our model of group learning', in D. Boud, R. Cohen and D. Walker (eds) *Using experience for learning*, Buckingham: Society for Research into Higher Education (SRHE) and Open University Press.

Katz, J.H. (1978) *White awareness: a handbook for anti-racism training*, Norman: University of Oklahoma Press.

Katzenbach, J.R. and Smith, D.K. (1993) 'The discipline of teams', *Harvard Business Review*, vol 71, no 2, pp 111-20.

Kets de Vries, M.F.R. (1989a) 'The leader as mirror: clinical reflections', *Human Relations*, vol 42, no 7, pp 607-23.

Kets de Vries, M.F.R. (1989b) *Prisoners of leadership*, New York: Norton.

Kets de Vries, M.F.R. (1990) 'Leaders on the couch', *Journal of Applied Behavioral Science*, vol 26, no 4, pp 423-31.

Kets de Vries, M.F.R. (1991) *Organisations on the couch*, San Francisco: Jossey-Bass.

Kets de Vries M.F.R. and Miller, D. (1985) *The neurotic organisation*, London: Jossey-Bass.

Kim, D.H. (1993) 'The link between individual and organizational learning', *Sloan Management Review*, vol 35, no 1, pp 37-50.

Kofman, F. and Senge, P.M. (1993) 'Communities of commitment: the heart of learning organisations', *Organizational Dynamics*, vol 22, no 2, pp 5-23.

Kolb, D. (1984) *Experiential learning*, Englewood Cliffs: Prentice Hall.

Kotter, J.P. and Schlesinger, L.A. (1979) 'Choosing strategies for change', *Harvard Business Review*, March/April, pp 106-14.

Krantz, J. (1990a) 'Commentary on the Barrett and Cooperrider article', *Journal of Applied Behavioral Science*, vol 26, no 2, pp 241-43.

Krantz, J. (1990b) 'Group relations training in context', in J. Gillette and M. McCollum (eds) *Groups in context*, Reading, Mass.: Addison-Wesley.

Kyle, N. (1993) 'Staying with the flow of change', *Journal for Quality and Participation*, vol 16, no 4, pp 34-42.

Lessem, R. (1993) *Business as a learning community: applying global concepts to organizational learning*, London: McGraw Hill.

Lewin, K. (1951) *Field theory in social science*, London: Harper and Row.

Lincoln, Y.S. and Guba, E.G. (1985) *Naturalistic inquiry*, London: Sage.

Lindsay, C. (1994) 'Things that go wrong in diversity training: conceptualisation and change with ethnic identity models', *Journal of Organizational Change Management*, vol 7, no 6, pp 18-33.

Lowery, M. (1995) 'The war on equal opportunity', *Black Enterprise*, vol 27, no 7, pp 148-54.

Lukes, S. (1974) *Power: a radical view*, London: Macmillan

Lukes, S. (1986) *Power*, Oxford: Basil Blackwell.

Lundberg, C.C. (1995) 'Learning in and by organizations: three conceptual issues', *International Journal of Organizational Analysis*, vol 3, no 1, pp 10-23.

MacKeracher, D. (1995) *Women and life narratives: a story about a story*, unpublished paper: Faculty of Education, University of New Brunswick, Canada.

Maddock, S. (1995) 'Rhetoric and reality: the business case for equality and why it continues to be resisted', *Women in Management Review*, vol 10, no 1, pp 14-20.

Manpower Services Commission (1987) *YTS Equal Opportunity Code*, TFSL 45, Sheffield: Manpower Services Commission.

March, J. (1991) 'Exploration and exploitation in organizational learning', *Organization Science*, vol 2, no 1, pp 71-87.

Marris, P. (1986) *Loss and change*, London: Routledge.

Marshall, J. (1995) *Women managers moving on: exploring career and life choices*, London: Routledge.

Marshall, C. and Rossman, G.B. (1989) *Designing qualitative research*, London: Sage.

Marsick, V.J. and Watkins, K.E. (1994) 'The learning organization: an integrative vision for human resource development', *Human Resource Development Quarterly*, vol 5, no 4, pp 353-60.

Martin, L. (1994) 'Power, continuity and change: women manager's experience in local government', in M. Tanton (ed) *Women in management: a developing presence*, London: Routledge.

Matejka, K. and Ramona, J. (1993) 'Resistance to change is natural', *Supervisory Management*, vol 38, no 10, pp 10-11.

McGill, I. and Beaty, L. (1995) *Action learning: a guide for professional, management and educational development* (2nd edn), London: Kogan Page.

McKendall, M. (1994) 'A course in workforce diversity: strategies and issues', *Journal of Management Education*, vol 18, no 4, pp 407-23.

Menzies-Lyth, I. (1990) 'Social systems as a defence against anxiety (revised)', in E. Trist and H. Murray (eds) *The social engagement of social science, vol 1.*, London: Free Association Books.

Mies, M. (1993) 'Towards a methodology for feminist research', in M. Hammersley (ed) *Social research*, London: Sage.

Mifsud, A. (1990) *Guidelines for trainers: a trainers manual*, Staff Development Organisation, Office of the Prime Minister, Malta.

Miller, E. (1989) 'The "Leicester" model: experiential study of group and organizational processes', London: Tavistock Institute of Human Relations Occasional Paper No 10.

Miller, E. and Rice, A.K. (1967) *Systems of organisation*, London: Tavistock.

Morgan, G. (1983) *Beyond method: strategies for social research*, London: Sage.

Morgan, G. (1986) *Images of organisation*, London: Sage.

Mumford, A. (1992) 'New ideas on action learning', in *Approaches to action learning*, University of Keele: Mercia Publications.

Nanton, P. (1995) 'Extending the boundaries: equal opportunities as social regulation', *Policy and Politics*, vol 23, no 3, pp 203-12.

Nkomo, S.M. (1992) 'The emperor has no clothes: rewriting "race in organizations"', *Academy of Management Review*, vol 17, no 3, pp 487-513.

Nord, W.R. and Jermier, J.M. (1994) 'Overcoming resistance to resistance: insights from a study of the shadows', *Public Administration Quarterly*, vol 17, no 4, pp 396-409.

O'Connor, C. (1993) 'Managing resistance to change', *Management Development Review*, vol 6, no 4, pp 25-29.

Oldham, M. and Kleiner, B.H. (1990) 'Understanding the nature and use of defense mechanisms in organisational life', *Journal of Managerial Psychology*, vol 5, no 5, pp i-iv.

Ontario Management Board Secretariat (1992a) *Employment Equity Annual Report, June 1991-May 1992*, Toronto, Ontario.

Ontario Management Board Secretariat (1992b) *Employment Systems Review Manual: Part one*, Toronto: Queen's Printer for Ontario.

Ontario Management Board Secretariat (1992c) *Employment Systems Review Manual: Part two, Technical guide*, Toronto: Queen's Printer for Ontario.

Ortony, A. (ed) (1979) *Metaphor and thought*, Cambridge: Cambridge University Press.

Palmer, B. (1979) 'Learning and the group experience', in W. Lawrence (ed) *Exploring individual and organisational boundaries*, Chichester: John Wiley.

Pateman, C. (1985) *The problem of political obligation: a critique of liberal theory*, Oxford: Polity Press.

Patton, M.Q. (1990) *Qualitative evaluation and research methods* (2nd edn), Newbury Park: Sage.

Pedler, M. and Boutall, J. (1992) *Action learning for change*, Eastwood Park, Glous.: NHSTD Publication.

Pedler, M., Burgoyne, J. and Boydell, T. (1991) *The learning company: a strategy for sustainable development*, London: McGraw Hill.

Pettigrew, A. (1987) *The management of strategic change*, Oxford: Basil Blackwell.

Phillips, A. (1995) *Terrors and experts*, London: Faber and Faber.

Pines, M. (1993) 'Interpretation: why, for whom and when', in D. Kennard, J. Roberts and D.A. Winter, *A work book of group-analytic interventions*, London: Routledge.

Plant, R. (1987) *Managing change and making it stick*, London: Fontana.

Pollert, A. (1985) *Unequal opportunities*, Birmingham Trade Union Resource Centre Publishing: West Midlands YTS Research Project.

Race Relations Act (1976) London: HMSO.

Reason, P. (1988) *Human inquiry in action*, London: Sage.

Reason, P. (1994) *Participation in human inquiry*, London: Sage.

Reason, P. and Marshall, J. (1987) 'Research as personal process', in D. Boud and V. Griffin (eds) *Appreciating adult learning*, Kogan Page.

Reason, P. and Rowan, J (1981) *Human inquiry: a sourcebook of new paradigm research*, Chichester: John Wiley.

Revans, R. (1971) *Developing effective managers*, London: Longman.

Revans, R. (1983) *The ABC of action learning*, Bromley, Kent: Chartwell, Bratt.

Reynolds, L. (1994) 'Understand employees' resistance to change', *HR Focus*, vol 71, no 6, pp 17-18.

Roberts, J. (1996) 'Management education and the limits of technical rationality: the conditions and consequences of management practice', in R. French and C. Grey (eds) *Rethinking management education*, London: Sage.

Ross, R. and Schneider, R. (1992) *From equality to diversity: a business case for equal opportunity*, London: Pitman.

Sackmann, S. (1989) 'The role of metaphors in organisation transformation', *Human Relations*, vol 42, no 6, pp 463-85.

Samuels, A. (1993) *The political psyche*, London: Routledge.

Sarbin, T.R. (1986) 'Emotion and act: roles and rhetoric', in R. Harre (ed) *The social construction of emotions*, Oxford: Blackwell.

Schein, E.H. (1985) *Organizational culture and leadership*, San Francisco: Jossey-Bass.

Schein, E.H. (1993a) 'How can organizations learn faster?: the challenge of entering the green room', *Sloan Management Review*, vol 34, no 2, pp 85-92.

Schein, E.H. (1993b) 'On dialogue, culture and organisational learning', *Organisational Dynamics*, vol 22, no 2, pp 40-51.

Schon, D.A. (1979) 'Generative metaphor: a perspective on problem-setting in social policy', in A. Ortony (ed) *Metaphor and thought*, Cambridge: Cambridge University Press.

Senge, P. (1990) 'The leader's new work: building learning organizations', *Sloan Management Review*, vol 32, no 1, pp 7-23.

Senge, P.M. (1991) *The fifth discipline: the art and practice of the learning organisation*, London: Century Business.

Sex Discrimination Act (1975) London: HMSO.

Sheridan, A. (1980) *Michel Foucault: the will to truth*, London: Tavistock.

Siim, B. (1988) 'Towards a feminist rethinking of the Welfare State', in K.B. Jones and A.G. Jonasdottir (eds) *The political interests of gender: developing theory and research with a feminist face*, London: Sage.

Smith, K.K. (1982) 'Philosophical problems in thinking about organisational change', in P.S. Goodman et al, *Change in organisations*, San Francisco: Jossey-Bass.

Smith, K.K. and Berg, D.N. (1987) *Paradoxes of group life*, San Francisco: Jossey-Bass.

Smith, P.B. (1980) *Group process and personal change*, London: Harper and Row.

Smith, R., Gaster, L., Harrison, L., Martin, L., Means, R. and Thistlethwaite, P. (1993) *Working together for better community care*, Bristol: SAUS Publications.

Snow, C.C., Miles, R.E. and Coleman, H.J. (1992) 'Managing 21st century network organizations', *Organizational Dynamics*, vol 20, no 3, pp 5-19.

Spero, M. (1994) 'Comments on: working at the boundary – the transference back and forth by Hirschhorn, L.', Summary Paper presented at the International Consulting Conference, South Bank University, London, January.

Stacey, R. (1993) *Strategic management and organizational dynamics*, London: Pitman.

Stanley, L. and Wise, S. (1983) *Breaking out: feminist consciousness and feminist research*, London: Routledge.

Steier, F. (1991) *Research and reflexivity*, London: Sage.

Stone, I. (1988) *Equal opportunities in local authorities*, London: HMSO.

Stringer, D. (1995) 'The role of women in workplace diversity consulting', *Journal of Organizational Change Management*, vol 8, no 1, pp 44-51.

Susman, G.I. and Evered, R.D. (1978) 'An assessment of the scientific merits of action research', *Administrative Science Quarterly*, vol 23, pp 582-603.

Thomas, V.C. (1994) 'The downside of diversity', *Training and Development*, vol 48, no 1, pp 60-62.

Torbert, W.R. (1981) 'Why educational research has been so uneducational: the case for a new model of social science based on collaborative inquiry', in P. Reason and J. Rowan (eds) *Human inquiry*, Chichester: John Wiley.

Torbert, W.R. (1991) *The power of balance*, London: Sage.

Torbert, W.R. (1994) 'Managerial learning, organizational learning: a potentially powerful redundancy', *Management Learning*, vol 25, no 1, pp 57-70.

Trist, E. and Murray, H. (1990) *The social engagement of social science, vol 1.*, London: Free Association Books.

Turner, B.A. (1981) 'Some practical aspects of qualitative data analysis', *Quality and Quantity*, vol 15, pp 225-47.

Ulrich, D., Von Glinow, M.A. and Jick, T. (1993) 'High input learning: building and diffusing learning capability', *Organizational Dynamics*, vol 22, no 2, pp 52-66.

Vince, R. (1990) 'The barriers to learning and change in public service bureaucracies', PhD. Thesis, University of Bristol.

Vince, R. (1995a) 'Learning about management: an analytic large group in a management development programme', *Group Analysis Quarterly*, vol 28, no 1, pp 21-33.

Vince, R. (1995b) 'Emphasising learning in management research', *Management Learning*, vol 26, no 1, pp 55-72.

Vince, R. (1995c) 'Working with emotions in the change process: using drawings for team diagnosis and development', *Organizations and People*, vol 2, no 1, pp 11-17.

Vince, R. (1996) 'Experimental management education as the practice of change', in R. French and C. Grey, *Rethinking management education*, London: Sage, pp 111-31.

Vince, R. (forthcoming) 'Behind and beyond Kolb's learning cycle', *Journal of Management Education*.

Vince, R. and Booth, C. (1996) *Equalities and organizational design*, London: Local Government Management Board.

Vince, R. and Broussine, M. (1996) 'Paradox, defence and attachment: accessing and working with emotions and relations underlying organizational change', *Organization Studies*, vol 17, no 1, pp 1-21.

Vince, R. and Kitusa, L. (1988) *The development of equal opportunity policy and practice: race and gender*, Avon Accredited Training Centre, Bristol Polytechnic.

Vince, R. and Martin, L. (1993) 'Inside action learning: the psychology and the politics of the action learning model', *Management Education and Development*, vol 24, no 3, pp 205-15.

Vinogradov, S. and Yalom, I.D. (1989) *Group psychotherapy*, Washington: American Psychiatric Press.

Watson, S. (ed) (1990) *Playing the state: Australian feminist interventions*, London: Verso.

Whyte, W.F. (1991) *Participatory action research*, Newbury Park: Sage.

Wickham, A. (1986) *Women and training*, Milton Keynes: Open University Press.

Willmott, H. (1993) 'Strength is ignorance; slavery is freedom: managing culture in modern organisations', *Journal of Management Studies*, vol 30, no 4, pp 515-52.

Wilson, D.C. (1992) *A strategy of change*, London: Routledge.

Yalom, I.D. (1985) *The theory and practice of group psychotherapy* (3rd edn), New York: Basic Books.

Young, K. (1990) 'Approaches to policy development in the field of equal opportunities', in W. Ball and J. Solomos (eds) *Race and local politics*, London: Macmillan.

Index